34

W9-CEI-288

Teaching English Language Learners

Strategies That Work, K–5

Katharine Davies Samway & Dorothy Taylor

SCHOLASTIC

New York • Toronto • London • Auckland • Sydney
Mexico City • New Delhi • Hong Kong • Buenos Aires

Figure 4.1. Dr. Sam Micklus, founder Odyssey of the Mind.

Acquiring Editor: Lois Bridges

Production Editor: Sarah Glasscock

Cover photographs: Asian girl with microscope © Fancy Photography/Veer;
African American boy writing & smiling at desk © Digital Vision/Veer;
Portrait of girl smiling w/braces © Blend Images/Veer;
High school students in chemistry class © Corbis. All Rights Reserved.

Cover design by Jason Robinson

Interior design by Sydney Wright

ISBN-13: 978-0-439-92647-8

ISBN-10: 0-439-92647-5

Copyright © 2007 by Katharine Davies Samway and Dorothy Taylor

All rights reserved.

Printed in the U.S.A.

1 2 3 4 5 6 7 8 9 10   40   12 11 10 09 08 07

Contents

ACKNOWLEDGMENTS

We are indebted to many, many people who have influenced us as teachers and/or helped us as we have written this book.

Over the years, we have had the good fortune to work with many gifted teachers, from whom we have learned so much, and we would like to first acknowledge our indebtedness to them— Marina Afentakis, Barbara Agor, Joan Albarella, Laura Alvarez, Sharon Amos, Edwin Aponte, Angie Barra, Joanne Basil, Jill Berg, Romeo Bryant, Fran Butler, Marsha Christiano, Stephanie Costner, Laurel Cress, Yolanda Dandridge, Jerry Dickson, Ellen Edes, JoAnne Edmiston, Audrey Fong, Maya Galperin, Isabel Hernandez, Mary Howlette, Jennifer Jones-Martinez, Jennifer Kim, Denise Leograndis, Musoko Luko, Kathy Maloney, Lynn McMichael, Mark Methven, Jen Meyers, Atsuko Nishida Mitchell, Todd Mitchell, Laurie Nussbaum, Gwen O'Dette, Mary Pippitt, Ali Rasheed, Doreen Regan, Marjorie Rosenthal-Foer, Rachel Rothman, Barbara Schmidt, Choji Shroeder, Lydia Stack, Carlyn Syvanen, Sharon Weight, María Wetzel, Robert Wiggenfeld, Beverly Wilkin, Gail Whang, and Mary Zimmer.

We would also like to thank the teachers who have shared invaluable resources with us while writing this book, and/or responded to our requests for situations that teachers encounter when working with ELLs—Jill Berg, Jerry Dickson, JoAnne Edminston, Lisa Gustafson, Elizabeth Jaeger, Karen Kane, Fran Magallanes, Lynn Matwijko, Erin McCarthy, Jen Meyers, Celeste Notaro, Bridgett O'Shea, Melanie Pyne, Rosalie Rienzo, Heather Rivera, Rachel Rothman, Kelly Shulman, and an anonymous teacher who responded to our survey and provided us with lots of very useful situations. Thanks also to Nancy Markowitz, Kris Pemberton, and Sharon Weight, for forwarding our request for situations to other teachers.

Several of the annotated book lists that we have included in the book are the consequence of the help that we received from Karen Peterman and Monica Vorac (librarians at Cecil County Public Library), Jill Berg, Jen Myers, Rachel Rothman, and Kelly Shulman—thank you for all your help.

Dorothy would like to thank Jan Kasik, who taught her students during the week that Dorothy took off to work on the book with Katharine. She would also like to thank Sherryl Weems and Debra Thompson for their support.

We have taught in several states, and we are indebted to our students in western New York, including Brockport, Buffalo, and Rochester; Brookline, Massachusetts; and Reston and Herndon in Virginia. We are especially grateful to Dorothy's adult ESL students at the Educational Opportunity Center/SUNY at Buffalo for their invaluable contributions to the chapter on communicating with parents.

Writing a book is a very time-consuming act, and would have been very difficult for us if we had not had the support of our families. In particular, Katharine would like to thank Tom Samway, who knows how important writing is to her, and epitomizes the supportive spouse. Dorothy would like to thank her parents, Hammersley and Ann Taylor, who knew she wanted to be a teacher even when she thought she didn't; Patricia Clay, Carol McKinney, Mary Jane Smith, and Jim Taylor; Don Pollock, the anthropologist, for expert advice on the sociolinguistic chapter; and Don Pollock, the husband, for too many kindnesses to list. We would both like to thank Don Pollock, the friend, who cooked us delicious meals and entertained us with lively stories over dinner when we spent several days working together on the book.

Our thanks also extend to the Scholastic staff, who helped bring this book into existence particularly editor, Lois Bridges, Sarah Glasscock, Jason Robinson, and Sydney Wright.

Introduction

Together, we have spent decades teaching and working on behalf of English language learners (ELLs), and it is work that we value enormously. We have found that working with ELLs and their families is very stimulating and rewarding, and through this work, we have been welcomed into the lives of our students, and we have learned through them how people from many different parts of the world think, communicate, and learn.

ELLs can be a tremendous asset to schools, but only when members of the school community view them that way. We recognize, of course, how challenging it is to try to communicate with a newcomer who does not yet know English (and whose native language we do not know). When this happens, we try to remind ourselves that any situation that we find challenging will almost always be much more challenging for the ELL student—after all, not only are ELL children in a new environment where they may not hear their home languages for hours at a time, but they are often separated from family members, friends, and familiar surroundings without sufficient time to say good-bye.

How we respond to ELLs can make a huge difference in how they feel about school and how other children respond to them. And, ultimately, it can have a huge impact on the learning of all of our students, both ELLs and non-ELLs. For example, when meeting a new student whose native language we cannot speak, we call upon some basic strategies that can help integrate the newcomer into the school and classroom community. We do this because we realize that ELLs will be learning more than the English language and content area material; they will also be learning the social and cultural norms of school life and life in the community at large, and peers can bridge that gap very effectively.

We hope that our book gives teachers who work with ELLs lots of strategies to use when they aren't sure what to do next. Though our focus is on ELLs, we firmly believe that effective strategies for ELLs are often effective for all students. This book emerged from working with ELL students and from working closely with many mainstream teachers and ESOL specialists (also called ESL or ELD teachers). The situations that we describe are genuine; they come from our experiences and those of other teachers. Although the book can be read from front to back, it does not have to be approached that way; it is designed so that teachers can dip into it as the need arises.

Each of the six chapters begins with background information on the overarching content of the chapter, followed by some general strategies. There are then several subsections, each with its own background, general strategies, specific situations, and targeted strategies for those situations. The table of contents lays out all the general strategies and specific situations.

We hope our readers will feel much more confident about working with ELLs once they have read this book. We also hope that all our readers feel the same enthusiasm and optimism that we feel when working with ELLs.

CHAPTER I

Sociocultural Issues

Often when we think about the needs of English language learners in our schools, we tend to focus on their linguistic needs. However, children do not come to us as clean slates ready for English language input. The social and cultural backgrounds of ELL students and their families greatly influence their school experiences, and schools must take sociocultural issues into account to successfully work with these children.

The learning styles of ELL students may be affected by their underlying assumptions about the nature of education, classrooms, and the authority of teachers. Students may be coming from cultures in which they were not expected (or allowed) to acquire significant levels of formal education. Students and their families may view schools as representatives of oppressive political regimes and may resist the well-intentioned efforts of teachers and school officials. Expectations about respect or personal demeanor may be highly variable, and assumptions about health and illness may sometimes differ from mainstream Western beliefs and practices.

Many students and their families may have come to the United States to escape war, oppression, or other hardships. Some have spent years in refugee camps, and many have suffered extraordinary traumas. Under such circumstances, the formal schooling of students and their families was interrupted or it may never have occurred. It is not unusual for political and tribal conflicts to carry over into classrooms and local communities in North America.

Regardless of how they arrived in this country, many ELL students and their families are dealing with economic hardships that affect the ways in which they participate in school. Students may be hungry; their clothes may not be new or of the current style; they may be lacking school supplies; and their parents and other family members may be working long hours and/or multiple jobs. The greater understanding teachers and schools have of these sociocultural issues, the better equipped they will be to achieve the goal of successfully educating ELL children.

Influence of Geopolitical Issues

In the past, immigrant students came to some school districts from well-educated, middle-class backgrounds, such as the first waves of Cuban and Vietnamese refugees in the early 1960s and 1970s respectively. In other cases, ELLs were the children of graduate students at local universities and they typically had been schooled in their native lands before coming to the U.S. Although middle-class immigrants continue to come to the U.S., now many more ELLs come from low-income homes. They have had little or no schooling due to a variety of factors, including economics (e.g., having to work to help support their families), geography (e.g., living in isolated areas that had very limited access to teachers), or war (e.g., leading to intermittent and interrupted schooling). In other cases, children who speak indigenous languages may have been schooled in a nonnative language, as often happens in countries such as Guatemala (where a majority of the population is of indigenous/Indian descent and speaks many different indigenous languages, including Mon). In these cases, it is common for teachers to arrive on a Monday and leave on a Friday, thereby further reducing the educational opportunities for local children.

Due to these socioeconomic factors, immigrants may enter U.S. schools with limited schooling in their native language. This factor alone—the level of education in the L1— plays a huge role in how long it takes to acculturate and acquire English language and literacy. Research shows that the more an ELL has been schooled in the L1, the greater the ease in acquiring English (e.g., Collier, 1989, 1992; Cummins, 1981; Thomas & Collier, 2001).

This is due, in part, to the way in which literacy skills and content knowledge transfer from the L1 to the L2. In addition, in many developing countries from which immigrants come, middle-class families have some familiarity with Western and U.S. culture through travel, the Internet, cable TV, movies, and print materials. In contrast, people from much humbler circumstances may have had very limited contact with English and Western customs; hence, they often need more time to adjust to a very different way of life.

General Strategies

Information is the key to being prepared to help newly arrived immigrant and refugee families. Local community support agencies, such as refugee resettlement agencies, can alert schools to anticipated arrivals of ELL families and provide culturally relevant information, including the educational backgrounds of arriving children. Once educators know which populations to expect in their schools, they can begin to gather information through the national resources listed on pages 14–16. Many immigrant and refugee families arrive with tremendous needs, and it is essential for schools to work with community agencies to coordinate efforts to meet the needs of these families. Patience, time, and a concerted consistent effort are the greatest means of support that teachers and schools can offer ELL children who have suffered traumas and had little or no schooling. Schools with large numbers or rapid rises in numbers of new immigrant and refugee families have found it useful to add some or all of the following staff members and programs:

- Parent liaisons, from the same ethnic backgrounds and language groups as the families, to provide a bridge between the school and the home

- Bilingual aides to support ELL students and classroom teachers

- ELL specialist support people to provide focused English Language Development (ELD) instruction

- After-school tutoring to provide one-on-one tutoring and homework assistance

- Volunteers to work one-on-one with ELLs on a regular basis

- Newcomer schools or classrooms to provide concentrated cultural orientation, ELD instruction, and sheltered content-area instruction, if it is not available in the L1

- Advocacy, particularly with regard to funding and standardized testing—
  it often helps to have access to extra funds for specialized ELD staff and
  programs, including professional development. Also, it is important to
  have the resources to act as advocates on behalf of ELLs, for example,
  regarding high-stakes testing waivers or test accommodations.

SITUATION 1 Why is it taking my more recent immigrant and refugee students so much longer to complete the English Language Development (ELD) program than the students I had a few years ago?

Targeted Strategy 1: Check into students' backgrounds.

How much formal education children have received in their native language
will greatly affect how quickly they progress in schools in North America.
In fact, a large-scale study by Thomas and Collier (2001) led the researchers
to conclude, "The strongest predictor of L2 student achievement is the
amount of formal L1 schooling. The more L1 grade-level schooling, the
higher L2 achievement." Asking questions about ELL children's backgrounds
will allow teachers to accommodate the needs of these children and adjust
expectations about how much time the students will need ELD support.
Some questions that teachers will want to ask parents or agency support
groups include the following:

- How much time did the child spend in school?

- Has the child's schooling been interrupted?

- When was the last time the child attended school?

- Did the child study in the home language?

- Is there a written form of the home language? If so, are the parents
  literate in the home language (or another language)?

- What kinds of trauma may affect the child's ability to concentrate?

Targeted Strategy 2: Teach students how to "do" school.

Students who have had little or no formal schooling are not just learning
a new language; they are also adjusting to the academic culture of school.
Sitting for long periods of time, using fine motor skills for writing with a
pencil or cutting with scissors, using computers, asking permission to leave

the room, and raising their hands to speak are a few examples of aspects of school that may be new to them. While teachers should uphold clearly stated standards of behavior for all children, they also should be prepared to explicitly model and instruct children in school conduct and encourage the newcomers' peers to do so as well—peer buddies can be hugely helpful to newcomer ELLs.

Targeted Strategy 3: Contact community support organizations.

Community agencies and refugee resettlement groups can provide information about new groups of immigrants and refugees entering the community and may also have in place support services for families, such as helping with basic living needs, transportation, or after-school tutoring. If these services are not in place already, agencies can work collaboratively with schools to write grants and look for other ways to support these services.

Targeted Strategy 4: Enroll students in after-school programs.

Students who have had little or no education in their home countries often benefit greatly from after-school tutoring and homework assistance. Refugee resettlement agencies, community support groups, and schools can work together to secure the financial resources to support these programs.

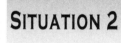 **SITUATION 2**   Which countries, languages, and cultures are we likely to see in the next few years in our schools?

Targeted Strategy 1: Contact national organizations.

Information about national trends in immigration, refugee resettlement, and secondary migration within a specific country can be obtained from the following organizations, which can often provide information about where to find local organizations.

- *Cultural Orientation Resource Center (COR)*
  The center is housed at the Center for Applied Linguistics (CAL), and offers orientation resources for refugee newcomers and service providers throughout the United States and overseas.
  www.cal.org/co/

- *National Clearinghouse for English Language Acquisition and Language Instruction Educational Programs (NCELA)*
  NCELA is funded by the U.S. Department of Education's Office of English Language Acquisition (OELA). It is authorized to collect, analyze, synthesize, and disseminate information about language instruction, educational programs for limited English-proficient children, and related programs.
  www.ncela.gwu.edu

- *U.S. Department of Homeland Security*
  The department produces data and statistics on foreign nationals who have been granted permanent residence or are applying for asylum or refugee status.
  www.dhs.gov/ximgtn/statistics

- *Church World Service (CWS)*
  CWS is the relief, development, and refugee assistance ministry of 35 Christian denominations (Protestant, Orthodox, and Anglican) in the United States.
  www.churchworldservice.org

- *Episcopal Migration Ministries (EMM)*
  EMM carries out a national program of refugee resettlement through a public/private partnership with the U.S. government.
  www.ecusa.anglican.org/emm.htm

- *Catholic Charities USA*
  One of the largest social service networks in the United States, Catholic Charities assists local agencies in refugee resettlement and provides networking opportunities, national advocacy, program development, training and technical assistance, and financial support.
  www.catholiccharitiesusa.org

- *Association of Jewish Family and Children's Agencies (AJFCA)*
  This organization is composed of more than 140 Jewish family and children's agencies and specialized Jewish human service agencies in the United States and Canada. Member agencies assist Jewish refugees and immigrants.
  www.ajfca.org/facts.html

- *Center for Applied Linguistics (CAL)*
  CAL is a private, nonprofit organization working to improve communication through better understanding of language and culture.
  www.cal.org/index.html

- *U.S. Committee for Refugees and Immigrants (USCRI)*
  The committee addresses the needs and rights of refugees and immigrants.
  www.refugeesusa.org

Targeted Strategy 2: Contact local agencies.

Local community support groups and refugee resettlement agencies are the best sources of information for and about immigrants and refugee families. The national agencies listed above often have information about where to find local services. Teachers can also contact community centers within their locale's ethnic community.

Targeted Strategy 3: Locate resources about ethnic groups.

Most of the agencies mentioned above have information available about ethnic groups that are currently in schools and slated to arrive in the near future. The Center for Applied Linguistics (CAL) regularly publishes profiles of the history and cultural background of refugee populations. Family members of ELL students can also share information about their cultures and recommend readings about their countries and cultures.

Conflicts Between Students

Any time that communities—including schools and classrooms—undergo change, there is the potential for conflict. Increased numbers of ELL students bring with them the opportunity to enrich a school's and community's global understanding. They also bring the potential for cultural clashes and misunderstandings, even in the elementary grades. Conflicts may arise between ELL students and the native English-speaking population or among groups of ELL students. These conflicts can be grounded in race, religion, nationality, ethnic background, gender, or other factors.

Many refugee children and families have lost family members and homes because of ethnic or tribal warfare. Not surprisingly, these rivalries and hostile feelings often carry over to their new country. Once families arrive in the U.S., the stress of poverty, cultural shock, and poor living conditions can fuel conflicts that manifest themselves in aggressive behavior and, sometimes, gang warfare.

All children need to feel safe in their schools. It is the school's responsibility to understand the nature of the conflicts, but also to take quick action to prevent all forms of physical and emotional aggression, eradicating them as quickly as possible when they do occur. See Appendix A (pp. 270–271) for a list of books and Appendix B (p. 272) for a list of videos on teasing and bullying. These resources can help stimulate discussions.

General Strategies

Although schools and teachers cannot change sociopolitical realities, they *can* make it clear that all cultures, races, ethnicities, and religions are welcome in the school, and that prejudice of any kind is not tolerated. And they can teach children strategies for dealing peacefully with anger, hurt, and prejudice. Below, we list some general strategies for schools and teachers, followed by more developed strategies for dealing with some of the most frequently encountered sociocultural issues affecting schoolchildren in North America.

- *What schools can do:*
  - ⋆ Produce clear, strong guidelines and rules about teasing and bullying
  - ⋆ Create strong relationships with community agencies and law enforcement agencies
  - ⋆ Provide professional development on conflict resolution
  - ⋆ Have parent liaisons and PTOs address conflict issues
- *What teachers can do:*
  - ⋆ Learn about potential tribal or ethnic conflicts between populations in the school
  - ⋆ Talk with students regularly about bullying and teasing
  - ⋆ Collaborate to generate norms about interpersonal communication, including bullying and teasing
  - ⋆ Include community building and conflict reduction/resolution into classroom activities on a regular basis
  - ⋆ Talk and read about different cultures
  - ⋆ Address conflicts head-on

SITUATION 1 My mainstream students aren't very welcoming of ELLs; they don't like having to work with ELLs in small groups.

Targeted Strategy 1: Set up projects in which ELLs are the experts.

Projects in which ELLs can contribute significantly include those that allow for the inclusion of information about their native countries. Rather than placing undue attention on ELLs, it is often a good idea to do this kind of sharing in small groups, where all students are responsible for sharing their customs and analyzing what they have in common, as well as their distinct experiences and customs. For example, when exploring life from an inclusive, multicultural perspective, ELL students can teach others in their group about the following:

- Words and phrases in their native language, such as the following:
  - Greetings and expressions, such as *hello, good-bye, thanks, no thank you, please*
  - Directions, such as *come with me, over there, please give me, have a seat*
  - Objects in the school and classroom, such as *ball, table, chair, book, paper, rug, pencil*
- A game, dance, and/or song from their country
- A special holiday or celebration in their culture, country, or family
- Famous people from their country
- The geography, climate, and animal life in their native geographical region (e.g., the equatorial rain forest areas in South America and Southeast Asia, and deserts or river regions in the Middle East and Africa)

Targeted Strategy 2: Support ELL student presentations.

ELL specialists can work with mainstream teachers to develop units in which ELL students visit classrooms around the school to present information about countries and cultures which the students in the classroom are studying. For example, a school in Montana celebrates its cultural diversity every year with International Day (Reed & Railsback, 2003). Each classroom hosts a nation, such as China, Mongolia, Russia, or Venezuela. Students from those nations speak about the customs, languages, music, geography, and special interests of their cultures. Students sample the country's foods, "travel" to the country using a passport, participate in a parade of flags, and sing to international music in the gym.

Targeted Strategy 3: Set up language-appropriate cooperative learning roles.

Playing a role in the classroom, such as timekeeper or errand runner, can help ELL students feel part of the group while lessening the pressure to perform beyond their linguistic ability. Illustrating, labeling, taking photographs, playing a musical instrument, sewing, cooking, and designing are other nonlinguistic ways that ELL students can contribute to group projects. However, care must be taken that they don't get stuck in these less linguistically demanding roles once they become more fluent in English.

Targeted Strategy 4: Group students carefully.

It is best to carefully consider with whom to place ELL students so that all students in a group can benefit from the cooperative learning experience. In many cases, ELL students can benefit from being included in heterogeneous groups of students. At other times, it may be useful to group students homogeneously by native language so they can support each other and clarify each other's learning in their first language. ELL students who have established comfortable working relationships with support buddies can be placed together, especially if the task is new to the ELL student.

SITUATION 2 — Some of my newcomers are bullied by other students.

Targeted Strategy 1: Use community-building activities.

Children who see themselves as part of a community are more likely to be respectful, responsible, and caring of each other. Some community-building school and classroom activities include the following:

- Cross-age tutoring programs. See Samway, Whang, and Pippitt's *Buddy Reading: Cross-Age Tutoring in a Multicultural School* (1995) for a detailed discussion of how to design, implement, and maintain a cross-age buddy reading program.

- Cooperative learning games in which students have to prepare each other to be successful. Here are the rules for one such game, Numbered Heads:
  - ★ Form teams of up to four students. Give each student a number from 1 to 4.
  - ★ Generate questions for each team. It's best to create questions that have multiple answers, so that each student with the same number can legitimately answer it (e.g., in a study of plant life, questions could include, *What are the parts of a flower?* and *What do plants need to flourish?*).
  - ★ The students work together to figure out the answers so that each team member can verbally answer the questions.
  - ★ Call out a number, such as 3. Each student with that number gives an answer. (It's a good idea to tell students in advance that they won't get credit for providing more than one answer.)
  - ★ A team gets two points for a correct answer and one point for a partial answer.

- Class meetings (e.g., working collectively to solve a problem in the classroom, such as children not sharing materials or excluding others from games at recess)
- Icebreakers, such as the following:
  - *Alliterative names*:
    - —With the class, brainstorm adjectives that can be used to describe people.
    - —Students have a few minutes to brainstorm adjectives they might use to describe themselves—this can be done alone or with a group of peers.
    - —Then students go around the class circle introducing themselves by adding an alliterative adjective (e.g., Dorothy might say, "I'm daring Dorothy," and Katharine might say, "I'm considerate Katharine").
    - —If time permits, have students go around a second time explaining why and how they decided on their adjectives.
  - *You may not know this about me*:
    - —Share some information about yourself that students may not already know. For example, Katharine has shared the following:
      - I won the outstanding athlete silver cup when I was in high school.
      - When I was in elementary school, I used to visit my relatives in the summer and help my uncle deliver milk in glass bottles from his little van.
      - I hiked the three highest peaks in Scotland, England, and Wales in 24 hours.
    - —Pairs of students have about five minutes to interview each other to learn more about their partners.
    - —Pairs take turns introducing each other, sharing one item that was discussed in the pair share.
  - *Let me tell you about our team*:
    - —The purpose of this activity is to help students find what they have in common, rather than how they are different (Vicens, 1995). It can also be a good activity when groups are new to each other, that is, a way for them to begin to form a cohesive group.
    - —Give students a set of the following prompts and designate an amount of time for them to figure out what they have in common:
      - Our team likes (*an activity*) _____. (e.g., soccer)
      - We have lots of (*an object*) _____. (e.g., soccer shirts)

- We (*do this activity*) _____ (*frequency*) _____.
  (e.g., play soccer/twice a week)
- Above all, (*this activity*) _____ makes us
  (*adjective*) _____. (e.g., strong)
- We are a very (*same adjective*) _____ team. (e.g., strong)

—Group members practice introducing their group to the rest of
the class. This can be a choral reading, or group members can
take turns in reading one of the sentences. An unassisted,
memorized introduction can also be very effective.

—Then groups take turns introducing themselves to the rest of
the class.

⋆ *What do we have in common?*:

—In this activity, students have a designated amount of time
(e.g., five to ten minutes) to generate a list of things that they
have in common. The winning team is the group that comes up
with the greatest number of things that are not shared by other
groups. Students we have worked with have listed walking to
school; gender of siblings; eye color; enjoyment of reading,
summer, or swimming; and a favorite video game.

⋆ *Liars' (or Actors') Club*:

—See Chapter 3 on Oral Situations for a description of this
activity (pp. 97–98).

- Literature study circles focus on books written by authors from
  underrepresented groups.

  ⋆ See Samway and Whang's *Literature Study Circles in a Multicultural
  Classroom* (1996) for a detailed discussion of how to implement and
  maintain successful, small-group book discussions with children from
  diverse cultural and linguistic backgrounds, and how this approach
  helps students deal with conflict.

  ⋆ For a list of authors and illustrators from underrepresented groups, see
  Appendix G (pp. 288–292).

  ⋆ For information about booksellers and distributors of books about
  diverse cultures and books written in languages other than English, see
  Appendix F (pp. 286–287).

- International festivals

  ⋆ These celebrations can be held during the day or in the evening so that
  parents can attend. Students can do the following in advance:

    —Practice dance performances, including traditional dances from
    different cultures or countries

—Rehearse musical performances, using modern and/or traditional instruments

—Prepare fashion shows of traditional clothing; write a script describing the clothes for the narrator

—Draw pictures of the geographic location where they were born

—Make maps of their native lands

—Write invitations to family and community members

—Identify music to be played at the festival

—Make labels for artifacts that will be displayed and food that will be served

★ We have found that ELL families are eager to share their favorite traditional foods and welcome the opportunity to share their cultures in this way. The best school international festivals that we have attended have included the following:

—Performances by children (e.g., dancing, playing music, putting on a fashion show, putting on skits)

—Displays of labeled artifacts that come from the diverse cultures in the school. These displays often help enormously in initiating conversations.

—Food from diverse cultures

—Attendance of all age groups—very young children can act as icebreakers for many adults who feel uncomfortable talking with strangers, but will do so when they see a very small child.

—School faculty and staff make a concerted effort to welcome and interact with family members.

⦿ School-wide murals also contribute to a sense of community. Students, school faculty and staff, parents, and community members can collaborate on designing and painting the mural.

⦿ School counselors are often excellent resources for community-building activities, such as Character Counts (www.charactercounts.org) or The Caring School Community (www.devstu.org/home.html).

Targeted Strategy 2: Set up norms for tolerance.

On a regular basis, discuss tolerance and bullying with the class. Post norms for behavior, explanations of what bullying is, and what to do if you see bullying or are bullied. Some strategies for dealing with bullying include the following:

⦿ *If you are being bullied:*

★ Don't keep it to yourself—tell an adult (e.g., a teacher, parent, coach, or playground supervisor).

* Stay calm and try not to show that you are scared or angry, as bullies tend to feed on reactions.
* Ignore or walk away from the bully
* If ignoring doesn't work, tell the bully to stop (e.g., *Stop that! That's not funny* or *How would you like it if someone did that to you?*).
* Don't fight back—a bully can't be bullied into changing his or her actions. Also, it's dangerous.

* *If you see bullying*:
  * Refuse to join in, because bullies thrive on an audience—if you aren't part of the solution, you're part of the problem.
  * Be a friend—if you know someone is being bullied, offer to walk or play with that person at recess or sit with him or her at lunch.
  * Walk up to the person being bullied and say, *Can I help?*
  * If offering to help doesn't work, get adult help—if you aren't part of the solution, you're part of the problem.

Targeted Strategy 3: Teach ELL students language for addressing bullies.

In the classroom, role-play bullying behavior and how to respond to it. Teach phrases such as, *Stop that, I don't like it*, or *Please leave me alone*. Include examples of what to do if you see someone else being bullied. (Please review the previous strategy for more details.)

Targeted Strategy 4: Monitor high-incidence bullying areas.

Bullying is most likely to occur outside of the classroom. Schools should take care to have an observant adult presence in high-incidence areas, such as playgrounds, cafeterias, and hallways.

Targeted Strategy 5: Prepare class for ELL students.

Teachers can prepare their classes for newly arriving ELL students by providing information about them, their language, and their country. In the following discussion excerpt, a teacher prepares his class for a new student from Somalia:

Teacher: Tomorrow a new student is joining our class. Her name is Zuhour. She comes from Somalia. Does anybody know where Somalia is? Can you show me on the map? It's in Africa. Who can show me Africa?

(Pat comes to the map and points to Africa.)

Teacher: Okay. Now, Somalia is in East Africa. Let's look at the eastern part of Africa and see if we can find Somalia.

(Emily comes to the map, searches in the general area indicated by the teacher, and points to Somalia.)

Teacher: Right, that's Somalia. That's where Zuhour was born. Somalia has been having a war for many years, and because of the war, Zuhour and her family had to leave her country. How do you think she and her family felt about leaving her country?

Javier: I think she feel sad.

Ahmed: Maybe scared?

Teacher: I think you're both probably right. When Zuhour and her family left Somalia, they went to Kenya. Let's see if we can find Kenya on the map.

(Teodoro comes up to the map and, with some help from the teacher, points to Kenya.)

Teacher: In Somalia, Zuhour probably spoke a language called Somali, but in Kenya she learned another language. That language is called Kiswahili. Do you think it was easy to have to learn another language suddenly?

Students: Nooo! Uh-uh!

Teacher: I agree. Now she's here in our town. How do you think Somalia and Kenya are different from here?

Rebecca: Maybe it's colder here? And we speak English.

Teacher: Yes, it is colder here. Zuhour won't be used to that. And, yes, she'll have to learn English. That will be her third language. Does anybody here speak three languages?

(Homa raises her hand.)

Homa: I speak Farsi, a little bit of French, and English.

Teacher: Right. You're trilingual, Homa. People who are trilingual speak three languages. We can help Zuhour learn English, so she can become trilingual, too. When Zuhour comes to our class tomorrow, you may notice that she's wearing a scarf on her head. Most people in Somalia are Muslim. Women and girls wear scarves on their heads so that they don't show their hair. It's part of the Muslim religious custom. Many people show their religion by things that they wear or do. Can you think of some other ways that people show their religion?

María: My grandma gave me a cross on a chain for my birthday because we're Catholic.

Teacher: Right, that's one way to show your religion.

(The teacher then shows pictures of children wearing crosses, yarmulkes, and turbans, and the class discusses the religions they're associated with.)

Teacher: In this country, everybody is free to practice their religion, and it's important to respect everyone's religion. Zuhour has already lived in two different countries and learned two languages. Now she'll be living in a new country and learning a new language. I think we'll be able to learn a lot from her. And we can help her learn about us. How can we help her?

(The discussion continues.)

Targeted Strategy 6: Include diverse racial and ethnic groups in the curriculum.

It is important to routinely include diverse racial and ethnic groups when studying all areas of the school curriculum, including literature, history, science, and art. The following appendices offer resources that can be very helpful to teachers who are diversifying their school and classroom libraries:

- Appendix C (pp. 273–283): Books for children about diverse cultures
- Appendix D (p. 284): Videos for children about diverse cultures
- Appendix E (p. 285): Books for children about diverse, alternative health practices
- Appendix F (pp. 286–287): Booksellers and distributors of books about diverse cultures written in English and other languages. Some of the books are bilingual (i.e., written in English and another language).
- Appendix G (pp. 288–292): Authors and illustrators from underrepresented groups. The bibliography is organized by ethnic group.

Targeted Strategy 7: Establish conflict-reduction/conflict-resolution programs.

Programs to reduce conflict, such as the three described below, can be implemented by one classroom or an entire school.

- TRIBES (Gibbs, 2007) is a process for enhancing learning and human development by creating communities where all students feel included, accepted, and safe. Four agreements are honored: attentive listening, appreciations/no put downs, mutual respect, and the right to pass. Students learn a set of collaborative skills so they can work well together in long-term groups (tribes). More information about the TRIBES process can be found at www.tribes.com/how_tribes_learning_works.htm.
- Peacemakers is a set of lessons that teaches the value of peaceful behavior. Students study the social skills needed to avoid conflict. Peacemakers includes lessons in anger management, problem solving, empathy, assertiveness, conflict resolution, and peer pressure resistance. Students also recognize how their own behavior might provoke other children. More information about Peacemakers is available at www.applewoodcenters.org/frames_page_prevention.htm

- Positive Action Program (PAP) teaches that actions influence feelings, which influence thoughts. Parents and community members work with teachers to enhance students' self-concepts so that they behave more responsibly and perform better academically. PAP includes training in conflict resolution, diversity education, ethics, values, responsibility, life skills, and leadership. More information is available at www.positiveaction.net.

Targeted Strategy 8: Survey parents.

Some schools that are proactive against bullying send out questionnaires to parents asking about any incidences of aggressive or threatening behavior their children may have encountered. These questionnaires not only clarify a schools' stance on bullying, but also give parents an opening to discuss bullying behaviors with their children. Questionnaires to parents of ELL children should be translated into their native language, and parent liaisons can make follow-up phone calls to parents who do not respond.

SITUATION 3 — My ELL students are teased because of their clothing and school equipment.

In *Our Own Stories* (Dresser, 1993), a young Vietnamese girl writes about her first day of school in the U.S. when she mistakenly wore a nightgown to class. She describes how confused she felt when the other children in the class laughed at her, and how embarrassed she felt when an Asian teacher explained to her that what she thought of as her "dress of lace" was actually a nightgown for sleeping. It is not uncommon for ELL children to find themselves in situations where their dress, school bags, or other equipment are inappropriate or different from those of other children. For example, we have known immigrant boys who have come to school wearing clothing or school equipment that is viewed in North America as girls' clothing (e.g., wearing a pink jacket, backpack, or sneakers). ELL families and school staff need education and cultural understanding in order to avoid the kinds of teasing and embarrassment that result from cultural differences or misunderstandings. Many of the issues discussed in Situation 2 surrounding bullying can be helpful in dealing with teasing behavior. The following are additional strategies:

Targeted Strategy 1: Address teasing head-on.

Norms against teasing should be talked about and posted in the classroom. Teachers should include teasing prevention lessons as a regular part of their curriculum. These lessons should include discussions about the difference between friendly and hurtful teasing. See Appendix A and Appendix B (pp. 270–272) for books and videos dealing with teasing and bullying—these resources can help stimulate discussions. Teachers can also conduct role-playing activities in which children take the part of someone being teased, someone doing the teasing, silent bystanders, and friends who intervene. The discussions that surround these types of activities can go a long way in educating children about the consequences of hurtful behavior and how to prevent teasing.

Targeted Strategy 2: Address issues of inappropriate dress and school equipment in parent orientations.

Parent orientations or handbooks are good places to discuss standard clothing and school equipment. For example, immigrant families may not be familiar with backpacks for children and places where they can be purchased inexpensively, including secondhand stores.

Targeted Strategy 3: Contact religious groups and social agencies for support.

Refugee resettlement agencies and community groups can discuss issues of appropriate dress and school equipment with client families. These groups often accept and distribute donations of clothing and other school items. Religious groups are another resource for clothing and school supplies. If these groups are presented with a list of needed school supplies, many are willing to fill individual backpacks for children in needy families.

Dissonances Between Community Expectations and School Practices

Most people have opinions, even strong opinions, on what school should look like and what it should do; this is true of immigrant and refugee families, also. In large part, this is due to school experiences that we have had, both positive and negative, and these form the basis for how we perceive that schooling should be conducted. For immigrant and refugee families, for whom life in North America is often filled with frustrations, conflicts, diminished resources, and reduced status, school may be one of the few situations over which they feel they have some knowledge, or even expertise.

Add to this reality the fact that classroom practices vary a great deal around the world. For example, in many developing countries, where classes are huge, (e.g., 50 to 100 students in one class), a didactic, transmission approach to teaching is often the norm, including rote learning, memorizing, and chanting lessons. If children and their families are familiar with this mode of instruction, it can be very challenging for them to adjust to more learner-centered approaches that they may encounter in North American schools.[1]

Another type of dissonance occurs when teaching practices in North America are much less progressive or learner-centered than those of the home country. For example, in Japan and Korea, there is a strong tradition of an inquiry approach to mathematics learning that is often missing in North American classrooms. Similarly, when children come from countries where students have been exposed to high levels of math and science instruction, it can be very alarming to both parents and students when the content demands are reduced in North American schools.

A third area of dissonance that is often encountered revolves around teacher-student dynamics, and there is a wide range of specific dissonances. For instance, some parents have come from countries where corporal punishment is the norm and they don't understand why teachers don't smack or physically punish children who have transgressed. In many countries, classrooms are relatively quiet, and when the teacher speaks, he or she gets the undivided attention of students. So, it is of great concern to immigrant families when they see what appears to be chaos in the classroom and children appear not to be paying attention. When children come from cultures where being quiet and deferential and not expressing an opinion to an adult are considered good behavior, it is hard for some parents to see their children chastised for being unassertive and quiet. When children encounter these huge differences in expectations and behavior, it can be very confusing and lead them to behave inappropriately.

General Strategies

Understanding the dissonance is the first step toward dealing with it. For example, what does the teacher expect as opposed to what does the student expect? And what are the underlying causes of these expectations? Flexibility on the part of the teacher and the ELL student and families may sometimes be the solution. For example, we have encountered the following situations and arrived at solutions that make sense to both the home and the school:

- Teachers changed homework policies so that children who were babysitting or going to work with their parents had an extended time to complete assignments.

---

[1] A transmission model of teaching/learning is, of course, still common in North America, particularly when mandated, scripted textbook teaching is the norm, as has become increasingly common in the United States in the last five years, since the passing of the No Child Left Behind Act (NCLB).

- The parents of a sick child who had been visiting traditional healers, but remained quite sick, agreed to take their child to a physician practicing Western medicine who consulted with the traditional healers.

- Teachers adopted certain practices used by school systems in other countries, such as an inquiry approach to math.

There are times, however, when practices commonly used in some cultures, such as spanking or beating, are unacceptable or illegal in North America, and schools and community organizations must make that very clear to immigrant families.

Schools should make every attempt to respect and tolerate religious differences, such as Muslim girls wearing headscarves or Sikh boys wearing turbans and bracelets. In order to inform their classes about unfamiliar customs and practices, teachers can invite parents or other guest speakers into classrooms to share aspects of their cultures. This can be extended to the entire school community through a school-wide international festival, which can provide an excellent avenue for discussions about cultural differences (and similarities).

SITUATION 1 My students do not like doing group work where all students get the same grade.

Targeted Strategy 1: Explain the purpose of group work.

When students object to one grade for an entire group, it is important to explain to them the following:

- Why they are being asked to do group work—e.g., to learn from and with peers, and to learn to work together

- The importance of doing one's fair share of the work, but that contributions may not be identical because group members have a range of skills and talents

Targeted Strategy 2: Arrange multifaceted group work.

Make sure that group work is multifaceted so you can accommodate different learning styles and talents. Also, encourage students to use audio and visual materials, including multimedia and PowerPoint presentations. Be prepared to teach the students how to use these tools, if they are not familiar with them. In addition to traditional cooperative learning roles, new ELL students can contribute to group work by illustrating, labeling, designing, sequencing, organizing, producing music, running errands, and providing information in their native language (if translators arc available).

Targeted Strategy 3: Teach non-ELL students strategies for working effectively with ELLs.

Non-ELLs can get frustrated when ELL peers don't understand or have a hard time completing academic tasks quickly or accurately, unless they are given strategies for working with ELLs. Such strategies include the following:

- Allowing enough time for ELLs to process questions and requests and to formulate responses

- Using gestures and pictures to explain things

- Listening attentively

- Paraphrasing what they hear

Targeted Strategy 4: Group students carefully and monitor progress regularly.

Group students very carefully, making sure that ELLs are in groups where they can succeed. Observe groups carefully by moving around the classroom. Watch and listen, at close range and from a distance. It is important to monitor groups regularly, so check in on their progress and ask about their future plans frequently.

Targeted Strategy 5: Teach students how to recognize, raise, and deal with problems.

Social skills do not magically appear when cooperative learning strategies are employed. Instead, social skills must be taught to students just as purposefully and precisely as academic skills. It is essential to be explicit about the kind of behavior you expect. Strategies that can foster successful group work include:

- *Making sure that students understand group work expectations*
   Shown below are some basic norms, which all students will do:
   - Contribute and help
   - Listen carefully to others
   - Encourage everyone in the group to participate
   - Praise helpful actions or good ideas
   - Ask for help, if needed
   - Check to make sure everyone understands
   - Stay on task

- *Modeling what these behaviors look like*

  Simple role-playing that includes appropriate and inappropriate behaviors can be very effective. We have noticed that students seem to better internalize appropriate behaviors after brainstorming these behaviors in a role-play.

- *Having students evaluate their behavior*

  If group members are not behaving appropriately, it can be helpful to do the following:

  - Assign someone to the gatekeeper role—this person has the responsibility of ensuring that behavioral expectations are met.
  - Have everyone in the group evaluate each other.

- *Allowing time for reflection and debriefing*

  Following group work, it is essential to allocate time for debriefing so that problems such as students not being prepared, goofing off, or putting down group members can be presented and solutions discussed and modeled through role-plays.

Targeted Strategy 6: Prepare a contract.

It is often useful to have the group prepare a contract together, listing the roles for each member of the group, along with deadlines (and signing off on it). At the end of the group work activity, ask students to assess the effectiveness of the group, as well as the contributions and work of each group member. It is important to spend time with students before beginning group work to develop a set of guidelines for effective group work. At this time, it is important to discuss how "same" is not necessarily "equal." It is not reasonable to expect a newcomer to be able to do the same kind of research that native speakers might do, but he or she can have other important roles, such as illustrating or labeling text that has been developed by other group members. Emphasize that all group members need to work hard for themselves and on behalf of the entire group—students can anonymously rate each other's contributions, and the teacher can give a group grade and individual grade based on feedback from group members. See Figure 1.1 (p. 32) for a form to use for this purpose.

Targeted Strategy 7: Don't always grade group work.

Although it is important for students to learn to work together, not all group work has to be graded.

Figure 1.1 Group Project Contract

Project: _____ Date: _____

Tasks to be completed	Person responsible	Due date	Signature

Names of Group Members:

Assessment of Group

How well do you think your group worked together?

Not very well: _____   OK: _____   Very well: _____   Superbly: _____

Please explain your rating:

What were the strengths of your group work?

What were the limitations of your group work?

Please rate each member of the group, including yourself:

Group member	Contributions	Difficulties encountered

SITUATION 2 Many of my ELL students never look directly at me when I am talking with them, which can sometimes feel awkward and sometimes downright rude.

In many countries around the globe, including China and Latin American countries, a sign of respect, particularly when being chastised, is to lower one's eyes and avoid eye contact. This situation, however, is just one of many cultural differences affecting classroom behavior that teachers may encounter when working with ELL students. Recognizing and understanding typical behaviors is not stereotyping. Behaviors are part of a larger culture and should be understood within that cultural context, rather than viewed as isolated behavior that may be perceived as strange.

Targeted Strategy 1: Understand cultural differences.

Understanding cultural differences helps to prevent misunderstandings about behavior that is thought to be rude. See Appendix H (pp. 293–294) for a list of behaviors that may appear to be rude or strange in North America, but reflect standard conduct in other parts of the world. In addition, the Cultural Orientation Resource Center at the Center for Applied Linguistics (www.cal.org/topics/rc/index.html) produces culture profiles to promote understanding of new refugee populations. Culture profiles provide short introductions to the history and cultural background of refugee populations. Local refugee resettlement and community service agencies are other good resources for cultural information.

Targeted Strategy 2: Explain your feelings.

Just as it is incumbent upon the teacher of ELL children to understand behaviors that are culture based, it is equally incumbent upon them to teach norms and practices in the new culture. Often, the most effective response is for teachers to be clear and explicit about their own expectations or those prevalent in North American society. Teachers can respectfully explain to ELL children and their parents their feelings about specific behaviors. As ELL students become part of a mainstream class, everyone in the class must be prepared to adapt and broaden his or her understanding. However, like language learning, cultural understanding does not happen spontaneously; it is a process that takes time and effort.

SITUATION 3 — My students come to school really tired because of family responsibilities.

Many parents of ELL children are in this country without the support of family or friends. Single parents or parents who work two or three jobs sometimes have no recourse but to have older children care for younger ones, or to take their children to work with them rather than leaving them at home unsupervised.

Targeted Strategy 1: Visit homes and talk with the family.

Parents may not realize how late hours and lack of sleep affect their children's school day. Teachers and parents may be able to come up with a solution, such as seeking the assistance of a neighbor or friend for child care or exploring social service agency support.

Targeted Strategy 2: Provide a napping place.

Schools or teachers can provide a quiet place, such as the nurse's office, for children who have family responsibilities and are extremely tired.

Targeted Strategy 3: Encourage children to talk and write about their experiences.

Teachers should recognize the value in the experience gained by children shouldering family responsibilities. Despite the difficulty of their circumstances, children who accompany their parents to their evening jobs are getting an up-close look at what a real job is like, and are seeing connections between what they learn in the classroom and real life. They can also see their parents' commitment to the family. Children looking after younger siblings are learning nurturing, patience, and decision-making skills. Encouraging children to talk and write about these experiences will help them make connections between what they are learning in the classroom and the skills they are using at home, and may help them deal with issues that arise as a result of these responsibilities.

SITUATION 4 — The parents of my ELL students are resistant to their children receiving mental health services.

Mental illness is a taboo subject in many countries, including in North America. To suggest that an individual has a mental illness may be insulting, stigmatizing, or incomprehensible to members of many cultures. Behavioral disorders may be viewed as spiritual problems or a physical illness. Care should thus be exercised in conveying any suggestion of mental illness or psychiatric disorder as an explanation for problematic behaviors.

Targeted Strategy 1: Meet with the parents and a mental health worker.

If you suspect that a student has a mental health condition, it is important to consult with the parents and ask if they have noticed the problematic behavior(s). If they say yes, ask them to explain what they think is the cause of these behaviors. Explanations of inappropriate behavior may include spirit possession, in which case families should be encouraged to seek the assistance of traditional healers in the community. Traditional healers are best equipped to work within a family's belief system, but are usually sensitive to the need to refer people to other medical services provided by, for example, official health care providers. Teachers and school mental health workers may want to read *The Spirit Catches You and You Fall Down* (Fadiman, 1998) for a sensitive and insightful account of the misunderstandings that can occur between people with traditional views of illness and those who follow western medicine.

Parents' denial of the existence of any problematic behaviors could be a fearful reaction to years of maltreatment from repressive political regimes in their home country. In these cases, it is best to encourage the parents to be alert to signs of the problematic behavior and to seek permission to have the child evaluated by an appropriate professional. Make it clear to parents that you are looking out for the child's best interest and that treatment may include traditional healers or caregivers from the family's native culture.

Targeted Strategy 2: Contact ethnic community groups.

Ethnic community groups are one of the best places to gather information about how to address mental health issues in schools. They can also provide referrals for traditional healers.

Targeted Strategy 3: Contact local refugee and immigrant agencies.

Refugee and immigrant agencies are also helpful resources about mental health issues. It is likely that these groups are dealing with similar issues with their client families, and it is best for all groups to work together with local mental health providers to best serve the needs of immigrant and refugee populations.

SITUATION 5 The families of my ELL students use practices, such as coining or beating, that are culturally unacceptable or illegal in North America.

While we must be alert to any instances of child abuse or neglect and act accordingly, it is helpful to be aware of culture-specific medical and other practices that may appear to be abusive, but actually are simply reflective of different medical practices. For example, coining, a common healing practice in Southeast Asian communities, leaves bruises on the back and other parts of the body, and there have been instances where parents have been falsely accused of child abuse. For this reason, it is helpful to explain to parents why these practices may be misunderstood.

Targeted Strategy 1: Learn about the cultural practices of students.

Cultural profile resources, mentioned previously (www.cal.org/topics/rc/index.html), include information about customary practices, including health practices, of refugee and immigrant populations. In addition, the University of Washington in Seattle offers an excellent Web site (www.ethnomed.org) that contains information about cultural beliefs, medical issues, and other related issues pertinent to the health care of recent immigrants. Two books that offer insights into cultural aspects of health care are *Culture, Health and Illness: An Introduction for Health Professionals* (Helman, 1994) and *Refugee and Immigrant Health: A Handbook for Health Professionals* (Kemp & Rasbridge, 2004).

Targeted Strategy 2: Read about alternative medical practices around the world to your class.

Reading about alternative medical practices around the world helps ELL children feel more comfortable about their families' traditional beliefs and encourages classroom discussions of different ways of viewing the world. See Appendix E (p. 285) for a list of children's books about alternative health practices.

Targeted Strategy 3: Address issues in parent orientations and handbooks.

Parents of ELL children need to know about how traditional healing practices may be misunderstood. They also need to be aware that some practices, such as beatings, may be culturally acceptable in their countries, but are illegal in North America. This information should be provided in the native language of the parents.

Targeted Strategy 4: Work with parent liaisons or community groups.

Teachers and schools can work together with community groups and other social and law enforcement agencies to help parents understand the legal implications of unacceptable practices. At the same time, these groups can work together to prevent misunderstandings on the part of social support agencies, law enforcement officials, and health care practitioners. Parent liaisons, in particular those who are members of the same ethnic group, can play a crucial role in these cultural awareness activities.

CHAPTER 2

Listening Situations

Listening is often viewed as a passive skill. However, listening requires active processing of the sounds, stresses, intonations, grammar, and meaning of the message being conveyed. Listening can be one of the more difficult demands of learning a new language, because the learner cannot always plan for or anticipate the topic being discussed. Although the results of listening are not always visible, it is imperative that teachers pay particular care that their ELL students are understanding what is being taught since, in the normal course of a day, listening is used nearly twice as much as speaking and four to five times as much as reading and writing (Rivers, 1981). In addition, listening can affect speaking and literacy, including vocabulary development, phonemic awareness, and comprehension (August & Shanahan, 2006; Fillmore & Snow, 2000; O'Malley & Valdez-Pierce, 1996). Students who can't hear sounds will almost certainly have difficulty producing them in speech or writing, or decoding them when reading. Listening to read-alouds has been found to be particularly beneficial to ELL students' language development (Krashen, 2006). Some other key issues that teachers of ELL students should keep in mind are:

- ELL students are more likely to listen actively if they are interested in or have background knowledge of the topic.

- Colloquial language and reduced forms, such as *didyaknow?*, can make comprehension difficult.

- Visual support (e.g., gestures, pictures, videos, realia[1]) foster comprehension.

- ELL students benefit from moving from one-step or other simple listening tasks to more complex, multistep tasks.

- Cultural expectations can affect listening efforts (e.g., a student who has recently arrived from a refugee camp may misunderstand when a teacher is talking about camping).

- Anxiety can affect a student's ability to listen.

Students Don't Understand or Don't Show They Understand

Recognizing whether newcomer ELL children understand what is being said to them is particularly challenging since many children go through a one- to six-month or longer silent period in which they do not respond orally. These silent newcomers can sometimes get lost in the busyness of classroom routines and instruction; however, it is essential for ELL children's language development that teachers communicate with them during this silent phase. Rather than pressuring the child to speak before he or she is ready, teachers can use other ways to gauge whether the child understands them. As ELL children move from the silent phase to oral communication, teachers can help them understand by using various speaking strategies and visual supports. Stephen Krashen (1985), one of the leading experts in second language acquisition and development, describes the need to provide second language learners with "comprehensible input + 1" (often referred to as *i + 1*). In other words, the ELL child should understand what is being said, and then be challenged slightly to extend or expand upon that understanding. Following are some ways in which teachers of ELL students can support this understanding and growth.

General Strategies

- Speak clearly, using a slightly slower pace than when speaking with native speakers—but make sure *not* to exaggerate your speech or increase the volume.

---

1 *Realia* refers to three-dimensional objects from real life that are used in classroom instruction, including tools, materials, utensils, furniture, food, and clothing.

- Provide visual cues through gestures, drawings and pictures, video, facial expressions, and writing.

- Encourage students to respond physically by pointing to or moving objects, acting, or role-playing.

- Say things in more than one way. Sometimes students may recognize one word for an object or concept but not another.

- Don't avoid colloquialisms or reduced forms, but take the time to stop periodically and give short summaries of key topics in which speech is slowed slightly and enunciated carefully. However, do not use unnaturally stilted language or speak louder.

- Write key words or phrases on the board.

- Avoid background noise or white noise, whenever possible, as this can interfere with comprehension when listening to a less familiar language.

- Place students in a quiet location where you can easily make eye contact with them.

- Assign buddies and encourage buddy or pair shares.

- Provide listening activities on the Internet or on audiotapes.

SITUATION 1
I'm not always sure if my ELL student understands me. How can I or others in the school check for understanding?

Targeted Strategy 1: Demonstrate understanding through actions or gestures.

Students who are not yet able to communicate orally can often show that they understand by pointing to an object or demonstrating an action. Total Physical Response (TPR) is a popular method of teaching languages (Asher, 2003). With TPR, students respond to commands that require physical movement. For example, the teacher can lead ELL students through a series of actions, such as this morning routine:

- Open the front door.
- Walk down the hall.
- Enter the classroom.
- Take off your coat.
- Sit at your desk.
- Take out your journal.

ELLs develop a receptive knowledge of these commands as the teacher demonstrates them. After demonstrating the action a few times with the teacher, the students can be asked to perform the actions by themselves. The teacher checks understanding by seeing if the ELL student is correctly performing each action. In addition to physically performing actions, students can be asked to point out objects in a drawing or show emotions through smiling or frowning. Colorforms (reusable vinyl stickers) or magnetic boards are useful tools for setting up more complex scenarios, such as going to the airport or choosing food at the cafeteria.

Targeted Strategy 2: Have students retell.

Ask the ELL student to retell a story or directions. Students working at a basic level can be asked to retell a story using pictures and may only give single words or short phrases for each picture, while more advanced ELLs can be asked to recap the story without visual aids. For example, ELL students with varied levels of proficiency in English listened to the story of Rumpelstiltskin on the BBC Web site (www.bbc.co.uk/cbeebies/rolymo/library/stories/rumple.shtml). They then responded to the pictures from the Web site (www.bbc.co.uk/cbeebies/storycircle/printablestories/rumpel), which reflected their different levels of proficiency in English (see Figure 2.1).

Student's English Language Level	Picture 1 (What the student said)	Picture 2 (What the student said)	Picture 3 (What the student said)
Basic	*girl*	*sad*	*man*
Intermediate	*Father tell king daughter make gold.*	*Daughter very sad and little man help her.*	*Little man make gold from straw.*
Advanced	*A father telled the king his daughter able to make gold from straw.*	*The daughter isn't able to make straw, but Rumpelstiltskin he offer to help her.*	*He spins straw into gold if she will guess his name.*

Figure 2.1: Student Responses to Rumpelstiltskin Pictures

Targeted Strategy 3: Translate into the native language.

One of the most expedient ways of transmitting important directions or key points when teaching is to translate them into the ELL student's native language. Many teachers believe that using a child's first language will inhibit development of English. On the contrary, the use of the first language can mediate tasks, so that students are better able to complete a task in the second language (e.g., Samway & McKeon, 1999, 2007; Storch & Wigglesworth, 2003). Some key issues to keep in mind when translating for ELL students include the following:

- Translators can be the teacher, an aide, or a peer who speaks the same language.

- Translation should be used mostly for beginner ELL students and then only to get across key concepts or essential instructions.

- Plan times when translation can be built into instructional time. Think-Pair-Shares (Lyman, 1981), described on p. 42, or table talks in which students explore new ideas or summarize materials presented, are good times to encourage the translation of important ideas.

- Expect and allow for the use of the native language when two or more students share a language.

- Don't overburden peer translators, and never ask a peer translator to translate sensitive or confidential information.

Targeted Strategy 4: Ask students to draw.

Have students draw pictures or symbols to demonstrate an understanding of school rules and classroom norms, classroom instructions, content area information, or even emotions. For example, a teacher working on animal classification might ask students to fill in a chart by placing the names of the animals under their correct classification (e.g., *dog* is a *mammal*). While native English-speaking children would typically write the word for the animal on the chart, the ELL child, who might not know the names of these animals in English, could draw a picture of the animal.

Targeted Strategy 5: Have students write.

Students who are unable to express themselves orally can sometimes express themselves in writing. Asking a student to write a short summary of a concept taught or make a list of important words can be particularly helpful to older children, especially if they are able to use a bilingual dictionary or electronic translator.

SITUATION 2 When I ask my ELL students if they understand, they often nod or say "Yes," but I then find out that they didn't understand.

ELL students can be embarrassed to admit that they don't understand something, especially if they think everyone else understands or if they come from a culture in which it is considered impolite to ask questions or appear different in any way. In some cases, students actually think they *did* understand, but because of their lack of linguistic sophistication or cultural background, they did not fully understand or misinterpreted the message. Rather than asking ELLs if they understand, teachers can implement the strategies described earlier to ensure their ELL children have understood them. What follows are some additional strategies for making sure ELL children understand without embarrassing them in front of their peers.

Targeted Strategy 1: Provide private time.

Provide a regular time in the day when the ELL student or students can work with the teacher, the aide, or a volunteer tutor. Encourage the students to make a note of questions or issues they didn't understand to discuss at this time. In addition, the teacher or tutor can use this time to go over any problems the child has encountered in class.

Targeted Strategy 2: Use Think-Pair-Share.

Think-Pair-Share is a cooperative discussion strategy (Lyman, 1981).

- First, students are prompted by the teacher to think about a question or observation. For example, a teacher introducing a unit on Antarctica can show it to students on a map and ask, *What do you think the climate is like in Antarctica?*

- Second, pairs of students talk about their answers or thoughts. For example, if the ELL child does not recognize the word *climate*, he or she can ask his or her partner.

- Finally, the pairs share their thinking with the rest of the class. Because they have had the opportunity to clarify the task, ask about unknown words, and talk about this topic with partners, ELL children may feel comfortable enough at this stage to share what they think with the whole class. If they do not want to share with the whole group, they will still have had the opportunity to participate in the activity and express their thoughts with a smaller audience.

SITUATION 3

My ELL student constantly says, "I don't understand," or says, "I don't understand" before I even finish the sentence.

The ELL child who tells you he or she doesn't understand, without appearing to make an attempt to understand or whose body language exhibits fear, may be an anxious child. Anyone who has entered a new environment in which they are not able to interpret the culture or language around them can understand the feelings of fear that ELL children sometimes experience. Research has shown that the less anxious and more relaxed the second language learner, the better they are able to learn the language (Dulay, Burt, & Krashen, 1982). Hence, the first step in dealing with anxious ELL children is to put them at ease. Rather than barraging the child with additional questions or information, it is better to smile and show that you are not concerned. Reassure the child that being able to express that one doesn't understand is actually a positive sign of developing language. The following strategies can help put ELL children at ease and move communication forward.

Targeted Strategy 1: Communicate nonverbally.

Hold out your hand for the child to take or guide him or her with a gentle hand on the shoulder, showing through pantomimes what you are trying to communicate.[2] Or ask another child to show the ELL student, as in the following scenario:

Teacher: Ali, you can go to the computer now and use the headphones to listen to The Rosetta Stone.

Ali: I don't understand.

Teacher: (*The teacher gently steers him to the computer.*) Brian, please help Ali load The Rosetta Stone and show him how to use the headphones. (*Brian joins Ali at the computer and uses words and gestures to explain what to do.*)

Targeted Strategy 2: Encourage children to demonstrate understanding.

Showing what they are able to understand gives ELL children confidence. When ELL children say, "I don't understand," encourage them to show you

---

[2] As always, take cues from the child about how and where to touch him or her to avoid any cultural taboos. See Appendix H (pp. 293–294) for information about taboos on physical contact.

what part of the message they *did* understand, as in the following example:

Teacher: Milagros, can you draw a triangle on the board?

Milagros: (*shakes head*)

Teacher: María and Tan, would you come to the board with Milagros. (*The teacher guides Milagros with a hand on her shoulder to join María and Tan and gives all three children a piece of chalk.*) Let's all draw a line like this. (*The teacher draws the first line of a triangle and the children follow suit.*) That's the first line of the triangle. María, what are we drawing?

María: Triangle.

Teacher: Yes, María, we're drawing a triangle. Now, let's draw the second line of the triangle. (*The children follow the lead of the teacher in drawing a second line.*) Tan, what are we drawing?

Tan: We drawing triangle?

Teacher: Right, Tan, we're drawing a triangle. Now, let's draw the third line of the triangle. (*The teacher and all three children draw a third line.*) Milagros, what are we drawing?

Milagros: Triangle.

Teacher: That's right, Milagros, a triangle. You've drawn a beautiful triangle!

Targeted Strategy 3: Have students retell.

As in the earlier example with the story of Rumpelstiltskin, on p. 40, ELL students can be invited to retell a story. The teacher can encourage the retell by pointing to illustrations and asking, "And what else?"

Targeted Strategy 4: Ask students what they heard you say.

More advanced students who appear to be using *I don't understand* out of habit can be asked, *What did you hear me say?* This question will also help the teacher better understand where communication broke down. What follows is an example of how this question can be used effectively:

Teacher: Today we're going to begin studying how to identify trees. First, we're going to go outside and find as many different leaves as we can. Then we're going to come inside and learn how to identify the leaves. That's one way to identify trees. Now, put on your jackets and line up at the door.

Jin: What? I don't understand.

Teacher: Jin, what did you hear me say?

Jin: I hear "jacket."

Teacher: Okay. Why do you need your jacket?

Jin: We go outside.

Teacher:	Right. Why are we going outside?
Jin:	I don't know (*shrugs shoulders*).
Teacher:	We're going to look for leaves from different trees. So we can identify trees. Put on your jacket and I'll show you.

SITUATION 4

We sometimes have difficulty communicating behavioral expectations to our ELL students, and I'm not sure how to handle it when ELL children misbehave.

It is essential that all children, including ELLs, understand the expectations for behavior and safety in a school. Education is highly esteemed in most countries around the world, and school personnel find that, in general, ELL children are very respectful of adult school figures. Sometimes ELL children come from school backgrounds that impose much stricter rules than children find in their new North American school. In these cases, the ELL child may be confused about exactly where the behavioral boundaries are, or assume that there are no boundaries at all. In other cases, the ELL child may not have attended school before and has no familiarity with the relatively structured environment of a school and classroom. Teachers or other school adults can sometimes feel frustrated when they can't communicate behavioral expectations to their ELL students. Anticipating the need to explain rules of behavior and safety to ELL children is the best way to prevent future problems. The following strategies suggest ways that teachers and other school staff can not only communicate with ELL children, but also establish a relationship with them to avoid potential problems or conflicts.

Targeted Strategy 1: Include expectations and behavioral issues in orientation.

Offer an orientation specifically for ELL children and their parents. If possible, invite bilingual translators to assist in these orientations. If professional translators are not available in the school district, invite parents to bring a bilingual friend. When sharing information, it is best to do so in short segments, followed by translations. Also, after sharing information on a particular topic, it is helpful to allow time for questions and comments, rather than waiting until the end of the entire presentation. Visuals, such as charts, labeled diagrams and objects, and role-plays or dramatizations can bring a presentation alive and make the content more accessible to parents and children. In addition to talking about expectations for school and classroom behavior, it is also a good idea to introduce key school personnel, not just the principal and vice principal, but the school nurse, secretary, home-school liaison, playground aides, and so on. Having snacks available after the presentation allows for continuing conversations—at such times, members of the school faculty and staff should mingle with parents, introducing themselves, inviting feedback and suggestions, and answering any questions.

Targeted Strategy 2: Create a bilingual school handbook.

Give students and parents a school handbook printed in English and their native language. The handbook should include names and contact information for district and school faculty and staff members, as well as norms and expectations regarding appropriate and inappropriate behavior, including consequences of inappropriate behavior.

Targeted Strategy 3: Make an expectations and norms poster.

Bilingual staff or older bilingual students can make bilingual posters of school and classroom expectations and norms. Posters can include a picture depicting the appropriate behavior, along with a heading and short description in English and the target language(s) of the related acceptable and/or unacceptable behavior. If the poster is laminated, it can be used many times for different purposes (e.g., post it in a hallway or in classrooms to act as a reminder and take it to a newcomer orientation meeting to inform new students and their parents).

Targeted Strategy 4: Teach common facial expressions and gestures for expressing emotions.

Children from other cultures might not understand the typical ways in which North Americans express disapproval, such as wagging a finger, frowning, knitting eyebrows, or shaking the head. Other gestures that ELL children may not understand are those for "come here," a dismissive wave of the hand for "go away," and pointing directly at someone or using thumb points (as a coach might use to indicate "you're out of here") for "leave," which are expressed differently in other countries. In Brazil, for example, the gesture for "come here" looks very much like the "good-bye" wave in North America. And in Japan, the North American gesture for "come" (palm turned up and hand waved to one's self) is rude. Also, other gestures that express positive messages in North America carry different, negative meanings in other countries. For example, the circling of the thumb and forefinger to mean *that's great* has negative sexual connotations in some cultures, including in Puerto Rico; crossed fingers for "good luck" means "dirty" in Japan; and the thumbs-up gesture is considered very rude in some African and Middle

Eastern countries. Although teachers don't need to learn the meaning of every international gesture, they should make sure that ELL children understand the positive and negative meanings of gestures that they might encounter and/or use.

Targeted Strategy 5: Incorporate role-play.

In class, practice responding to reprimands, admonitions, and cautions through role-play. Children can prepare skits based on scenarios, such as a cafeteria aide reprimanding a child for throwing food—one child plays the role of the cafeteria aide, while another plays the role of the child. These role-plays allow ELL children to recognize forms of reprimands, as well as learn ways to show that they don't understand or to apologize for inappropriate behavior.

Targeted Strategy 6: Use peer translators.

Ask a peer who shares the child's language to explain what the student is doing wrong. However, don't put a peer translator in the uncomfortable role of delivering any form of reprimand or punishment. Any punitive actions should come from an adult, and an adult translator or parent should explain the rationale for such measures to the child.

Targeted Strategy 7: Talk with someone who knows the child.

In cases when it is suspected that the ELL child may actually understand reprimands in English, but is using his or her ELL status to avoid following classroom or school norms and expectations, it can be very helpful to talk with someone who knows the child. The child's ELD teacher, a bilingual aide, a parent advocate, or the child's parents may be able to provide insight into the situation. Perhaps linguistic or cultural gaps hindered the child's understanding in that particular situation. If there is general consensus that the child probably did understand the reprimand, these resource people can often suggest ways of dealing with the child and avoiding problems in the future.

Targeted Strategy 8: Help develop a relationship between school staff and ELL children.

Provide ways for ELL children to meet school staff so that ELL students will know who different adults in the school are and what they do when they encounter them outside the classroom. Invite staff, such as the nurse, cafeteria workers, office secretaries, and custodians, into the classroom to talk about what they do, or send small groups of students to interview and photograph them. Place photos with names on a bulletin board so children will recognize the faces and names. Make a point of introducing ELL students to staff members. Sometimes, the names of nonnative English speakers can be difficult for native English speakers to pronounce. However, as children are much more likely to respond positively to adults who use their name when speaking to them, it is worth helping school staff members learn how to pronounce their names.

Students Don't Understand Directions

When ELL students enroll and enter their first North American classroom, there are many aspects of school life they might find confusing. Beginning ELL students typically do not have the language to express that confusion or ask for clarification. If the teacher does not share the ELL student's native language, explaining or giving directions to that child can be difficult. ELL students entering the classroom with little or no English will commonly develop an understanding of directions in the following stages:

Stage 1	Understands little or no spoken English, but can understand pictures, gestures, dramatizations, and translations of directions into the native language.
Stage 2	Understands simple directions with continued support of pictures, gestures, and dramatizations. Understands best when sentence structures and words used are simple, and repetition and paraphrasing are used frequently.
Stage 3	Understands complex directions broken down into simple steps. Understands best when given time between each step to check for understanding and to clarify any confusion.
Stage 4	Understands complex directions with little or no support.

Figure 2.2: Stages in Understanding of Directions

Movement from one of the above stages to the next is not always clear-cut and depends on many factors, such as the background knowledge or familiarity the ELL student has with the task at hand or how much of the vocabulary or key concepts the student recognizes. Even ELL students who come to the classroom with some facility in English can become confused at times because of cultural differences between how schools and classrooms work in their native country and North America. For example, in some countries, students would never be asked to work in pairs or small groups, whereas in other countries, all class work, including tests, are collaborative efforts. Hence, an ELL child's look of confusion when asked to perform some tasks may not be because they do not understand the directions, but simply because he or she has never been asked to do the task in that way.

General Strategies

Using consistent classroom routines and language can help considerably in ELL students' understanding of what is happening in the classroom (Curran, 2003; Tabors & Snow, 1994; Wong-Fillmore, 1985). The following types of routines can be particularly helpful:

- Keeping to a scheduled time for activities helps children know what to expect (e.g., writing workshop is from 9:30–10:15 each day, followed by math).

- Designating specific locations for certain activities, such as share time at the rug and guided reading at the round table, adds to the ELL child's sense of security about what to do in each location.

- Using consistent language helps them transition more easily from one location to the next (e.g., "It's share time. Let's go to the rug" or "It's guided reading time for Alex, Marco, Alma, Hamid, and Gloria. Let's go to the round table.").

- Marking schedule times for activities on the board and conspicuously noting any changes to the schedule.

In addition to these classroom routines, teachers can help ELL children understand oral instructions by:

- Using repetition or redundancy when giving directions. For example, "You need to interview a family member tonight about his or her earliest memory. So, choose one of your parents. Or a grandparent, a brother, a sister, an aunt, or an uncle. Someone in your family (*walk over and point to a bilingual chart of family members on a wall*). And ask them to think back (*put finger to temple in the sign for thinking*) to their earliest memory (*point backward while emphasizing "earliest memory"*). Was it when they were a baby? (*point to a picture of a baby on the chart*). Was it when they were a young child? (*point to a picture of a young child on the chart*). And then ask them to tell you about it. And keep notes (*use a gesture to indicate writing on a sheet of paper*) on what they told you so you can share with us tomorrow (*point forward while emphasizing "tomorrow"*).

* Use simple structures and avoid complex structures (e.g., "Today it's cold outside. Please put on your coat" instead of "Since it's cold outside, don't forget to wear your coat when you go out to recess.").

* Leave time so you can give students the opportunity to ask questions.

In addition to these general guidelines, the following specific strategies address particular issues that may arise in the different phases of understanding referred to earlier.

SITUATION 1   My ELL student doesn't understand simple directions.

Targeted Strategy 1: Teach standard gestures for directions.

As we mentioned previously, ELL students may not recognize standard North American gestures for directions, such as "come here" or "stand up." They may have learned a different set of gestures for these commands. *The ESL Miscellany* (Clark, Moran, & Burrows, 1981) is a valuable resource of standard gestures for many common commands.

Targeted Strategy 2: Use consistent visual or oral cues for lesson transitions.

Some kindergarten teachers use musical sounds to indicate to their students that it is time to stop one activity and move to a different one. The following cues require little or no language but, when used consistently, signal to the ELL student, and all students, that they are expected to stop one activity and prepare for the next one:

* Sounds, such as ringing a bell, playing a chord on the piano, or upending a rain stick

* Verbal cues, such as *Time to line up for lunch*

* Visual cues, such as holding up a hand or counting silently to five with the fingers on one hand

Targeted Strategy 3: Change the physical location for different activities.

Students who regularly begin the day sitting at individual desks, clusters of desks, or tables as they write in dialogue journals can move to the rug area for share time, to round tables for guided reading instruction and small-group work, and back to their individual desks, clusters of desks or tables for whole-class math instruction. This will give them a clear understanding of what to expect at each location. Even if the ELL child does not understand all of the language that takes place at each of these locations, he or she will be better able to understand what kind of instruction to expect and what kind of language to listen for.

Targeted Strategy 4: Use pictures, gestures, or realia.

Demonstrate what it is you want students to do through pictures, gestures, or realia. For example, a math lesson with one or more beginner ELL students might begin in this way:

Teacher: Take out your math books (*Holds up math book*).

Teacher: Open your books to page 26 (*opens book and holds it up to show the correct page*). That's page 26. Two (*pause*) six (*walks around the room, making sure students are on the correct page*).

Teacher: Today we're going to learn about measuring. You'll need a ruler (*holds up a ruler*). Please take out your ruler (*walks around the room, making sure everyone has a ruler*).

Teacher: We're going to measure the red triangle on page 26 (*holds up book and points to the red triangle*).

Teacher: We're going to measure the bottom of the triangle (*demonstrates by pointing to the bottom of the triangle*). This is the bottom of the triangle. Put your finger on the bottom of the triangle (*checks to make sure all students' fingers are in the correct place*).

Teacher: I'll show you how to measure the bottom of the triangle. (*Using an overhead projector, the teacher demonstrates the correct placement of the ruler on the triangle and then walks around the room, checking on students.*)

The lesson continues with the teacher pointing and demonstrating at each step, and then walking around the room, checking to make sure that all the students are following the procedures correctly.

Targeted Strategy 5: Write directions.

When giving oral directions, also write them on the board. Designate a specific area for homework instructions (e.g., in the top right quadrant of the whiteboard) and ask children to write these assignments in a homework notebook.

SITUATION 2 My ELL student doesn't understand complex directions.

Due to the linguistic and cultural demands of working in a new language, ELL students often need more time than native English-speaking students to process information. This is especially true when ELL students are learning content material that is unfamiliar to them. If ELL students are still working to understand the beginning of a complex set of instructions, they will not be able to pay attention to any information that follows and can easily become lost or confused. In addition to the strategies mentioned earlier, teachers can use the following strategies to help their ELL students navigate complex directions.

Targeted Strategy 1: Teach clarification strategies and when to use them.

Teach ELL students how to ask for clarification or how to express that they don't understand. Make a poster with common expressions, including the following:

- *Excuse me. I didn't understand.*

- *Can you repeat that, please?*

- *Can you explain what _____ means?*

- *Can we go back to number 1?*

Practice using these expressions, and also practice when it's an appropriate and inappropriate time to ask for clarification (e.g., it's usually not a good idea to interrupt and ask for clarification when the teacher is already clarifying a point or when another student is speaking).

Targeted Strategy 2: Break down directions into smaller steps.

Complex directions are easier to follow if the teacher breaks them into smaller steps and checks for understanding at each step. It also helps to use terms such as *first*, *second*, *third* to make the steps sequential. For example, to complete an experiment about how plants store water, the teacher can begin with these step-by-step instructions:

- First, take a cup from the table.

- Second, go to the sink.

- Third, fill the cup with water.

- Fourth, return to your desk.

- Wait until everyone has his or her water.

After everyone has water, the teacher continues giving directions.

Targeted Strategy 3: Describe a drawing.

This activity can be done in pairs, with the teacher, or with one student giving directions to a small group of students. Only the person giving the instructions sees the picture or set of symbols, which they describe as the other students draw in response to the directions. For example, as Student A looks at the picture shown in Figure 2.3 and describes it to Student B, they might negotiate understanding as follows:

Student A: Draw circle.

Student B: (*draws large circle in the middle of the page*)

Student A: Not so big. Make it little smaller. Move it down the paper.

Student B: (*draws smaller circle*)

Student A: Draw a small circle on top of big circle—like a head.

Student B: (*draws small circle on top of larger circle*)

Student A: Put two (*pause*) like this (*draws triangle in the air*).

Student B: Triangles?

Student A: Yes! Draw two triangles inside small circle—like eyes.

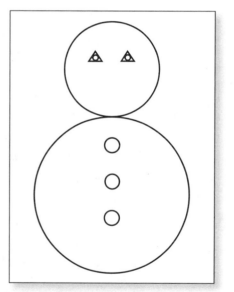

Figure 2.3: Drawing

The conversation continues until the drawing is complete.

Targeted Strategy 4: Read maps.

Sharing a map, the teacher or a student guides a partner or group members from a starting point to a destination, as in the following example:

You are at the gas station.
Turn left out of the gas station onto Davis Street.
Turn right onto West Avenue at the post office.

Go through the intersection at West and Elm.
Stop at the building on the left, next to the school.
Where are you?

See other activities for pairs in *Back and Forth: Pair Activities for Language Development* (Palmer, Rodgers, & Olsen, 1985).

Targeted Strategy 5: Give a simplified summary.

When giving directions that are likely to be difficult for ELL learners to follow, stop periodically and give a more simplified summary to help them stay on track. The bold text in the example below shows what the teacher added for the benefit of ELLs:

> *Next week, when we go on the field trip to the Museum of Science, we won't begin at our usual time. The bus is leaving at 8:00, so you should be here by 7:30.* **Let me repeat. Monday we go to the Science Museum. Come to school early. Come to school at 7:30 in the morning.**
>
> *You should wear comfortable shoes because we're going to be there for several hours and it's a large museum. There are more than 30 exhibits and you won't be able to sit down.* **So remember—wear sneakers or shoes for walking. (Teacher points to sneakers and demonstrates walking and getting tired.)**
>
> *At the museum, we will divide into groups of four. Everyone will have an opportunity to see all of the exhibits and do the dinosaur activity. We won't be back in time for lunch, but you can either bring your lunch or buy food at the cafeteria at the museum.* **Bring your lunch or bring money for lunch.**
>
> *When we return at 2:00, we'll go to our classroom to wait for dismissal.* **We come back to school at 2:00 in the afternoon. Do you have any questions?**

In this scenario, important information should also be written on the board and sent home to parents, preferably in their native language.

SITUATION 3   My ELL student doesn't pay attention when I'm giving directions.

ELL students often become accustomed to tuning out of classroom conversations, especially when they are not actively engaged in learning. The best way to get them to tune back in is to actively involve them.

Most of the above strategies for understanding directions require some kind of action on the part of the student. In the following strategies, students are also actively involved.

Targeted Strategy 1: Assess background knowledge.

Elicit from students what they already know about the activity before beginning to give directions. If the ELL student has a general idea of what he or she is supposed to be doing, it will be easier to follow directions or instructions. For example, if students are expected to read information or watch a video about Martin Luther King, Jr., and make a timeline about his life, hold up a picture of him, and ask students if they know who he is. Write his name and other facts contributed by the students on the board.

Targeted Strategy 2: Model steps and the final product.

Show students what you expect them to do and what a finished product, or similar finished product, should look like. In the example of the Martin Luther King, Jr., timeline mentioned above, after eliciting information about him, add dates to some of the facts. Draw a timeline on the board, and demonstrate how dates and facts can be added to it. Then ask a couple of students to come to the board and add more dates and facts.

Targeted Strategy 3: Introduce jigsaw listening.

Jigsaw listening is an activity in which each student has only one part of a set of directions and must work with a group to construct the complete set (Gibbons, 2002). The directions can be provided through pictures, in writing, by the teacher, or on audiotape. For example, if students are conducting an experiment with Queen Anne's lace to investigate how flowers store water, each student can be given one of the following directions on a slip of paper:

- Take a flower from the vase on the table.
- Take a container from the table and fill it with water.
- Take a bottle of food coloring from the table.
- Put four drops of food coloring in the container.
- Put the flower in the container.
- Write your group's name on the container with a marker.

Each student then reads his or her direction as the others listen. Then students discuss the best way to put the directions in order. The activity can only be completed through a combination of listening and following each student's directions.

Targeted Strategy 4: Craft activities.

Craft activities, such as making corn husk dolls when studying colonial life, or tissue paper fish for Chinese New Year, provide a here-and-now focus for listening, and the finished product provides a strong motivation for listening carefully to instructions.

Students Don't Understand Content Materials

Teachers of ELL students might be perplexed when their students converse easily with other children on the playground and have no difficulty understanding and answering questions about weekend or after-school activities, but appear lost and confused during social studies or language arts lessons. Researchers in second language acquisition have found that children learn social language more quickly than academic language (e.g., Cummins, 2000). The first set of skills, basic interpersonal communicative skills (BICS), is what children use when they chat with friends or teachers about subjects they are already familiar with and hear about every day. Children usually acquire these skills within the first two years of using the new language. Developing cognitive academic language proficiency (CALP) involves a deeper and more demanding task of understanding content area material with which ELL children may have had little or no exposure, even in their first language. These more cognitively demanding academic skills can take up to ten years to acquire. It is important for teachers to understand why seemingly bilingual children struggle with subject matter, and how to support them in their development of academic language. The following strategies are for helping ELL children with content area listening tasks.

General Strategies

- Write key words or phrases on the board. Avoid writing in cursive as ELL students often have difficulty reading it.

- Provide a pre-listening activity that explains the purpose for the listening activity, draws on students' background knowledge of the topic, and introduces key words and phrases they will hear. For example, before showing a video about tornadoes, a teacher can demonstrate the meaning of *rotate* by asking a student to turn around. She can draw a picture of clouds and show a diagram of clouds forming into funnels as she writes the words *rotate*, *clouds*, and *funnel* on the board. She can also ask students if they have ever seen a tornado in person or on television and ask them to describe what they have seen.

- One way to provide an active listening role for learners is by asking them to respond physically (e.g., raise their hands or hold up a card), or in writing (e.g., put information on an input chart or fill gaps in a cloze exercise[3]). Prior to showing a video about tornadoes, a teacher can show a map of North America and ask students to listen carefully to the video to find out which parts of the country have many tornadoes. She can tell them that, after watching the video, they will draw a picture of a location before and after a tornado hits it.

- Encourage students to make audio recordings of lessons.

- Provide support in the native language whenever possible. For example, translate key words or phrases, or help students who are literate in their first language to find translations of the reading materials in their native language.

- Provide students with different kinds of listening activities, such as small group and pair work. For example, students could work in small groups to place a symbol for "frequent tornado activity" on a map. Working in pairs, they could draw before-and-after pictures showing the impact of tornadoes, with one student drawing "before" pictures and the other student drawing "after" pictures.

SITUATION 1   My students don't understand my read-alouds.

Targeted Strategy 1: Give background information.

Before beginning the read-aloud, go over key ideas or words from the story. If it is a chapter book, show pictures of important characters or scenes.

Targeted Strategy 2: Do a story walk-through.

Begin a read-aloud by walking students through the book. For example, while many North American children are familiar with E. B. White's *Stuart Little* (1974), many ELL children are not. A walk-through of the book, beginning with the cover, will help establish Stuart as a mouse with humanlike characteristics and attributes, who lives with a human family.

---

[3] A cloze activity is one in which students predict words that are missing in a written passage and fill in the blanks with words. See Appendices L–P, pp. 299–303, for examples of cloze activities.

Showing other pages with illustrations can introduce other characters (e.g., his brother, George, and his parents), and explain incidents in the book, such as Stuart going down the drain to retrieve his mother's ring.

Targeted Strategy 3: Focus on illustrations.

Pointing to various objects and characters as you read picture books captures ELL children's interest and helps them learn the words that describe what they are seeing in the book. For example, as a teacher we know read *Jack and the Beanstalk* (Kellogg, 1997), she pointed to characters and objects the first time they appeared (e.g., Jack, his mother, the cow), then invited children to point to the various figures and objects as she continued reading the story, as the following excerpt illustrates:

Teacher: Boun, can you show us Jack in this picture? (*Boun points to Jack.*)

Teacher: Right. Tanya, where's the beanstalk? (*Tanya points to a tree.*)

Teacher: That's a tree, Tanya. Here's the beanstalk. (*The teacher points to the beanstalk. Then she turns the page.*) Can you show us the beanstalk on this page, Tanya? (*Tanya correctly identifies the beanstalk.*) That's right. That's the beanstalk.

As a teacher reads chapter books to a large class, using an opaque projector, overhead transparencies of illustrations or scanned pictures on a computer help make the read-aloud more comprehensible to ELLs. For example, an ESL teacher we know was reading *James and the Giant Peach* (Dahl, 1961) to a group of students, and she showed an overhead illustration of the two evil aunts and the various insect characters, which the class referred to in its discussion of the text.

Targeted Strategy 4: Invite children to chime in.

Many children's books have repetitions or chants.[4] As ELLs become familiar with these stories and chants through repeated readings, they can join in on the refrains. For example, in *Tikki Tikki Tembo* (Mosel, 1968, 1989), the older Chinese son's very long name is repeated several times. Dorothy encourages students to chime in with the son's long name each time it is read. Another story well-loved for its chant is *The Gingerbread Man* (McCafferty, 2001). Children can join in chorally the first time it is read. In a second read-through, they can take turns individually providing chants, such as *Run, run, as fast as you can. You can't catch me, I'm the gingerbread man.*

Targeted Strategy 5: Act out scenes.

Picture book or chapter book read-alouds often lend themselves to acting out scenes. For example, in *The Gingerbread Man*, students can line up according to

---

[4] A list of patterned/predictable books that have worked well with ELLs can be found in Appendix I (p. 295).

the order of the characters chasing the gingerbread man. In a historical chapter book, such as *Grasshopper Summer* (Turner, 2000), set just after the Civil War, students can act out Billy's grandfather blowing his bugle or the family building its sod house in the Dakota Territory.

Targeted Strategy 6: Watch the video.

Teacher read-alouds often include books that have been made into movies that many native-English-speaking children have seen, but ELL children may not have. It is helpful to provide time prior to the read-aloud for ELL children to view the movie of the book in its entirety, or in segments, if it's a longer book. The children will especially benefit if a fluent English-speaking buddy views the movie with them and helps clarify things, when necessary.

Targeted Strategy 7: Encourage reading along during read-aloud.

When children have access to a copy of the book being read aloud, they can follow along in their own copy, which gives them insights into many features of written text and reading aloud. For example, they can see how fluent reading sounds, how sound/symbol correspondences work, and how words and phrases look and are pronounced. This is particularly important for ELLs. We have seen a teacher use this strategy very effectively. She has several copies of the read-aloud book available and students take turns following along in a copy. What usually happens is that other children cluster around the student whose turn it is to hold the book and they follow along, too. If the ELL child is literate in his or her native language, it is also useful to encourage the child to read a translation, if it is available.

Targeted Strategy 8: Preview and summarize or paraphrase.

For books or sections of books that have especially difficult language, it helps to preview the scene in a few short, easy phrases. For example, we observed a teacher reading *Any Small Goodness: A Novel of the Barrio* (Johnston, 2003). She prepared the students for the description of the teacher, Ms. Pringle, by alerting them to abstract terminology she thought her students might have difficulty with. She also asked them to be prepared for a related follow-up conversation, as the following excerpt shows:

Teacher: Listen carefully while I read this section about Arturo's teacher, Ms. Pringle. He says that "she's got 'excessive sparkle.'" Something that sparkles is very shiny or bright. As I read this section, think about why he describes her that way. What else does he say about her?

SITUATION 2 My ELL students have difficulty with phonics instruction because they don't seem to hear the differences between sounds.

English language learners do not benefit from teaching that isolates parts of language, such as letters and words, before they have developed a meaningful context for them. For example, if children are asked to look at pictures of a lake, a cape, and a bat, and locate the words that have the long /a/ sound (*lake* and *cape*), ELL children are likely to be lost because they may not know the names of these objects. Even if the ELL child knows the word for an object, he or she may not hear the sounds in English like a native English-speaking child might. For example, asked to discriminate between *ship* and *sheep*, the ELL child may not hear the difference. Classroom activities that support English language should always help ELL children understand the meaning of the words and sounds that they are hearing.

Targeted Strategy 1: Use poems, songs, and jazz chants.

Listening to poems, songs, and jazz chants helps ELL children develop an understanding of the sounds, syllables, stress, and intonation of English. Children can listen to and join in on the following:

- Audiotapes of jazz chants developed specifically for ELL children by Carolyn Graham (1985, 2002)

- Rhyming songs, such as "There Was an Old Lady Who Swallowed a Fly"

- Rhyming poems, such as those written by Shel Silverstein (Go to Shel Silverstein's Web site at www.shelsilverstein.com for his animated reading of some of his poems.)

Targeted Strategy 2: Have students work with minimal pairs flash cards.

Minimal pairs are pairs of words that are identical in pronunciation, except for one phoneme (e.g., *rot* and *lot* or *pen* and *pin*). After listening to a song, chant, or poem, ELL children and their buddies can create flash cards of minimal pairs to practice. For example, after reading *Sheep in a Jeep* (Shaw, 1986), the children can make flash cards with words such as *sheep*, *steep*, *jeep*, and then test each other with the cards for a few minutes.

SITUATION 3
My ELL students understand me when I talk about things that they are familiar with, but they look totally lost when I teach science or social studies.

Targeted Strategy 1: Pre-teach or provide background information.

Bring in pictures or objects to help students understand key vocabulary and concepts prior to beginning a unit. For example, an ESL teacher we know did the following with her ELL students prior to beginning a unit on the Jamestown colony:

- Showed the students a map of the world

- Helped students locate England and Virginia, and wrote these place names on chart paper

- On the map of the world, moved pictures of ships from England to Jamestown, while talking about events surrounding this movement

- Showed pictures of the English settlers—again, writing important words on the chart paper (e.g., *John Smith*, *John Rolfe*, *James River*, *settlement*, *settlers*)

- Had a conversation with students about how they had come to North America

- Asked students to compare their arrival to the arrival of the English settlers

Targeted Strategy 2: Introduce hands-on activities.

Hands-on activities help ELL students acquire knowledge and vocabulary, and can help enormously in the development of reading and writing skills. Hands-on learning can also be used for assessment purposes by enabling teachers to measure both factual knowledge and comprehension. See figure 2.4 below for hands-on subject area projects and activities that we have found to be particularly helpful in supporting ELLs.

Math	counting, measuring, weighing, estimating, sorting
Social Studies	taking photos, painting or drawing pictures and murals
Science	conducting experiments, going on scavenger hunts, recycling, caring for animals, classifying information
Language Arts	creating books, making puppets, collaboratively developing skits

Figure 2.4: Subject-Area Hands-On Activities

Targeted Strategy 3: Allow time for pair shares and table talks.

It is very important to provide time for students to talk with a partner or in small groups about what they have just learned. For a lesson on the Amazon, for example, the teacher might begin by holding up a picture of the Amazon Jungle and asking, *What do you see here?* Subsequent pair-share questions or table discussions could focus on *How many animals do you see in this picture? Which ones are you familiar with? What kind of place is this? Where might we see a jungle like this? Why are there so many plants in the jungle?*

Targeted Strategy 4: Use charts and graphic organizers.

Charts and graphic organizers, such as KWLH (*What I Know, What I Want to Learn, What I Learned, and How I Learned What I Learned*), Venn diagrams, and timelines help children focus their listening. For example, children watching a video about the Amazon jungle can complete a KWLH chart prior to watching the video, and then complete a Venn diagram after they have watched it.[5] (See Figure 2.5.)

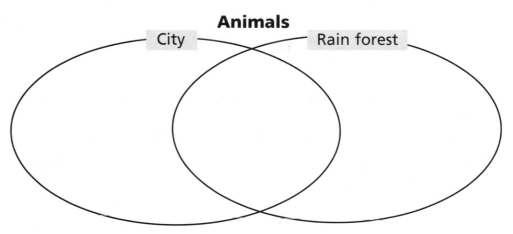

Figure 2.5: Venn Diagram for Amazon Jungle

Targeted Strategy 5: Have students work with sentence strips.

One way to actively engage ELL students in learning content material is through an activity in which they are given a series of sentences to put in the correct order. Sentence strips can be used in science to help students understand the order of processes (see the bean seed example that follows) or in social studies to reference dates and time. For example, when studying the conditions needed for plants to grow and thrive, Dorothy did the following with a small group of students:

---

[5] Additional strategies are discussed in Chapter 4, Reading Situations.

Teaching English Language Learners: Strategies That Work, K–5

- Explained the purpose of the experiment

- Demonstrated how to plant a bean seed in a small container

- Asked the students to plant their own bean seeds

- Discussed with students the steps they took to plant their seeds

- Recorded these steps (not necessarily in the correct order) on the chalkboard

- Gave each student a sentence strip and asked them to record one sentence on the strip (a different sentence per student)

- Asked students to put the sentences in the order in which the experiment was conducted (See Figure 2.6 for an example of unscrambled sentence strips.)

- Gave each student a strip to memorize

- Took away the strips and asked the students to put themselves in the correct order by listening to the other children recite their sentences.

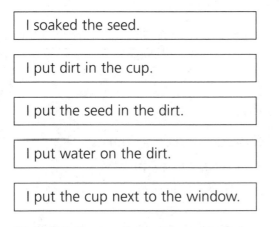

Figure 2.6: Sentence Strips Arranged in Order

Targeted Strategy 6: Work with sentence halves.

To build comprehension of subject matter material and learn key facts, it can be helpful to ask students to listen for their sentence partners or other halves.

- Give one half of a group of students the beginning of factual sentences and the other half the end of these sentences. (See Figure 2.7 for an example of sentence halves, which comes from a unit on Thomas Edison.)

- Student 1 reads the beginning of a sentence out loud.

- Students with ending sentences must listen carefully to know if they have the end of that sentence. The student with the ending for that sentence reads it out loud.

- This process continues until all of the sentences have been read.

- After pairs read all of the sentences, have them physically put sentences together on matte board or a poster.

My name is	Thomas Edison.
I was born in	1847.
When I was 14,	I published my own newspaper.
I invented	the lightbulb and the phonograph.
My nickname was	the Wizard of Menlo Park.
When I died,	the lights in the U.S. were dimmed for one minute.

Figure 2.7: Sentence Halves

SITUATION 4

Sometimes I look at my ELL students' faces and they are blank, exhausted and/or confused—as if they've stopped listening.

Entering a new culture and learning a new language is physically, cognitively, and emotionally demanding. In addition to the stresses of the school environment, ELL children may be experiencing similar tensions at home, as parents and siblings adjust to their new environment as well. Also, refugee children may be suffering symptoms from traumatic events they've experienced. (See Chapter 1 for an in-depth discussion of sociocultural issues affecting ELLs and related useful strategies.) Some common physical reactions to these stresses are tiredness, sleeplessness or oversleeping, headaches and stomachaches, and susceptibility to illness. The emotional effects can include anxiety, irritability, aggressiveness, and depression. As mentioned previously, stress and anxiety can have a significant effect on an ELL child's language development. When ELL children show signs of

listlessness, irritability, or anxiety, it is best to provide them with
a time-out from the more rigorous demands of learning.

Targeted Strategy 1: Use physical activity.

Children who have spent little or no time in a classroom and are
unaccustomed to sitting for long periods of time often benefit from
physical tasks, such as the following:

- Stapling papers

- Running errands

- Erasing the chalkboard

- Tidying a closet

- Collecting or distributing books

- Posting information on a bulletin board

- Putting pictures on the wall

   Care must be taken, however, that ELL children do not spend long
periods of time doing these tasks once they are accustomed to school life
and/or when they no longer need emotional time-outs.

Strategy 2: Offer a less linguistically demanding activity.

From time to time, invite students to do something they especially enjoy
or they have done before that has more limited linguistic demands than
they typically encounter in school. Some less linguistically demanding
activities include:

- Computer games

- Word searches

- Picture matches

- Listening to stories

- Watching videos

- Listening to songs and chants

CHAPTER 3

Oral Situations

I t is interesting that, when many of us think about using language, we first think of speaking or oral communication. However, speaking is not necessarily the first form that communication takes in second language learners, particularly in young children. Rather, ELL children's first steps toward communication often involve actions (e.g., responding to a request to sit down or open their books), gestures (e.g., pointing to the apple instead of the orange to indicate their choice) or facial expressions (e.g., crying or smiling).

Children's oral development progresses in stages, as do all other aspects of second language development, and the first stage for many children is silence. Although ELL children may be silent at first, their oral language development depends upon rich sources of oral language from those around them. As children emerge from the silent stage and begin to speak, they need to hear and read meaningful language that is progressively more complex. They also need to participate in social and academic conversations. Because their ability to use the phonological system and grammatical structures in English is not complete and they do not have extensive English vocabulary, they must know that those around them will make every attempt to understand their offers of communication with interest and questions, not with criticism or corrections. And, finally, they need to know that as they are developing full academic and social competence in English, their home language is supported and respected.

Students Aren't Speaking English

Language learners often go through a silent period at the beginning of learning a new language. Figure 3.1 gives an overview of second language production stages.

Stages	Characteristics	Approximate Time Frame
Preproduction	Responds nonverbally	0–6 months
Single-word production	Responds with a single word (e.g., *yes, no, come*)	3 months–1 year
Early production	Combines 2 or 3 words (e.g., *Pencil on floor, Where teacher?*)	6 months–1 year
Speech emergence	Uses phrases (e.g., *I see it there. Where you going? Time for lunch.*)	1–3 years
Intermediate fluency	Uses sentences	3–5 years
Advanced	Uses complex discourse	5–10 years

Figure 3.1: Stages of Second Language Production*

*Information drawn from *The Natural Approach* (Krashen & Terrell, 1983)

During this silent period of language development (referred to as "preproduction" in Figure 3.1), the learner is listening, observing, and absorbing the language, but is not yet ready to produce oral language. Although this stage can last from a few hours to several months, it can last for up to a year; this depends on a number of factors, including age, personality, cultural background, and learning environment. Some studies have indicated that this silent period may be beneficial to the language learning process (Dulay, et al., 1982).

Although learners are not producing oral language at this stage, it does not mean that they are not processing it. Observant teachers may note how emergent language learners closely watch their classmates, mimicking their behavior or silently mouthing words and phrases to themselves. In fact, parents of ELL students have reported to Dorothy that this stage can be one of the most exhausting periods of language learning as the learners carefully monitor everything around them while they try to blend in and assimilate to their new environment. Teachers can help their ELL students at this stage of language development by including them in classroom activities in nonverbal ways, such as asking them to point to a picture, close the door, or hand out papers. Pressing ELL children to speak in this early stage of learning will not speed up the language learning process. Rather, children benefit most from a classroom environment in which they feel safe enough to take the risk of speaking when they are ready. Nonverbal communication, such as smiling, learning a few words in the child's home language, and developing a system of friendly, helpful classroom buddies to act as peer support will not only make ELL children feel more comfortable and foster their receptive language learning, but will also provide the kind of safe environment in which they feel free to risk speaking when they are ready.

General Strategies [1]

General Strategy 1: Ask students to do classroom tasks that are physically active.

It is important to engage ELLs who aren't yet speaking English in the life of the classroom, and to ask them to complete tasks that do not rely on talking, but on physical actions, is one way to accomplish this goal.

---

[1] Many of the general strategies in this section are addressed very thoughtfully in a Los Angeles County Office of Education video, *So, They Don't All Speak English.*

For example, they can pass out paper, collect books, hand out playground equipment at recess, and open and close the door before and after lunch. Through these activities, students learn vocabulary and come to feel they have a meaningful presence in the classroom. At first, it may be essential to accompany the request with gestures and a demonstration in order to make the task comprehensible. Also, the teacher and student may complete the task collaboratively the first time it is done in order to make the task clear.

General Strategy 2: Develop a buddy system.

Entering an entirely new environment can be overwhelming for any child, and assigning a few buddies to the new student is a strategy that we have found to be very worthwhile. Buddies can include students who share the emerging speaker's language, but a shared language is not necessary. Also, it is advisable to assign more than one buddy to a newcomer student— buddies can be assigned for different activities or different times of the day. It is important that buddies are taught how to work with ELLs. Helpful hints for setting up a buddy system to work with newcomer ELL students are available at www.everythingesl.net/inservices/buddies.php.

General Strategy 3: Ask students to run errands.

Teachers can ask students to deliver notes or lunch orders outside of the classroom. When newcomer ELLs go on these errands, it is important that they are accompanied by a buddy to help navigate the school and its often unfamiliar personnel and routines. These activities help students learn about other parts of the school and enable them to get to know other people in the school.

General Strategy 4: Use puppets.

Familiar or endearing puppets, such as animals or the internationally well-known Sesame Street characters, often help young children relax. Frequently, children will talk to a puppet before they speak to adults. In addition to commercial puppets, children can make their own finger puppets or popsicle-stick figures. The following activities are some examples of how to use puppets to actively engage ELL students in ways that require little or no speaking on their part—both the teacher and other students can interact with ELLs while doing these activities:

- Telling stories to accompany pictures drawn by the student

- Telling stories using wordless picture books (See Appendix J, pp. 296–297, for a list of wordless picture books.)

- Telling stories using picture sequence cards

- Talking about photos in magazines or books, particularly about events that are familiar to the student

- Giving directions (e.g., *draw a circle*, *put an X under the circle*)

- Acting out stories or situations, such as classic fairy tales (e.g., *Little Red Riding Hood*) and patterned language books (e.g., *The Monster's Party*)

- Role-playing conversations, such as introductions, going to the doctor, and playing with children on the playground

- Giving and responding to directions—puppets can be used as the medium for both giving and responding to simple directions, such as *shut the door*, *throw the paper in the trash can*, and *open the book*. As ELLs become adept at completing simple directions, more complex direction can be given, such as *pick up the pencil and put it on the table*.

- Acting out songs, rhymes, and poems, including those with a counting refrain (e.g., "Ten Little Pumpkins")

General Strategy 5: Employ art, science, drama, and P.E. activities.

These activities are particularly helpful because they require high levels of physical activity, and don't require nearly as much expressive language as other subjects. Keep in mind that demonstrations and gestures will still be required when explaining tasks to newcomer ELLs.

SITUATION 1 I have students who have been in the country for almost six months, and they still won't speak in class. They only nod or smile when I ask questions.

It is not uncommon for newcomer ELLs to *not* speak for several months. The following strategies can help facilitate communication during this stage.

Targeted Strategy 1: Post pictures of classroom routines and objects.

Posting pictures of classroom routines and objects will allow both children and the teacher to point to what they need or what action is called for. For example, a teacher can ask children to point to a picture of a lunch box or a cafeteria tray to find out if they have brought their lunch. If a child appears to be sick, a teacher can use a labeled picture of the human body, and point to the part that is typically associated with a medical condition while using facial expressions and gestures to show pain (e.g., pointing to the stomach and saying *Do you have a stomachache?*, pointing to the ear and saying

Do you have an earache?, or pointing to the throat and saying *Do you have a sore throat?*). The child can point to where it hurts. Drawings should be culturally diverse and include situations or objects that ELL students will recognize (e.g., rice balls, beans and rice).

Targeted Strategy 2: Use Total Physical Response with patterned books.

Total Physical Response (TPR) is a method of developing language and vocabulary through actions (Asher, 2003). The teacher (or another student) recites a series of actions while performing them and invites the ELL student to do so as well (e.g., *stand up, sit down, sit on the chair, sit on the rug, jump, jump on the rug, pick up a pencil, put the pencil on the chair, put the pencil on the rug*). Putting actions to words helps students retain them. Patterned-language big books are particularly useful for pairing words with actions.[2] The following is an example of how teachers can use a patterned big book to incorporate TPR:

- The teacher reads the big book version of *The Monsters' Party* (Cowley, 2001) and acts out a monster's activities (e.g., *This monster likes to dance*).

- On a second reading, all the children act out the monsters' various activities.

- Other related activities include the following:
  - The teacher asks children to show the page on which the monster dances, sings, and so on.
  - After children are assigned different monsters, they stand up and do the activity of that monster when it appears in the text.
  - Children make monster puppets by coloring and cutting out figures on cardboard and attaching them to popsicle sticks. The puppets imitate the actions of the monsters as they appear in the book.
  - ELL children who aren't yet speaking can be partnered with a speaking buddy, who can ask questions, such as, *Which monster likes to sing?* The ELL child can then turn to the correct page. In turn, the "silent" ELL child can mimic one monster and the other child can turn to the correct page.

- The teacher asks children what they can do at a party and children demonstrate activities, such as twirling around and playing the piano.

- Students can make their own *Monsters' Party*–inspired picture books, using activities from the book and adding their own. The teacher can write the

---

[2] Big books are large-format books with enlarged print and a predictable feature, such as a refrain or a series of actions that are introduced with the same phrase.

pattern on the board, along with a list of activities, and the teacher or buddy can help the ELL student with words for any new activities they add to the book.

Targeted Strategy 3: Introduce hands-on projects.

Hands-on projects, such as science experiments, designing or building structures, and making papier-mâché figures, are excellent activities for ELL students during their silent period. Through these activities, students can learn content-area vocabulary and demonstrate their understanding of oral directions.

One example of a hands-on science project that is beneficial for ELL students in the preproduction speech stage involves investigating the life of a plant by planting and nurturing a bean seed. The procedure for this experiment is explained below.

- *Day One*: Show students a lima bean pod, a lima bean, and a poster of the parts of a bean seed and how seeds grow. Talk about this process in simple language, but use the appropriate terms (e.g., *seed*, *stem*). Students soak several beans in water for one day.

- *Day Two*: Students use a magnifying glass to examine the outside of the bean and draw a picture of the bean in their Life Cycle Journals. They then split the seed in half and look for the parts of the seed (e.g., the seed leaves, the embryonic or immature root, the seed coat or outer shell, and the seed leaves). They draw a picture and label the parts of the seed. Figure 3.2 shows a sample drawing.

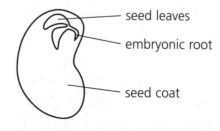

Figure 3.2: Parts of a Bean Seed

- *Day Three*: Students plant two bean seeds in separate paper cups, placing one cup in the sun and one away from the sun. They then draw and write about their actions in their Life Cycle Journals. (If students are literate in their native language, they can use this language in their journals. Although the teacher may not be able to read the entries, family members can often help students learn the correct terminology; also, students often feel very proud when they can share their journals with others who speak their native language.)

- *Subsequent Days*: Students continue to make daily observations of their bean plants in their journals. Observations can include noting how long it takes each plant to sprout, measuring the height of plants, and noting the appearance and number of new leaves. Finally, students can make Venn diagrams comparing bean seeds planted in light and bean seeds deprived of light. Figure 3.3 shows a sample.

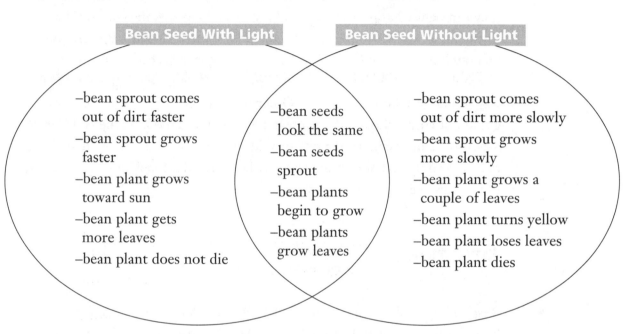

Figure 3.3: Venn Diagram: Bean Seed Experiment

Targeted Strategy 4: Take photos.

Students can use inexpensive cameras to take photos of family members, friends, and/or neighborhood locations. They can then point to items such as the tree, their house, their mother, their baby sister. Alternatively, the teacher or a partner can point to items and ask questions, such as "Is this your little brother?"

Targeted Strategy 5: Build scenarios on magnetic or felt boards.

Magnetic or felt boards allow students to build entire scenarios while still in the preproduction stage of speaking. Teachers or buddies can give TPR kinds of instructions (e.g., *Move the airplane onto the runway*, *Put the carrots in the grocery cart next to the peas*). As children's understanding increases, they can answer more complex questions and follow more complex directions. For example, when working with a magnetic board of a house, the teacher can ask questions such as *Where do you think the baby should sit?* When working with a board of a desert environment, students can be directed to add some animals that can live in a desert.

Targeted Strategy 6: Tell a story while manipulating Cuisenaire rods.

Cuisenaire rods, the slim, colored, rectangular rods that were developed for teaching mathematics, are also good resources for language development as they can be used as props in storytelling. (Like puppets, the rods offer a psychological buffer for children in the preproduction stage.) For example, in a retelling of *Little Red Riding Hood*, the longest rods can be set up to resemble the woods through which Little Red Riding Hood passes on her way to her grandmother's house. Other rods can be used to represent the grandmother, her house, the wolf, and Red Riding Hood. As the children listen to a story being read aloud or told to them, they can manipulate the rods accordingly. (Later in the chapter there are additional strategies for using Cuisenaire rods.)

SITUATION 2 I have a student who answers with only yes/no answers.

Responding in short, one-word answers is a developmental stage for ELL learners and is to be expected. As their language comprehension increases, students can be encouraged to expand their responses and even initiate conversations by providing them with situations where they can authentically produce a more extended response. Sometimes a yes or no answer is indicative of caution, so ELLs need to be in an environment where they feel they can increasingly take risks. It is important that activities and communication are focused on the extension of speech, not correction.

Targeted Strategy 1: Make use of chants, songs, and poems.

Many children who are reluctant speakers happily sing along or chime in with chants and poems. These group activities allow students to develop the rhythms, stress, and intonation of English. Carolyn Graham (1985, 2002) has created books of rhythmical chants, songs, and poems to illustrate the natural stress and intonation patterns of conversational American English. Her books and recordings of the chants, although created specifically for ELL students, can be enjoyed by all children. In a typical lesson, students listen to the recording, go over any unknown words, and then practice reciting the chant line by line. After they are comfortable with the words and rhythm, they recite the whole chant chorally and can add clapping or other forms of rhythm (e.g., patting the desk or tapping pencils together). Many of the chants have choral responses so that a group can be divided in half for call-and-response types of experiences. Also, students or pairs of students can do solos or duets. After working with jazz chants, students can modify them or create their own. For example, a modification of Graham's chant "Snow is Hot" follows:

> *Rain is wet.*
> > *Very wet!*
> > *Very wet!*
> *Gets you soaking wet.*
> > *You bet!*
> > *You bet!*
> *Got to go inside.*
> > *Go inside!*
> > *Go inside!*
> *Got to get dry.*
> > *That's why!*
> > *That's why!*

Many poems, songs, and books lend themselves to excellent practice with the rhythms and sounds of English. For example, Shel Silverstein's poems[3] and Dr. Seuss books are examples of texts that many children love to listen to and recite.

Targeted Strategy 2: Provide wordless picture books.

Illustrations in wordless picture books provide a rich backdrop for children to add their own words. For some children, the absence of words in a book frees them to produce their own. For example, Dorothy read *Goldilocks* to a group of ELL first graders and followed this reading by showing them *Deep in the Forest* (Turkle, 1992), an alternative wordless *Goldilocks* story in which a small bear enters a human family's cabin in the forest while they are away. Reading *Goldilocks* to the children first gave the ELL students words and phrases that they were able to use when narrating *Deep in the Forest*, such as *bear* and *Who's been sitting in my chair?* After a first "read through," in which the children contributed words and lines that they remembered from *Goldilocks* (e.g., "He taste the Papa cereal, but it too hot"), the students reread the book, with each student narrating a page. Later, pairs of students took turns being the bear and Goldilocks.

---

[3] Shel Silverstein reads some of his own poems at www.shelsilverstein.com.

Another teacher we know has students work in pairs to present a wordless picture book to the class, using the following procedure:

- Pairs choose a wordless picture book. (A list of wordless picture books is provided in Appendix J, pp. 296–297.)

- After reviewing the book, students collaborate on developing a narrative script. The teacher's role is to check in with pairs and provide words and phrases that they might need for their narrative scripts.

- Students take turns presenting their narratives (and books) to the class. One student holds the left side of the book and narrates the pages on the left side. The other student holds the right side of the book and narrates the pages on the right side. Pairs alternate narrating double-page illustrations.

Targeted Strategy 3: Hold class circle time.

Whole-class circle or share time is often when ELL children begin to produce more than one or two words, possibly because this is an occasion when they are most likely to be in command of the topic of conversation. It is also when ELL children have the opportunity to listen to others talk about experiences they may be familiar with (e.g., going to a popular restaurant, celebrating a birthday, getting new shoes) (Taylor, 1999). During the silent or preproduction period, ELLs may be using circle time to mentally collect words to use in the future. For example, a newcomer ELL child whom Dorothy taught pointed to her shoes and announced "new shoes" during circle time after hearing several children proudly show and talk about their new shoes. Teachers can encourage ELL children to expand upon their one- or two-word responses during share time.

- Ask follow-up questions that require more than a yes or no response (e.g., *What does your new sofa look like? What happened after the bee stung you? Why did you go to Ohio?*).

- Invite children to ask each other questions (e.g., *What did you eat at McDonalds? What color is your bicycle?*).

- Ask students to bring in artifacts or photos from home to talk about (e.g., pictures of family members and objects from their home country, such as embroidery or wooden figures). At home or at school, students can be given time to practice talking about these artifacts to help them with needed vocabulary and to increase their confidence about speaking to the whole class.

* Occasionally announce a topic in advance (e.g., your favorite season, somebody who is important to you) so that students have time to develop ideas and figure out words and expressions prior to sharing time.

Targeted Strategy 4: Tell a story with the help of Cuisenaire rods.

A set of Cuisenaire rods usually consists of ten wooden, four-sided, multicolored rods that range in size from 1 square centimeter to 10 centimeters. They were developed for use in schools to teach fractions and other aspects of math. Gattegno (1972) introduced them as a language teaching tool in a methodology he termed the Silent Way, which is grounded in the theory that language is best learned when the teacher intervenes as little as possible. Teachers using the Silent Way communicate with just a few words and occasional mimes and gestures, but encourage their students to create and manipulate language through the use of Cuisenaire rods and/or color charts. Rods can represent sounds, words, and grammatical points or people, places, and objects. The rods give students something to visually and physically manipulate without fear of overly critical responses from teachers. The rods are usually manipulated by a small group of students. For example, we observed a teacher use the rods in the following way:

* The teacher pulled out a tall rod, said, "Principal," and handed it to a student.

* She pulled out a slightly shorter rod and said, "Teacher," and handed it to another student.

* She pulled out a few shorter rods, handed them to students and looked at the group quizzically. The students responded, "Students."

* The teachers spread out her hands to the students and to the table to indicate that they should begin to manipulate their rods.

* The student with the teacher rod said, "Good morning, students, please sit down."

* The students with the student rods placed their rods in rows around the teacher.

* The student with the principal rod placed it at the edge of the table and said, "Knock, knock."

* The student with the teacher rod said, "Please come in, Mr. Black."

* The teacher with the principal rod said, "Good morning, students. How are you?"

- The students responded, "We're good, Mr. Black. How are you?"

- The conversation proceeded with Mr. Black announcing that today was Book Day so all the students got to go to the library to receive a free book.

Cuisenaire rod activities allow ELL children to use their imaginations while working with the words and structures they know and building language cooperatively with other learners. Later in this chapter, we will explain how these rods can be used to introduce grammatical points.

Targeted Strategy 5: Do information gap activities.

Information gap activities are usually done in pairs. They are activities in which one student has information that the other student doesn't have, or both students have information that their partner doesn't have. Students must negotiate the communication to gather all of the information needed to complete the activity. These activities provide structured ways for ELL students to begin extending speech and can take many different forms, including the following:

- **Describe a drawing:** One student looks at a simple picture and describes it to his or her partner. The partner draws the picture that the student describes. (See Chapter 2, Listening Situations, p. 53, for an example and a detailed description of this activity.)

- **What's the difference?:** Partners look at pictures of scenes that are almost identical, but have slight differences; however, they do not look at each other's pictures. For example, in Student A's picture, a woman is wearing a striped dress. In Student B's picture, the same woman is wearing a flowered dress. Students must describe their respective pictures to find the differences and then circle each difference, as the following example illustrates:

  Student A: I have woman in my picture. Do you have woman in your picture?

  Student B: Yes. Is the woman wear thing in her ear?

  Student A: No. Does she have dress?

  Student B: Yes. Does the dress have little round thing on it, to close?

  Student A: Yes. (*The students continue in this way.*)

  Usually, the teacher tells students the number of differences so partners know when they have found all the differences. Also, it helps if the teacher walks around the room to provide support and suggestions if students get stuck. These conversations generate a lot of vocabulary that may need to be clarified later (e.g., the *thing in her ear* is called an *earring* and *little round thing on it, to close* is a *button*). An alternative for students who may find this activity too difficult is to have them look at their pictures together and collaboratively locate and list the differences.

Look Again Pictures (Olsen, 1998) is a book filled with "what's the difference" scenarios. Another excellent source for picture differences and other information gap activities is *Back and Forth* (Palmer et al., 1985). It includes several reproducible pages of short, interactive information gap activities divided into four parts: pronunciation and listening discrimination, describing a picture, describing abstract forms and shapes, and language or word puzzles.

Targeted Strategy 6: Introduce *Toss and Talk.*

An engaging way to talk about targeted subjects (e.g., animals, playground equipment, household objects, the seashore) is Toss and Talk. The procedure for introducing this strategy follows:

- Cover a small, soft box (e.g., an empty tissue box) with fabric.

- Using sturdy rubber bands, attach pictures to the six sides of the box.

- Students sit in a small circle and take turns gently tossing the picture-covered box to each other. When a student catches the box, he or she has to say something about the picture according to the location of his or her fingers on the box (e.g., a thumb or index finger on a picture).

Alternative Toss and Talk: Toss a Globe
This activity can be played with a soft globe. Students are asked to give some information about the country that their thumb (or finger) touches or points to.

Alternative Toss and Talk: Toss the Seasons
One teacher we know glues pictures of seasons to the sides of tissue boxes and asks students to say something about the picture facing them. When students catch the box, they name the season that is facing them and then say something about what they like to do in that season (e.g., *It is spring.* or *I like to go to the park*).

As you can probably imagine, there are unlimited alternatives for Toss and Talk activities. We have learned that, for these activities to remain enjoyable, it is important to keep them short (e.g., a maximum of five minutes at a time).

SITUATION 3   I have a student who cries when I speak with him.

Entering school for the first time can be quite frightening and overwhelming for any child. For ELL children who have had little or no exposure to English, it can be much more so. When the grandson of a friend of Dorothy's was 3 years old, he spent all of his time with Russian speakers. One day, driving in the city, his parents and grandparents couldn't find the address they were looking for, so they stopped, rolled down the window, and asked a man on the street for directions. As the man was giving his father directions, the young boy, Misha, asked his grandmother why he couldn't understand the man. "He's speaking English," she replied. "Close that window and stop talking to that man," Misha told his father. Clearly, Misha's first encounter with English was a bit disturbing to him, but he was surrounded by close family members. Imagine how difficult it must be for school-age children who, in addition to dealing with a new language, may be experiencing school for the first time, or encountering a very different type of school experience than what they were accustomed to in their home countries. Stress related to cultural shock (as well as the traumatic experiences that some students have had to deal with) can result in depression or overt signs of sadness in ELL students. Children who constantly cry or manifest other signs of depression should be referred to a mental health worker—Chapter 1 addresses these sociocultural issues in greater depth. However, occasional crying when students first enter school is not that unusual, and teachers can help children overcome these periods of sadness. Here are some strategies that schools and teachers can use to support newcomers as they adjust to their new lives.

Targeted Strategy 1: Request help from bilingual aides or peers.

If a newcomer child is not able to communicate with teachers, the best resource is someone who speaks the child's language, such as a bilingual aide, older sibling, or another student. Someone who speaks the same language can elicit the source of the child's distress, which can then be addressed.

Targeted Strategy 2: Let children work with puppets.

As mentioned previously in this chapter, puppets often relax children and help them express their feelings. As an ESOL pullout teacher, Dorothy often used puppets when she introduced herself to young ELL children.

Sesame Street characters, such as Big Bird or Cookie Monster, are known around the world, and Dorothy would take these puppets with her when she went into classrooms or to meetings with ELL children. She introduced a puppet and herself and invited the child to do the same.

Teachers can also use puppets to ask ELL children about how they are feeling. In addition, we have found that it is a good idea to hand a puppet to a child or have a puppet speak to the child if he or she seems particularly tired or sad.

In addition to television characters and animals, puppets should represent different races and nationalities.

Targeted Strategy 3: Assign buddies.

Assigning a classroom buddy to a newcomer ELL helps lessen the shock of the new environment. It helps if the buddy speaks the same home language as the ELL child, but it is not necessary. Simply having a friend to play games with at recess or to sit with in the cafeteria can help ELL children feel more at home in their new settings.

Targeted Strategy 4: Incorporate music or art.

We have seen children stop crying immediately when someone begins to play a musical instrument or when they are given an instrument to play. Similarly, art is an activity that helps children through sadness. A child who misses his or her mother or father can be asked to draw a picture of the parent and other family members or to draw a picture for the parent.

Targeted Strategy 5: Encourage grandparents to volunteer in the classroom.

Children generally respond well to grandparent volunteers. These volunteers are often kindly and unthreatening and know how to soothe distressed children. Schools should encourage senior citizens from various ethnic communities to volunteer in schools. It should be stressed that limited English is not a barrier to becoming a volunteer. These "grandparents" can contribute in many ways to schools, particularly by reading to children in their native language, helping with art projects, or simply providing caring words of encouragement. Schools, in turn, may be doing immigrant senior citizens a favor, as we have heard from some seniors that they feel little sense of purpose in their new country because their children and grandchildren are busy working and going to school.

Targeted Strategy 6: Invite parents into the classroom.

Teachers can make a point of inviting parents into the classroom to participate in activities with children. Having a parent nearby or involved in the school day when a child first enters the school can help ELL children adjust to the new language and setting. Many parents of ELL children lead very busy lives and are not able to spend a great deal of time in school, but those who are able to should be encouraged to volunteer in the school or simply stop in at the beginning or end of the day so children can show what they are doing and connect their new school life with their home life.

Targeted Strategy 7: Employ animals and nature artifacts.

Animals in the classroom, such as hamsters, rabbits, or lizards, can be great stress relievers. Dorothy had two lizards and a collection of seashells in her ESOL pullout classroom, and new children often headed immediately to one or the other upon entering the room. If they could communicate in English, they would often ask what the lizard's name was or what it ate. If they were a newcomer, they would often simply point. Dorothy or the newcomer's classmates would respond and offer more information, such as the lizard's color or a description of the sticks and other objects in its cage. If the students migrated to the seashells, Dorothy would pick up the conch shell, put it up to her ear, and then put it up to the ear of the child. Children usually smiled at the sound, which is like the rush of ocean at the beach. Children often chose a seashell to take with them back to their mainstream classroom, generating conversation with the mainstream teacher and classmates.

One way of welcoming newcomers and providing less stressful opportunities to talk is to give them (and their buddies) responsibility for taking care of classroom pets, including giving food and water or cleaning the cages. Teachers with classroom pets should make sure that parents are aware of this, and that ELL children do not have allergies or other medical sensitivities. And, of course, all children should be taught proper hygiene for dealing with classroom animals (e.g., washing their hands before and after handling animals, and the proper disposal of animal waste), as well as how to handle the animals (e.g., how to pick up a hamster or rabbit).

SITUATION 4   I can't communicate with my ELLs because we don't have a shared language yet.

One of the questions ELD specialists are asked most frequently is "Do you speak all of the languages of your students?" closely followed by "How do you communicate with them if you don't?" There is no question that speaking the same language as one's students is ideal. That is why it is important for schools to have bilingual support specialists and parent liaisons who speak the same language as ELL children. However, to acquire English, ELL children also need opportunities to communicate in their new language. Providing a supportive relationship that accepts the stages of language development and helps students move forward through these stages is an important role for teachers to play for their ELL students. Anxiety is an inhibitor to language learning; hence, the most important initial communication tactic is to ensure that ELL children are comfortable with the teacher, their classmates, and their surroundings. Teachers should closely monitor their ELL children for signs of comprehension, and can use the following strategies to make sure they are connecting with students:

Targeted Strategy 1: Smile.

Children are sensitive to signs of distress or unease on the part of others. When communication breaks down or when an ELL newcomer speaks little or no English, it is natural for teachers (and sometimes English-speaking students) to feel frustrated. However, physical indications of those frustrated feelings, such as furrowed brows or sighs, will most likely make the child feel responsible. Keep smiling, and patiently continue to speak in a quiet (not raised) voice, and use gestures, pictures, or other means of connecting until the child understands.

Targeted Strategy 2: Have plenty of visual support.

Photographs, pictures, posters, realia, and gestures are all ways that help ELL children see what you want them to do or what you are referring to. Pictures or posters relating to important classroom events (e.g., removing objects from backpacks, going to the cafeteria for lunch, going to the playground at recess) can be displayed on the wall so that teachers can refer to them as needed. One way for teachers to indicate that students should open their books is by explaining what to do while elaborately opening a book and pointing to the page number, and then writing the number on the board. A teacher who notices that a child has a dull pencil can explain what to do by accompanying the verbal directions with gestures (e.g., touching the child's pencil, going over to the pencil sharpener and pointing to it, beginning to sharpen a pencil to show how it works, and then pointing to the child's pencil and the pencil sharpener). Whenever possible, anticipate specific communication needs and provide some kind of visual support—

it can make a big difference in whether newcomer ELL children understand even a little of what is happening around them, or whether they are completely confused.

Targeted Strategy 3: Provide picture dictionaries and bilingual dictionaries.

Picture dictionaries are essential tools for communicating with newcomer ELL children, and they are often helpful at much later stages of language development as well. Several publishers of books for ELL students publish picture dictionaries with pages grouped around specific themes, such as school, health, or clothing. Some of these picture dictionaries provide bilingual versions (e.g., English-Spanish or English-Vietnamese). (See Appendix K, p. 298, for a list of picture and visual dictionaries.) Older ELL children who are literate in their native languages can use bilingual dictionaries to look up words they want to communicate, or a teacher can look up the word they want to express in English and point to the word in the child's language. Keep in mind, however, that dictionaries have somewhat limited use as the same word may mean very different things (e.g., *cool*, meaning "not warm" and "excellent").

Targeted Strategy 4: Observe ELL students.

Pay careful attention to ELL children's faces to monitor their feelings. Notice what an ELL student is interested in, what he or she may want to talk about or knows, and then select a conversation topic that is meaningful to that child. For example, when visiting a kindergarten classroom, Dorothy noticed that Juanito went directly to the play area and chose a truck from a group of toys. His teacher went over to him and asked, "Juanito, do you like trucks?" He nodded. "Do you have a truck at home?" the teacher asked. Juanito looked up, smiled and nodded. "What color is your truck?" she asked. "Is it green like this truck?" Juanito shook his head, and pointed to a red car. "Oh, your truck is red," she responded. Juanito nodded. Later, during drawing time, the teacher selected a red crayon for Juanito, gave him the truck, and asked, "Would you like to draw a picture of your red truck?" He did. Juanito's teacher used his interest in the toy truck to initiate a conversation with him and continued to interact with him, despite the fact that he used minimal language. She asked questions that Juanito could easily respond to with a nod, a shake of his head, or a one-word response.

Targeted Strategy 5: Use actual names of people and objects rather than pronouns.

Make a point of learning the correct pronunciation of ELL children's names and use their names frequently when speaking to them or about them. In the conversation described in the previous strategy, notice that Juanito's teacher called him by name as she initiated the conversation. She regularly referred to the truck, always calling it by name instead of *it* or *this one* or *that one.*

Targeted Strategy 6: Focus on the present and the concrete.

It is difficult for a newcomer ELL child to talk about the future or the past because they don't have a frame of reference. When Juanito's teacher asked him about the truck, it was something they could both look at and touch. Juanito was able to point to something red to indicate that his father's truck was red. Then, when his teacher invited him to draw a truck, she showed him the red crayon and brought the truck to him.

Later that day, Dorothy noticed that the same teacher complimented a student on her dress. "That's a beautiful dress, Zalikha. I like the flowers on it." The teacher pointed to the flowers. Then she pointed to the flowers on her own sweater. "My sweater has flowers on it, too." The teacher was able to make the connection between the flowers because they were both wearing flowers. If the teacher had referred to the flowers on a sweater she had worn the day before, it is not likely that Zalikha would have made the connection.

Targeted Strategy 7: Establish a morning greeting and afternoon leave-taking routine.

ELL children flourish with routines (as do all children). A good way to make connections with ELL children is to establish a routine morning greeting and afternoon leave-taking. For example, some teachers greet children at the classroom door and give them the choice of a handshake or a hug as they enter the classroom in the morning. The teachers then do something similar at the end of the day, expressing explicit gratitude for what each child accomplished that day (e.g., *Thank you, Javier, for taking care of the math books*; *I appreciate how hard you worked in math, Mari*; *Make sure to tell your mom and dad about how you published your first book today, Lai*).

When greeting and interacting with children, it is important to be aware of cultural norms that may differ from our own. For example, many Western teachers gently touch children on the tops of their heads as a sign of caring, but in some cultures, it is not acceptable to touch the top of the head because it is considered a religiously symbolic part of the body. (See Chapter 1 on sociocultural issues for more information on this topic.)

Students Are Reluctant to Speak

As ELL students emerge from the silent and one- or two-word production stage, they may still be reluctant to speak in some settings. There can be many causes for this reluctance, including shyness, not having the words or grammatical structures for certain situations, or fear of making a mistake.

General Strategies

Children generally feel most comfortable speaking when they know something about the topic under discussion, and feel that they won't be laughed at. Reluctant speakers often feel safest when they are given structured situations with clear guidelines or patterns. Teachers can gradually transition reluctant speakers from these more structured activities to ones that require increasingly more spontaneous, unstructured talk on the part of students.

SITUATION 1 I have intermediate/advanced students who don't talk in class.

Targeted Strategy 1: Set up small groups.

ELL students who are reluctant to speak to a whole class are often more willing to contribute to small-group discussions and pair shares, especially when they are carefully paired with other students, including ELLs, friends, and other students who speak the same language.

Targeted Strategy 2: Thank students for their work.

A colleague of Dorothy's makes a point of regularly thanking her students for their hard work. Acknowledging that volunteering to read or speak or contribute an opinion is a courageous act and is appreciated can motivate students to volunteer again. It also seems to inspire other students to contribute as well. Teachers should be specific about what they are thanking students for (e.g., *Helping to stop litter is a great reason about why recycling is important. Thank you, Javier.*). Of course, all students in the class should be thanked on a regular basis for their contributions, not only ELLs.

Targeted Strategy 3: Treat questions with respect.

Teachers often implore students to ask questions if they don't understand. In reality, questions can be disruptive when asked at inopportune times, such as just before the bell rings or when the teacher wants to quickly finish up a lesson. Every question doesn't need to be answered immediately, but every question should be treated with respect. As in volunteering, asking a question, especially in front of other students, can require bravery on the part of any student, particularly ELL students. When a student asks a question, it is a good idea to acknowledge the value of the question (e.g., *Thank you, Omid, for asking that question. Probably many students don't know what the word* habitat *means. Let's find that word in our reading, and then we'll see if we can work together to figure out what it means.*).

If teachers do not have time to address a question when it is asked, they can still acknowledge that the question is important and emphasize that it will be answered, just not right at that time (e.g., *Wow! That's a big, important question you just asked, Fong, "What is a preposition?" That's going to take more time than we have right now to answer, but I'm going to make a note to myself to start by talking about prepositions in tomorrow's grammar lesson. Even though prepositions are small words, they carry important meanings.* And the teacher *did* make sure to return to prepositions the next day).

Not all questions that ELL students ask need to be addressed with the whole class. For example, ELL students may have questions about words or cultural issues that English-speaking North American children would be familiar with (e.g., *What's an amusement park?* or *What does "chimney" mean?*). In these cases, it's best to establish a consistent routine, one that addresses the ELL child's need to know, but doesn't disrupt the class. Ways to handle these more ELL-specific questions include the following:

- Set aside 15–20 minutes each day to meet with ELL children.

- Refer children to a picture dictionary.

- Ask children to jot down questions to ask their buddies later (quick sketches and/or words in the L1 or English can help jog their memories later).

- Using frequent Think-Pair-Shares[4] can also address ELL students' questions.

Targeted Strategy 4: Take advantage of picture talks.

Pictures give ELL children a visual support and focus for their talk. Some activities for ELL children involving pictures include the following:

- **Talk about what's happening in a poster or pictures**. These pictures can come from picture dictionaries, classroom posters, calendars,

---

[4] Think-Pair-Share is a cooperative discussion strategy in which students are prompted by the teacher to 1) think about a question or observation, 2) talk about their answers or thoughts with a partner, and 3) share their thinking with the rest of the class. This strategy is discussed in more detail in Chapter 2, Listening Situations, p. 42.

magazines, or the teacher's picture file of intriguing pictures. Talks can be open-ended (e.g., responding to the question, *What's happening in this picture?*) or more focused, (e.g., *What do you think the boy is saying?* or *Describe the different kinds of shops in the pictures and talk about what you might buy in each store.*).

Pictures can also be gathered from the Internet. A group of compelling pictures is available at Story-It: Language Art Resources for children and their teachers (www.storyit.com/Starters/picstart.htm). Although intended as story starters, they serve well as a basis for picture talks.

Another excellent source for picture talks is Alma Flor Ada and F. Isabel Campoy's *Blue and Green* (2000), which couples famous paintings by artists such as Diego Velázquez, Carmen Lomas Garza, Héctor Poleo, Roberto Benítez, and Luis Jasoon on one page with a short poem on the opposite page. Students can present both the picture and the accompanying poem. As a follow-up, students may choose to create their own poems in response to paintings or photographs that they select.

- **Create a series of pictures using digital photography.** Students can put the photos in the correct sequence and describe what is happening. For example, a student can photograph the sequence of events in making giant bubbles using the following steps:

  1. Mix the solution.

  2. Create a hoop with a clothes hanger.

  3. Fill a shallow tray with the solution.

  4. Submerge the hoop in the solution.

  5. Wave the hoop to create the giant bubble.

  6. Follow the bubble until it breaks.

After printing out the photos, students can put them in the correct order and explain each step either to a partner or to the class. Students can predict what will happen next if the final photograph is not included in the series (e.g., *The bubble going to fall on the floor and break because no more water.*).

Other activities that lend themselves to this type of sequential picture taking and discussion include the following:

- Making a sandwich or tortilla
- Making a pie (e.g., from picking the fruit to taking the pie out of the oven)
- Making clay or play dough figures
- Making a greeting card

* Making a paper bag mask
* Carving a pumpkin
* Planting a garden
* Playing a baseball inning (e.g., one player gets on first base, the next batter moves this player to third base, and the next batter hits a fly ball).

Depending upon the order in which the pictures are placed, there may be several "stories" to accompany each series of events.

* **Narrate a wordless picture book.** (See the suggestions for narrating wordless picture books that appeared earlier in this chapter, on pp. 75–76.)

Targeted Strategy 5: Create cross-age buddy reading programs.

In cross-age buddy reading programs, older students read to younger buddies. The older student becomes the knower or teacher, something that ELL children generally have few opportunities to be in their mainstream classrooms. These programs provide a great deal of oral practice on the part of the older students, the tutors, as they prepare for and while they work with their younger buddy (e.g., reading books ahead of time and discussing them with peers, and then discussing the books with their younger buddies). It gives younger ELL students who have a tutor an opportunity to receive one-on-one attention and English practice, and it provides a forum for them to ask questions and receive answers. ELL children who rarely speak in their own classrooms will often open up in this more intimate context. See Samway, Whang, & Pippitt's *Buddy Reading: Cross-Age Tutoring in a Multicultural School* (1995) for a detailed discussion of how to design, implement, and maintain a cross-age buddy reading program.

Targeted Strategy 6: Put a poem in your pocket.

Teachers and students don't have to wait for Poem in Your Pocket Day to share wonderful poetry, but it is one way to celebrate poetry with ELL students. This event was started in New York City to recognize National Poetry Month in April, but it is now celebrated in many schools around North America around that time. Named after the poem "Keep a Poem in My Pocket" by Beatrice Schenk de Regniers (White, Moore, & de Regniers, 1988), celebrants are encouraged to carry poems in their pockets and share them with friends, family, coworkers, and classmates.

On Poem in Your Pocket Day (or on any day of the year), students select a favorite short poem, practice reciting it, and then share it with the class or a small group of students. After reciting the poem, students explain why they chose this particular poem. They can select poems in English, a language other than English, or bilingual poems. Poems that are appropriate for children can be found at the children's section of the Poetry Archive Web site (www.poetryarchive.org/childrensarchive/home.do). Poetry about diverse cultures for children can be found in Appendix C on p. 281.

Targeted Strategy 7: Show books, pictures, and videos of familiar content.

Children are more likely to speak about topics with which they are familiar. Showing books, pictures, and videos of familiar content (e.g., about the native lands and cultures of ELL students) is one way of drawing out ELL children. It is important to read books or show videos to children that reflect multiple realities and experiences. Good books for this purpose include the following:

- UNICEF books, such as *Children Just Like Me* (A. Kindersley & B. Kindersley, 1995) and *A Life Like Mine* (D. Kindersley, 2002)

- Oxfam's books about the way people live around the world, such as *Come Home With Us* (Kubler & Formby, 1995b) and *Come and Eat With Us* (Kubler & Formby, 1995a)

- Books by Ann Morris, including *Bread, Bread, Bread* (1989), *Shoes, Shoes, Shoes* (1995), and the Grandma Remembers series, including *Grandma Francisca Remembers: An Hispanic-American Family Story* (2002)

- The Dorothy and Thomas Hoobler Family Album series, such as *The Chinese American Family Album* (1994a) and *The Mexican American Family Album* (1994b)

- Arthur Dorros's *This Is My House* (1992)

- Selby Beeler's *Throw Your Tooth on the Roof* (2001)

A comprehensive list of books and videos about diverse cultures can be found in Appendices C and D, pp. 273–284. When introducing these books and videos to children, ask them to think about what the book or video reminds them of and then follow up with a discussion. One follow-up activity is to create class books that capture individual children's family celebrations and experiences. Class books can show the following:

- How marriages are celebrated around the world or across families

- How birthdays are celebrated around the world and across families

- How the end of a season is marked around the world

- Celebrations that are particular to just one family. (We know a family that has a pig roast when a family member leaves for another country. Another family goes to a local restaurant when a child graduates from elementary school.)

Targeted Strategy 8: Go on field trips.

Field trips can serve two important purposes for ELL children. First, they can introduce children to places and activities they have not had an opportunity to experience, particularly since many families of ELL children work long hours and have little money to pursue excursions. For example, Dorothy and the other ESOL teachers at her school took a group of ELL students to visit the African Art Museum and Freer and Sackler Galleries at the Smithsonian Institution in Washington, D.C. Later, the classroom teacher of one of the children told Dorothy that when the child returned from the field trip, he talked excitedly for about an hour about what he had seen and done on the visit, including "The Peacock Room," painted by James McNeill Whistler; Japanese scrolls; and African sculptures and masks. The teacher commented that this child rarely spoke or shared information in class, and that this was the most animated he had ever been in class.

Field trips can also help ELLs connect with their homeland. For example, an ESOL teacher in Boston whom we know took her ELL students to visit the Museum of Science for an exhibit of Indian culture. In addition to seeing exhibits of cultural and artistic artifacts, there were artisans from India who worked on crafts, such as textiles and jewelry. One of the students, a very reserved Indian girl, Asha, eagerly talked about the exhibits and crafts to her classmates, explaining how her mother had a sari that looked like one on display and that she had seen many earrings similar to the ones the artisan was making. All of the students reacted excitedly to the henna hand painting since they remembered when Asha had come to school with her hands beautifully painted following a family member's wedding.

Some successful field trip destinations that we have visited include the following:

- The zoo

- Farms or orchards to pick apples, strawberries, and pumpkins, and take hayrides

- Factories (e.g., ice cream)

- Newspaper tours

- Supermarkets (especially those that sell international products)

- Farm markets

- Museums (natural history, science, space, art, and so on)

- Aquariums

- Musical concerts and performances

- Amusement parks

- Historical sites (e.g., Jamestown, Plimoth Plantation, historical village recreations)

- Nature parks and reserves (e.g., the Marin Headlands in Sausalito, California)

Paying for field trips is often a hardship for families of ELL children, so please see Chapter 6, Communication With Parents, p. 248, for ideas about how to financially support field trips.

SITUATION 2 My students are reluctant to make errors, so they only say what they're sure of or don't speak at all. They're overly cautious.

SITUATION 3 I have students who ask other students to speak for them.

Although these two situations manifest themselves in slightly different ways, both the causes and the strategies for addressing them are likely to be similar, so we are discussing them together. Reasons for hesitancy in speaking may be grounded in the individual's personality or cultural norms. Even though personality has not been found to have a long-term effect on second-language acquisition (Lightbown & Spada, 1993, 2006), research has indicated that low anxiety and a tendency to be outgoing do have a positive effect on L2 learners (Dulay et al., 1982; Wong-Fillmore, 1985). Self-confidence leads to sociability, which in turn results in communicative fluidity. Hence, an introverted or anxious child may be more reluctant to spontaneously engage in conversation than an extroverted or self-confident one.

Cultural factors may also come into play in children's hesitancy to speak when they are unsure about the accuracy of what they are about to say.

Some ELL students may come from learning environments in which accuracy is valued above experimentation. Particularly when learning another language, students may be used to reproducing accurate translations of texts and reciting scripted dialogues, rather than formulating opinions and responses, and realizing that making errors is part of the language development process.

The most important way that teachers can help ELL students overcome their fear of making mistakes is to show that they and others in the classroom appreciate all attempts at communication on the part of the ELL child. Teachers may find the activities for building classroom community addressed in the sociocultural issues of Chapter 1 helpful, as people often are reluctant to make mistakes when they feel that they are being criticized. In addition, many of the strategies described in Situation 1 may encourage students to extend their speaking beyond rote responses. The following activities also help transition students from structured to more unstructured speech.

Targeted Strategy 1: Try to speak the child's native language.

On occasion, ask the child how to say words or phrases in his or her native language. Label the room with words and phrases in the languages of ELL students and practice saying these words. You will likely mispronounce the words and make other mistakes, but this will show children how normal it is to make mistakes.

Targeted Strategy 2: Set aside one-on-one time.

Ask the student to do small classroom tasks that allow you to have one-on-one conversations and build a relationship. For example, putting books on the classroom library shelves can lead to a conversation about which book the child likes best, and feeding the classroom pet(s) can lead to a conversation about any animals the child has had.

Targeted Strategy 3: Encourage PowerPoint presentations.

Students can create PowerPoint presentations about some aspect of their lives (e.g., a pet, where they live, their friends), their native land (e.g., geography, food, history), or a content area (e.g., how to find a common denominator in fractions, important inventions). The slides of the presentation provide ELL students with a focus for speaking, but when classmates ask questions, students have the opportunity to speak extemporaneously. Extremely shy or reluctant students can give these presentations with a buddy.

Targeted Strategy 4: Initiate polls or oral questionnaires.

Students can be asked to answer questions and collect information about topics, such as favorite sports or how they get to school, and to create charts or graphs representing the information they collected. The following example of a "Favorite Sport" investigation illustrates this process:

- ⚹ Use pictures representing a wide range of sports to spark a brief class discussion of each sport (e.g., soccer, basketball, baseball, hockey). The pictures are displayed on the board or wall and labels for each sport are attached underneath.

- ⚹ Students generate questions they could ask each other, which are then written on the board. A discussion may be needed to explain the difference between closed questions, such as *Do you like soccer?* or *Is basketball your favorite sport?* and open-ended questions, such as *Why is hockey your favorite sport?*

- ⚹ In groups of five or six, students ask each other about their favorite sports. As they collect their answers, they fill in a chart with the names of the students in their group and their responses.

- ⚹ After each group has completed the survey, groups report back to the teacher. As the groups report their results, the teacher uses an overhead

FAVORITE SPORTS

Name	Favorite Sport
Tien	soccer
Abdul	basketball
Mathew	basketball
Sara	basketball
Jaime	baseball
Rosa	baseball
Boun	soccer
Ali	football
Abuk	soccer
Calum	soccer
Zuhour	volleyball
Danny	football
Mohamed	soccer
Elena	volleyball
José	football
Yu-Chun	basketball
Kim	soccer
Adan	soccer
Junko	basketball
Pilar	volleyball

Figure 3.4: Favorite Sports Results

projector to fill in all of the names of the students on a chart. In the end, it contains results for the entire class.

- Students fill in the missing information on their charts so that they also have a chart that includes information from all of the students in the class. Figure 3.4 on the previous page shows a completed example.

- In small groups, students figure out the number of students that chose each sport (e.g. in Figure 3.4, soccer: 7; basketball: 5).

- Groups report back to the whole class and make sure all their calculations are correct.

- The teacher reviews how to calculate percentages. (The number in a single category is multiplied by 100 and then divided by the total number of respondents. In the case of Figure 3.4, where 7 out of 20 students chose soccer, the calculation looks like this:

$$7 \times 100 = \frac{700}{20} = 35\%$$

- In small groups or pairs, students calculate the percentage of students who selected each sport.

- Groups report back to the rest of the class, and the class makes sure that all percentages are correct.

- Groups go to the Kids Zone Web site of the National Center for Education Statistics, Institute of Education Sciences, U.S. Department of Education (nces.ed.gov/nceskids/createagraph/default.aspx), and insert the names of the sports and percentages to create a circle graph similar to the one shown in Figure 3.5.

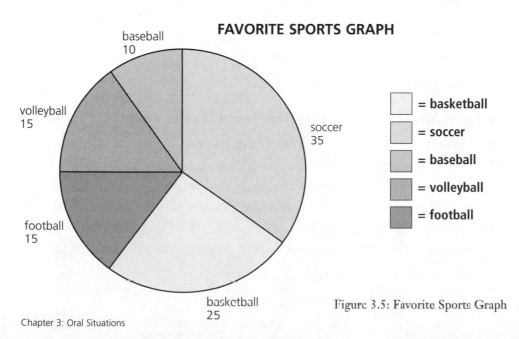

FAVORITE SPORTS GRAPH

baseball
10

volleyball
15

soccer
35

football
15

basketball
25

☐ = basketball
☐ = soccer
☐ = baseball
☐ = volleyball
☐ = football

Figure 3.5: Favorite Sports Graph

- The students print their circle graphs.

- In small groups or in a whole-class discussion, students can discuss why a sport is their favorite and why they think some sports are more popular than others among class members.

Targeted Strategy 5: Assign real-life projects.

Carolyn Syvanen (2000) provided a real-life learning experience for her intermediate and advanced ELL students through a school-wide recycling program. She designated one of her classes as the Recycling Team, whose responsibility it was to make presentations to other classes about the importance of recycling—explaining how to do it, distributing recycling containers, and collecting recyclables once a week. Speaking roles for the students included the following:

- Persuading others to recycle through class presentations

- Communicating with teachers and office staff about the recycling schedule

- Politely interrupting classes when they came to collect the recyclables

- Requesting needed supplies

- Informally chatting with office staff as they collected the recyclables

Other kinds of real-life learning experiences might include:

- Planting and maintaining a school garden

- Developing and maintaining an anti-litter campaign

- Developing fire-prevention awareness strategies (e.g., making fire safety posters and arranging for fire inspections)

- Running a school supply store

- Operating a worm farm for composting

- Producing a school-wide news show

Targeted Strategy 6: Encourage open-ended role-plays.

Open-ended role-plays offer a collaborative learning experience that can lead quiet students to develop enough confidence to speak up. As students work in small groups to create scripts in response to a prompt provided by the teacher, and as they listen to these scripted conversations, students are able to develop schema that they can draw on when they find themselves in similar situations in the future. Some possible role-playing situations include:

- Tell the school nurse that you don't feel well

- Introduce your parents to the teacher

- Explain to a store owner that you received the wrong change
- Set a time for a sleepover with a friend
- Explain to a teacher why you don't have your homework
- Ask neighbors if they have seen your missing cat
- Call 911 to report an emergency

It is possible to assign the same prompt to all groups and then compare their scripts, or groups can be assigned different prompts.

Targeted Strategy 7: Play the Liars' (or Actors') Club.

This activity provides students with an enjoyable pretext for speaking, as well as a way to learn about each other. It integrates many skills, all centered around practicing and using English (Wheeler, 1994). We have found that it works well to follow this procedure:

1. Explain to students that they are going to see how many good liars (or actors) there are in the class.

2. Provide an example by writing three sentences about yourself on the board (one of which is true and two that you make up), and asking the class to think a minute and then decide which of these sentences is true and which two are lies. For example, Dorothy might write:

   a. I rode an elephant in India.

   b. I learned to ride a bicycle when I was 40.

   c. I lived in the Amazon jungle.

3. Ask everyone to vote once for the sentence they think is true.

4. Count the votes for each sentence, and write the total number of votes next to the sentence on the board. Determine which sentence received the most votes.

5. If the class does not guess the true sentence (in the above example, the final sentence, *I lived in the Amazon jungle*, is the true sentence about Dorothy), this proves that the student (or teacher) is a good liar/actor and can be a member of the Liars' (or Actors') Club. The person's name is recorded underneath a heading, "The Liars' (or Actors') Club," and he or she becomes the first member of the club.

6. Once students understand the principle of the game, ask them to write three sentences about themselves—one true sentence and two made-up sentences. The teacher might want to give some examples of sentences that are too outrageous to believe, too easy to believe, or already known about them (e.g., *I visited the moon* or *I am in the fourth grade*).

7. It is a good idea to check students' sentences to make sure that they understand the idea of the game and that the sentences are understandable.

8. If the class is not too large, individuals can volunteer to try to become a member of the Liars' (or Actors') Club. In large classes, the teacher can divide the class into groups of three to five students, and the groups can choose the best sentences (keeping in mind that the true sentence must be true about the student presenting the information).

9. Individuals or groups write their three sentences on the board and read them out loud. The rest of the students vote on which sentence they believe to be true. (When groups have chosen one member to represent them, they do not vote when that member presents the sentences.)

10. A scorekeeper writes the votes for each sentence on the board, and the individual or group announces whether the class has correctly identified the one true sentence. If a majority of the class was not able to choose the true sentence, the individual or group members' names are recorded as members of the Liars' (or Actors') Club.

This activity usually generates many follow-up questions about the true sentences since good ones are usually a little offbeat.

Additional activities that help students get to know each other are included in community-building activities in Chapter 1, pp. 19–22.

Targeted Strategy 8: Have students prepare a list of topics.

Ask students to prepare a series of cards on which they list or draw topics they know a lot about. Working in small groups, students take turns selecting one of the cards from a group member's collection. That student then talks briefly about the topic and answers any questions.

Grammatical Structures

Making grammatical errors is a normal part of language development and learning. Research has shown that most errors that second language learners make are not the result of their native language, but are similar to the errors that young children make learning their first language (Dulay et al., 1982). As ELL children begin to speak, they gradually begin to develop an understanding of grammatical structures. Analysis of second language learners' development shows that their language use includes characteristics of their native language, some characteristics of the new language, and some characteristics that are common in all second language learning regardless of

This process is by no means static; language learners are continually adding to their knowledge base of how language works as they receive and interpret additional data in the form of language input through listening, reading, and writing in the new language (Krashen & Scarcella, 1982; Lightbown & Spada, 1993, 2006; Oller, 1979).

The following composite example of an ELL child's conversation with his teacher demonstrates how grammatical structures work in the developmental process of ELL learners:

Teacher: Did you do anything special to celebrate your birthday yesterday, Rafael?

Rafael: Sí, we wented to Chuck E. Cheese and we did have good time.

Teacher: Who went with you?

Rafael: Me mami y me papi y me two sister.

Teacher: Your older brother didn't go with you?

Rafael: No, she didn't not go. She working.

Teacher: Oh, that's too bad he couldn't go with you. What did you do at Chuck E. Cheese?

Rafael: Me y me two sister, we play game and we get ticket.

Teacher: What do you do with the tickets?

Rafael: We do using dem for get prize. I get car red and dinosaur. Rebecca get bunny rabbit y María get, uh. How you say muñeca?

Teacher: Doll. So, María got a doll. Did you eat pizza?

Rafael: Sí, we eat pizza, pero me mami she no eat pizza 'cause she no like. She eat chickens.

Teacher: It sounds like you had a good birthday.

Rafael: Sí, was good happy birthday.

In this example, we can see many of the typical developmental errors made by ELL students:

- Misuse of he/she pronouns (*No, she didn't not go* instead of *No, he didn't not go*)

- Incorrect use of subject/object forms of pronouns (*me mami y me papi y me two sister* instead of *my mami, my papi, and my two sister*)—though *me* could have been *mi*, meaning "my" in Spanish

- Omission of articles (*We did have good time* instead of *We did have a good time*)

- Omission of verb endings/inflections, e.g., the final *-s, -ed, -ing* (*two sister* instead of *two sisters*, *We play game* instead of *We played game*)

- Overuse of verb endings/inflections (*We wented to Chuck E. Cheese* instead of *We went to Chuck E. Cheese*)

- Overuse of the present progressive tense marker *-ing* (*We do using dem for get prize* instead of *We do use dem for get prize*)

- Misuse of auxiliary verb (*We did have good time* instead of *We had good time*)

- Use of *-s* on non-countable nouns (*she eat chickens* instead of *she eat chicken*)

- Omission of the pronoun *it* (*Was good happy birthday* instead of *It was good happy birthday*)

- Misuse of prepositions (*We do using dem for get prize* instead of *We do using dem to get prize*)

- Incorrect word order (*I get car red* instead of *I get red car*)

- Double negatives (*She didn't not go* instead of *She didn't go*)

- Incorrectly formed negatives (*Me mami she no eat pizza* instead of *Me mami doesn't eat pizza*)

- Incorrectly formed questions (*How you say muñeca?* instead of *How do you say muñeca?*)

- Use of native language for common phrases (*sí* for *yes*; *y* for *and*; *pero* for *but*)

- Overuse of common phrases (*was good happy birthday* instead of *was good birthday*)

In addition to the typical developmental errors represented in the above example, teachers of ELL students have noted the following:

- Mispronunciation of inflections, such as talk-ed for talk+t (*He talk+ed to me after school* for *He talk+t to me after school*)

- Mixed up modals and other verb forms (e.g., *I can will do that* for *I can do that* or *I must to not do that* for *I must not do that*)

Correcting ELL students' grammatical errors will not automatically change their language patterns, nor will explaining differences between English and the native language. However, an awareness of common grammatical acquisition order and language differences will help teachers of ELL students understand what to expect as their students develop their knowledge of the English language.

General Strategies

Research has shown that correction is not very reliable in helping students overcome errors (Dulay et al., 1982), so correcting students' grammatical errors should be done judiciously; instead, it is much more useful to focus instruction on a frequently occurring structure, particularly a structure that causes confusion for the listener. It is especially important that teachers *not* correct students' errors as they are emerging from the silent period and in situations in which they might be embarrassed in front of their peers or others. For example, in the following interaction, the teacher's response is likely to cause embarrassment and may make the student reluctant to speak any further:

Student: He have a book.

Teacher: No, that's not right. It's "<u>She has</u> a book." Say that after me.

A more effective way of dealing with the error is to clarify the confusion and model the proper usage, as the following illustrates:

Student: He have a book.

Teacher: Who has the book? <u>He</u>? (*pointing to Juan*) Or <u>she</u>? (*pointing to Patricia*)

It then would be helpful for the teacher to make a note that pronoun differences (*she/he*) and subject/verb agreement (*have/has*) would be good teaching points . . . and to follow up on them later.

Asking questions to clarify meaning in a conversation or instructional interaction is the most natural way to address grammatical confusion. For example, if an ELL child says, *My mother take me to school*, the teacher might ask, *Do you mean your mother took you to school this morning, or she's going to come and get you this afternoon?* These negotiations for meaning may not have an immediate effect on the ELL students' use of language, but as their language develops, they will begin to recognize the importance of subtleties in verb tense, correct pronoun use, and other aspects of grammar, and apply them in their own speech.

Since children acquire language by understanding messages—in other words, through receiving comprehensible input—teachers can play an important role by providing a rich array of language experiences. These experiences should be natural, not artificial, and include activities that children enjoy, opportunities to play with language, and opportunities to use language to process, create, and express ideas in ways that are cognitively stimulating. Grammar drills and explicit teaching of grammar points should have a limited role in the teaching of young ELL children. Instead, they can begin to recognize and use standard patterns of grammar through the following materials and methods. Each will receive fuller attention later in the chapter to show how they can contribute to the development of specific grammatical features.

- Jazz chants
- Shared reading/big books
- Language Experience Approach (LEA)
- Cuisenaire rods—the Silent Way

SITUATION 1 My students misuse pronouns. For example, they say "he" when they mean "she."

Targeted Strategy 1: Create a family book.

- Tell students that they are going to make a book about their family by drawing pictures and writing sentences.

- In groups, students talk about members of their families. Keep in mind that many ELL students view grandparents, uncles, aunts, cousins, and close friends of the family as members of their immediate family. Also, they may refer to the children of aunts and uncles as brothers or sisters, rather than cousins.

- Students orally describe one family member to the whole class.

- Students draw a picture of each family member.

- Underneath each picture, students write (or dictate) two or more sentences about that family member (e.g., *This is my mother. She has brown hair. My brother's name is Juanito. He is five years old.*).

- Students draw a front page that shows all their family members and write (or dictate) a title.

- They staple the pages together into a book, share their books with the class, and then take them home to share with their families.

Here is an alternative activity:

- Students write a book that focuses on family members' favorite things to do (e.g., *This is my grandpa. He loves to garden. This is my cousin. She likes to dance. This is my sister. She likes to swim and dive in the pool.*).

- Students borrow inexpensive cameras or Polaroid cameras to take pictures of their family members.

- Students bring in photos of their family members and use them to illustrate their books.

Targeted Strategy 2: Use Language Experience Approach (LEA) about a guest speaker.

Language Experience Approach (LEA) was developed as a way to produce reading materials that emergent readers could understand (Allen, 1976; Stauffer, 1970). Teachers take dictation from their students about a shared experience. This dictation, using the students' own words, then becomes their reading material. More details about Language Experience Approach and a lesson example are available in Chapter 4 on pp. 135–136. Following is an example of how teachers can use the Language Experience Approach to exploit the *he* or *she* pronouns after a visit by a guest speaker.

- Invite a guest speaker into the classroom to talk about his or her profession. (It's important to prepare guest speakers so they come with lots of visuals and realia to involve the students.)

- After the visit, create an LEA text with the class, in which the class collaborates to generate the text, which the teacher writes on chart paper.

  —Encourage each child to contribute a sentence to the text.
  —Write the sentences exactly as the children say them, including their nonstandard use of English (e.g., *Mrs. Yamada come to class. She wear kimono. He show tea ceremony.*).
  —Work with the students to correct the non-standard uses of English, particularly any misuses of pronouns (e.g., the use of *he* in the example above).
  —Read aloud the text as a whole group.
  —Invite individual students to read parts of the text.

Follow-up activities can include the following:

- Students act out the text using the LEA text as the script.
- Students write independently (as opposed to copying) in their journals about the guest speaker's visit.
- Small groups of children can generate follow-up questions for the speaker, and pose these questions in a letter or an e-mail.
- The class writes a thank-you letter to the speaker (this can also be collaboratively written as an LEA text).

Targeted Strategy 3: Create a gender Venn diagram.

Students read a book or watch a movie that has a sharp contrast between a male and female character. They then create a Venn diagram delineating the roles of the male and female characters. For example, students can watch *Children of Heaven*, an Iranian film about a boy who accidentally loses his sister's shoes (Majidi, 1999). Coming from a poor family, the brother and sister go to great lengths to avoid having their parents find out that the shoes are lost. After watching the film, children can make a Venn diagram similar to the following:

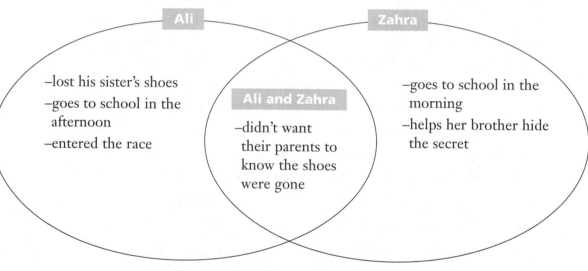

Figure 3.6: Venn Diagram: *Children of Heaven*

After creating the Venn diagram, students talk about the film, including what the brother did, what the sister did, and what they both did to overcome their dilemma (e.g., *Ali set Zahra's shoes down outside the market. He was upset when they were taken. Zahra wore Ali's shoes to school in the morning. She gave them to her brother in the afternoon.*).

Targeted Strategy 4: Use jazz chants.

Students can practice distinguishing between he/she pronouns with Carolyn Graham's jazz chants (see earlier references to jazz chants on pp. 74–75 for more information). Some of the chants that include explicit practice with the he/she pronouns include "Where's Jack," "I Asked My Father," and "Early Bird" (Tang & Loyet, 2003). Teachers can emphasize *he* and *she* by pointing to pictures of males and females as they recite the chants, and then inviting children to point to the pictures as the other children are reciting the chant.

An alternative is to have one boy and one girl stand up for the recitations of Jack or Mary in "Where's Jack," or the mother and father in "I Asked My Father."

SITUATION 2 — My students often omit the plural ending –s (e.g., they say "three book" instead of "three books").

Targeted Strategy 1: Stock the classroom with counting books.

There are many beautiful counting books that provide natural repetition of the final –*s* plural ending. One of our favorite counting books, *The Very Hungry Caterpillar* (Carle, 1979/1994), includes many basic concepts, including numbers, days of the week, and foods. Children can create and read aloud from spin-off books they make themselves, such as *The Very Thirsty Bear* in which, for example, the main character drinks one glass of water, two cups of cocoa, and three pints of milk.

Targeted Strategy 2: Introduce counting rhymes.

Counting rhymes provide good opportunities for using the plural –*s* ending. Many counting rhymes can be found on the Enchanted Learning Web site at www.enchantedlearning.com/themes/123.shtml. They are presented in rebus form and some, such as "Five Speckled Frogs," have animation. These rhymes do not have audio, so it is important that someone, such as a teacher, instructional aide, peer buddy, or volunteer, reads the rhymes to ELL students. After viewing the animated Web site, teachers can put the rhymes on a chart and create their own animated versions, with children acting out the parts.

Targeted Strategy 3: Teach a modified version of Simon Says.

A modified version of the game Simon Says is an enjoyable activity that helps ELLs discriminate between singular and plural forms of words. The children are asked to listen carefully to what Simon says. (The teacher initially takes this role.) If he says, "Touch your *ears*," they have to touch both ears. Students who touch only one ear are out. If he says, "Touch your *knee*," they have to touch only one knee. Students who touch both knees are out. After playing a few rounds, children can play the part of Simon.

SITUATION 3 My ELL students often confuse verb tenses. For example, they use the present tense instead of the past tense (e.g., "I go to school yesterday") or overuse the present progressive tense (e.g., "I am washing my face every day").

Targeted Strategy 1: Introduce focused picture drawing.

On Friday, the teacher asks the ELL students to draw a picture and talk about what they are going to do that weekend, as the example below shows:

Teacher: What are you going to do this weekend?

Deng: I going to park play soccer (*holds up a drawing of himself playing soccer in the park*).

Teacher: That should be fun. If the weather is nice, I'm going to the park, too, but I'm not going to play soccer. I'm going to take a walk in the park.

Marisol: I go shopping with my mommy for new shoes (*holds up a picture of her mother, herself, and a pair of shoes*).

Teacher: Oh, you're going shopping with your mother. I hope you find some pretty new shoes.

On Monday, the teacher reviews the pictures and asks students if they did what they planned to do.

Teacher: Let's look at your drawings and see if you did what you planned to do. What about you, Marisol?

Marisol: Yes, I buyed new shoes.

Teacher: You bought new shoes? Are they shoes for school?

Marisol: Yes, I bought new shoes, but they shoes for church.

Teacher: Deng, what about you?

Deng: I no can go park because it raining.

Teacher: Oh, that's a shame that you couldn't go to the park because it was raining. I didn't go to the park either. I hope we can go next weekend.

In the example above, the teacher provides opportunities for students to use the future and past tenses, but she does not overtly correct their errors. If the teacher routinely provides opportunities to use the two different tenses in a natural way, models the correct use of the tenses, and provides many examples of how and when to use the verb tenses through patterned books, songs, chants, poetry, and prose read-alouds, children will begin to recognize the patterns and consistently use the correct forms of the verb tenses.

se or overuse the present tense

essive tense (e.g., "He *walking*

He *walks* to the bus every day").

e that the present tense form of verbs

s for nonnative speakers to learn. On

erson singular verbs (e.g., *She plays*) in

er, while the *–ing* verb ending (e.g.,

ay et al., 1982). As a result, teachers

tudents using what sounds like the

aily routines (e.g., *She's never absent.*

of *She's never absent. She comes to school*

ion has been found to be the natural

arners typically take, correction,

nmar drills may change the ELL child's

speech patterns temporarily, but are not likely to have any long-term effect.
When ELL children use the *-ing* form of a verb instead of the present tense,
the best course for teachers is to concentrate on the communication and
clarify any misunderstandings. However, teachers can provide opportunities
for students to hear and use the present tense and, when they are
developmentally ready, they will begin to use it.

Targeted Strategy 1: Let students conduct interviews about daily routines.

Pairs of students interview each other about their daily routines or activities.
The students take notes about their partner's activities and report back to
the class (e.g., *Teshome gets up every day at 7:00. Miguel plays soccer on
Tuesdays.*). As a follow-up, teachers can orally quiz students to see how
much they remember (e.g., *Who plays soccer on Tuesdays? How many students
get up before 8:00?*).

Targeted Strategy 2: Have students interview school staff members.

This activity allows students to learn more about the people who work in
their school. Prior to beginning this lesson, the teacher should contact school
staff members to explain the purpose of the interviews (for students to learn
about the jobs and duties of school personnel), see who would be willing to
be interviewed by students, and find out the most convenient time for the
student interviews. The following steps have worked well for us:

- Students list as many school staff members as they can (e.g., secretary, nurse, principal, vice principal, cafeteria workers, custodians). If students are not familiar with many of these people, the teacher may want to begin this activity by taking a tour of the school, so students can informally meet these people and know where they work.

- Students brainstorm questions to ask so they can find out more about the jobs of these staff members (e.g., *What is your job title? When do you start work? What do you do first? What are some other things you do? What part of your job do you like best? Least?*)

- Assign small groups of three or four students to interview one school staff member.

- The small groups meet to select ten questions to ask the staff member. Students can select from the brainstormed questions or they may wish to modify or add questions that they think are better for that particular staff member. For example, if students are interviewing the school nurse, they may decide to ask, *What do you do if a child is sick and their parent isn't home?* Students interviewing the principal or vice principal might ask *What do you do if a student gets into a fight?*

- Then students choose roles for each group member (e.g., interviewer, tape recorder, note-taking recorder, photographer).

- Students interview the staff member, record the answers by hand and on a cassette tape or digital recorder, and take photographs of the staff member doing some aspects of his or her job and with the members of the group. (The teacher or a volunteer can take the group photograph.)

- The groups transcribe their notes and recordings and write up the results of their interviews (e.g., *Mrs. Johnson is the school nurse. She works in the clinic next to the principal's office. She takes care of children when they are sick. She takes their temperature to see if they have a fever. She calls their parents if they have a fever. She gives some students medicine. She likes her job. She says that she gets to meet many students and she likes to help them.*).

- Final presentations can take several forms. Groups can present their information orally to the class, write up their information for a class or school newspaper, and/or create a bulletin board.

Targeted Strategy 3: Play the circle game.

This circle game gives students an opportunity to use the present tense in its positive and negative forms. As a whole class or in small groups, students sit in a circle. The teacher explains that each student will draw a sentence from a box and read it out loud to the person to his or her left. The purpose of the game is to decide if the sentence is true or false (e.g., *The earth revolves around the sun*). If it is true, the student on the left simply agrees (e.g., *Yes, it does*). If it is false (e.g., *The earth revolves around the moon*), the student replies no, and explains what is true (e.g., *No, it doesn't. The moon revolves around the earth.*). If a student replies incorrectly, he or she is out of the circle. The game continues until only one child is left in the circle. If the student uses the incorrect verb form (e.g., *The moon revolving around the earth*), the teacher confirms that the answer is correct while supplying the correct verb form (e.g., *That's correct. The moon revolves around the earth.*).

SITUATION 5 Students omit modals (e.g., "I go to the game" for "I can go to the game") or mix up modals (e.g., "You have can go if you want to" for "You can go if you want to").

Modals are auxiliary words that are added to verbs to express ideas such as ability (e.g., *He can play the piano*), necessity (e.g., *All students must wash their hands before eating*), advisability (e.g., *You should take your book bag home*), expectations (e.g., *We ought to be there soon*), and possibility (e.g., *He might be sick*). The modal auxiliaries in English are: *can, could, had better, may, might, must, ought to, shall, should, will,* and *would* (Azar, 1989). Children typically attain full use of modal auxiliaries in the later stages of second-language development, although standard phrases or routines, such as *Can I go to the bathroom*, may be acquired fairly early.

Targeted Strategy 1: Review classroom or school norms.

At the beginning of the school year, teachers sometimes work with students to create a book or poster of norms for the class or for the school. A book might include entries such as *Students should listen to each other*. Once, as Dorothy's students were reviewing their school norms book, one of the students asked, "What about teachers? Don't they have standards?" Dorothy and the students decided to create standards for teachers as well, which included the following:

- *Teachers should correct students' homework promptly.*
- *Teachers should not chew gum.*
- *Teachers ought to respect students.*
- *Teachers should not interrupt students.*

Other norms books or posters can include those for parents and community workers such as, doctors, nurses, and police officers.

Targeted Strategy 2: Create skits or role-plays.

Teachers and students can work together to create situations in which students use modals to suggest and advise. Some examples of role-play situations include the following:

- A mother and child talk about a messy bedroom and what the child has to do.

- Someone buys an electronic device, but it doesn't work. A store worker must tell the buyer what to do.

- The coach hasn't let you play in the game. A friend advises you on what to say to the coach.

Targeted Strategy 3: Make use of patterned books.

Patterned books give students repeated practice with grammatical structures. In the big book *The Monsters' Party* (Cowley, 2001), each monster describes what it can do. Students get plenty of practice hearing and using this structure as they read and reread the book. In addition, follow-up activities, described on page 71, give students opportunities to use the structure, *I can _____*, to create sentences about themselves.

SITUATION 6 My student has difficulty forming negatives (e.g., "I *no* want play" for "I *don't* want to play").

Targeted Strategy 1: Play the chain game.

In the chain game, the first person begins with a sentence, such as "I want to go to ___ (e.g., Katharine might say, "I want to go to Nepal"). The second person either agrees with the sentence (e.g., Dorothy might say, "I want to go to Nepal, too") or disagrees and adds what he or she wants to do (e.g., Dorothy might say, "I don't want to go to Nepal. I want to go to Mexico."). This game can be played with many categories of words, including countries, food (e.g., *I want to eat _____*), sports activities (e.g., *I want to play _____*), clothing (e.g., *I like to wear _____*), and TV shows (e.g., *I like to watch _____*). Although not all children will necessarily be using the negative in this game, they will have many opportunities to hear the negative being used.

Targeted Strategy 2: Utilize jazz chants (again).

We've mentioned Carolyn Graham's jazz chants as an excellent device for learning the rhythms, sounds, and structure of language. One of the most compelling aspects of jazz chants is that they use rhythm and rhyme so powerfully that it's often hard to get them out of your head. (Katharine can still remember the "Sh!, Sh!, Baby's Sleeping!" chant decades after first hearing it.) One of the chants least likely to be forgotten is "I Love to Say 'I Won't'," which contains many negatives and can take the form of a call-and-response activity (e.g., one group of students reads one part and another group reads another part). Other jazz chants that use the negative are "I Bought a Cat for My Dog" and "Go Away!"

SITUATION 7 My students have difficulty forming questions.

The interview strategies discussed on pp. 107–108 provide many opportunities for ELL children to ask questions. Also, the chain game described on p. 110 can be modified to include questions (e.g., *I want to go to Nepal. Where do you want to go?*). Here are more strategies for helping students form questions.

Targeted Strategy 1: Create a poster of common questions.

Students can help create a poster of common questions they often ask in class. Creating the poster will help them form questions and, with pictures for visual support, can serve as a resource for newcomers to refer to when they need to ask questions. Some useful questions that teachers have included on posters follow:

* *Can you repeat that?*
* *How do I do that?*
* *May I go to the _____ (e.g., bathroom, office)?*
* *Can I borrow _____ (e.g., a pencil/marker, an eraser, the stapler)?*
* *Did you say _____?*
* *Where is the _____ (e.g., media center, nurse's office)?*
* *How do you say this word?*
* *When is _____ (e.g., lunch, P.E., computer lab)?*
* *What page are we on?*
* *Is it okay if I take _____ (e.g., the ball, a marker)?*

Targeted Strategy 2: Make a question word chart.

Some ELL students have difficulty distinguishing between question words (e.g., *who* question words are asking about people, *where* question words are asking about places). A poster with these words, some visuals, and examples can help ELL children know which word to use when they want to form questions. A sample poster is shown below.

Question Word Poster

Question Word	Function of the Word	Example
Who	People	Who lives in the White House? A: the President
What	Things	What is on the table? A: a book
Where	Places	Where does the President live? A: in Washington, D.C.
When	Time	When did you get up? A: at 8:30
Why	Reason	Why did you stand up? A: to get a drink of water
How	Process $2 + 2 = 4$	How did you get the sum of 4? A: adding 2 + 2

Figure 3.7: Question Word Poster

Teachers can also refer students to the poster when they become confused. For example, if a teacher asks, *Who picked up the book?* and a student answers, *On the shelf*, the teacher can point to "Who" on the question word chart.

Targeted Strategy 3: Manipulate Cuisenaire rods.

A common mistake that ELL students make in forming questions is reversing the order of the subject and verb. A visual way to help students become aware of that word reversal is to assign parts of speech to different colored

Cuisenaire rods.[5] Students then manipulate the rods to show an understanding of the subject-verb reversal. The following is taken from a lesson in which a teacher used Cuisenaire rods to demonstrate how to form questions beginning with a declarative sentence:

- The teacher says, "Luis is going to bed."

- The teacher picks up a red rod and says "Luis," and sets the rod on the table.

- The teacher picks up a white rod, says "is," and sets it on the table next to the red rod.

- The teacher picks up a green rod, says "going," and sets it next to the white rod.

- The teacher picks up a purple rod, says "to bed," and sets it next to the green rod.

- The teacher says the complete sentence again: "Luis is going to bed." She points to each rod as she says the word or words it represents.

- Next, she asks, "Is Luis going to bed?"

- As she asks this question, the teacher moves the white rod from its place between the red rod and the green rod, places it in front of the red rod, and repeats, "Is Luis going to bed?" as she points to each rod.

- The teacher follows this demonstration by saying a similar sentence (e.g., *Mary is eating lunch*). She sets the rods in their original pattern (red-white-green-purple) and repeats the sentence, pointing to each rod the word represents.

- Then she says, "Is Mary eating lunch?" and points to the rods, indicating by gestures that one of the children should move the white rod.

- One of the children moves the white rod to the front of the sentence.

- After practicing these sentences a few times, students can work in small groups with the rods to create their own sentences and ask questions.

- Teachers can follow up by asking students to write sentences and questions similar to the ones they have been forming with the rods.

An alternative to using Cuisenaire rods is to use colored cards with words written on them, and to manipulate the cards. A small group of students can practice manipulating the colored cards on a table and, as a follow-up, line up

---

[5] See page 77 for more information about Cuisenaire rods and how to use them for language development and practice.

the cards in front of them to form a sentence. As the teacher or the students recite the questions, the student holding the auxiliary verb (e.g., *is*) then physically moves to the front of the line with the card.

SITUATION 8 My students have difficulty conveying meaning because of their confusion about grammar use (e.g., "Sister he no look she bus go away" for "My sister missed the bus").

It's important to recognize that these types of misunderstandings result from the student taking the linguistic risk of communicating information that is beyond his or her ability to speak in English at that moment. Focusing on communication during these breakdowns is absolutely crucial for supporting ELLs because if we abandon the conversation, we are telling them that what they have to say isn't important or that they are somehow deficient.

Targeted Strategy 1: Listen and paraphrase.

When communication breaks down, try to figure out what the speaker means by picking out key words and concepts and paraphrasing what the student has said. Ask questions, and once the confusion is sorted out, respond to the content of the student's comment, as the following interaction illustrates:

Student: Sister he no look she bus go away

Teacher: Your sister?

Student: Yes.

Teacher: She went on the bus?

Student: No.

Teacher: She's not on the bus?

Student: Yes. Not on bus.

Teacher: Did she <u>want</u> to take the bus?

Student: Yes (*nods vigorously*).

Teacher: Did the bus come to the bus stop?

Student: Yes. Bus go away.

Teacher: But your sister wasn't on the bus.

Student: Yes.

Teacher: Ahh. Your sister missed the bus?

(*The student nods.*)

Teacher: Your sister missed the bus? Okay. But <u>you</u> (*points to the student*) say, "My (*points to self*) sister missed the bus."

Student: (*nods*) My sister missed the bus.

The teacher continues with the conversation, asking, "What happened to your sister?" and "Could she take a later bus?" Now that the teacher understands the gist of what the student is trying to say, she can deal with the situation of the sister missing the bus and its consequences. In other words, the teacher can figure out what the student wants to convey.

SITUATION 9   I correct my students' grammatical errors, but they continue to make the same mistakes.

It's a natural reaction for many people, including teachers, to try to correct a student when he or she uses incorrect grammar. However, it is important to remember that second language learners often acquire grammatical structures in a certain order. Also, studies show that correcting grammatical errors will not change that order and is likely to be ineffective. Modeling the correct structure will not change the child's language use either, but it is, nonetheless, useful to expose the child to the correct grammatical form. With language enrichment activities, the child will ultimately acquire the correct structure.

Pronunciation

When it comes to learning to speak a second language without an accent, there is no question that children have an advantage over adults. Unlike native language grammatical structures, which have limited influence on second language learners, the phonology, or sound system, of a child's first language does influence the new one. However, this influence does not last long for children. Research indicates that children first process the sound system of their new language through their first language. But, as they gradually acquire the sound system of the second language, ELL children's reliance on the native language disappears, and they develop accent-free pronunciation (Anderson, 2004; Krashen & Scarcella, 1982). Age plays a significant role in the ability to acquire the sound system of a new language. Although researchers have not yet explained exactly why age makes such a difference, studies indicate that puberty is an important turning point in learning to speak a second language without an accent (Dulay et al., 1985).

General Strategies

The most productive role that teachers can play in young ELL children's speech development is to provide them with many opportunities to listen to the sounds and rhythms of the new language, using the strategies already discussed here and in other chapters. Keep the following tenets in mind:

- Many young children go through a silent period of approximately one to six months in which they do not produce language, but take in the sounds and structures of the new language. It is important to talk and read to the child during this period, supplementing any message with pictures or other visuals to help him or her understand what is being communicated. (See Chapter 2, Listening Situations, for specific strategies.)

- Phonemes, the sounds in a language that differentiate meaning, differ from language to language. Listening to and participating in natural language activities, such as conversations, songs, poetry, chants, rhymes, patterned books, and prose are the best ways for ELL children to develop phonemic awareness in English.

- ELL children must develop phonemic awareness in English before they can begin to understand phonics, a way of teaching students to make connections between letter patterns and the sounds they represent.

- ELL students do not benefit from phonemic awareness and phonics exercises that are taken out of a meaningful context. For example, an exercise that asks an ELL child to look at pictures of a cat, a hat, a bat and a dog and select the picture for the word that doesn't have an /a/ sound requires the child to know the word that each of the pictures represents. In fact, the ELL child may pick the hat because it is not an animal.

SITUATION 1 Sometimes I can't understand my new ELLs when they speak because of their accents.

ELL children who have not been exposed to English prior to entering school may speak with an accent at the beginning. Teachers may notice that some ELL children pronounce *th* as *d* or *s* (e.g., *dis* for *this*, *sink* for *think*), insert an *e* before *s* (e.g., *espelling*) or use irregular stress or intonation when they speak. These irregularities in speech are probably the result of influences from the home language; however, in most cases, they will disappear after about a year's exposure to the new language and without any direct intervention from teachers. When communication breaks down because of an ELL child's pronunciation errors, teachers can help get the conversation back on track with the following strategies. As with breakdowns of understanding because of grammatical structures, it is important to respond to the content of the student's comment once the confusion is sorted out.

Targeted Strategy 1: Keep listening.

Rather than interrupting children when they pronounce a word or phrase in a way that you don't understand, continuing to listen to them often clears up the misunderstanding. For example, if a child responds to a teacher's question about what he or she did over the weekend with *I do no sing*, simply waiting for the child to elaborate or encouraging the child to continue by responding, *Yes?* the confusion may be resolved. If the child continues by saying, *It raining. I no play soccer. I no go to park. I do no sing*, the teacher understands that the child wanted to convey, *I did nothing*, and can respond appropriately.

Targeted Strategy 2: Ask strategic questions using gestures or drawings.

When a child's elaborations don't resolve pronunciation misunderstandings, teachers can ask questions and use drawings or gestures, as in the following conversation:

Sasha: My mom no let me eat *snakes*.

Teacher: Why is that, Sasha?

Sasha: She say they no good.

Teacher: Do you mean snacks, like potato chips (*gestures eating potato chips from a bag*) or snakes? (*sketches a picture of a snake and shows it to Sasha*)

Sasha: I mean *snakes*, like potato chips (*gestures eating potato chips*).

Teacher: Your mom is right. Snacks like potato chips are not good for you.

SITUATION 2 When we're doing phonics and phonemic awareness work, my ELL students can't produce certain sounds (e.g., /th/ as in *thing* or /v/ as in *vest*).

Targeted Strategy 1: Teach aural distinction before oral production of sounds.

Students must first be able to discriminate aurally between sounds in English before pronouncing them correctly. See Chapter 2, p. 60 for listening strategies to help students distinguish specific sounds in English.

Targeted Strategy 2: Show students how to articulate specific sounds.

Teachers can explicitly demonstrate how lips, teeth, and the tongue are used to create specific sounds in English (e.g., to pronounce /th/ as in *thing*, the tongue is placed between the upper and bottom teeth). The Web site, Phonetics: The Sounds of American English, www.uiowa.edu/~acadtech/phonetics/english/frameset.html, provides animated articulatory diagrams and audio and video of each sound spoken in context. Demonstrations of how to articulate sounds should be short, and teachers should avoid intense drilling or repetition.

Vocabulary

ELL students develop vocabulary through repeated exposure to new words and opportunities to use new words (e.g., through a wide variety of reading, intentional word-focused activities, and ongoing review) (Wallace, 2004). When first exposed to a new language, young children who lack strong literacy skills in their home language will develop their vocabulary through pictures, gestures, and actions. Educational television, in particular *Sesame Street*, has been shown to help young children learn new words (Rice, Huston, Truglio, & Wright, 1990). As teachers introduce ELL children to short texts through patterned books, poetry, and chants, they will begin to learn vocabulary through these resources. Reading aloud to ELL children, with support to ensure understanding (e.g., pictures, gestures, explanations), is essential to vocabulary development. Later, as children become literate in English, they will begin to learn new words and the concepts that go with them through literature and content-based texts. Children will develop the vocabulary for basic interpersonal communication skills, commonly referred to as BICS (e.g., the language used in the lunchroom, on the playground, and in casual day-to-day conversations), before they develop vocabulary associated with cognitive academic language proficiency, known as CALP (e.g., the language needed to fully understand age-appropriate subject area content material) (Cummins, 1981a, 1981b). The following are some general strategies to help ELL children develop the initial words they need for basic social interaction, and to transition them into learning the more cognitively demanding words they need for content-area studies. Also see Chapter 4, in particular pp. 137–156, for additional vocabulary development activities.

General Strategies

- At first, use gestures, pictures, realia, and labels to help children understand the meanings of the words you are using. For example, point to the chair as you ask them to sit down or hold up red and black markers when you ask which they would like to write with.

- Talk to ELLs about concrete subjects and help them connect words to objects. As you look at a drawing, say *That's a beautiful butterfly* while pointing to the butterfly, and *I like the way you gave it green wings* while pointing to the wings.

- Give ELLs many opportunities to interact with other students (e.g., in pairs, with peer buddies, with younger or older students through cross-age buddy reading, in small groups, as part of whole-group activities). Provide many different contexts, including different subject area studies, such as math and science; in specials, such as art, music, and physical education; at lunch; on the playground; in extracurricular clubs and sports.

- Ask parents to encourage their children to watch age-appropriate educational programs on TV.

- Read aloud to ELLs, using many different kinds of texts, including poems, chants, fiction, and nonfiction. See Chapters 2 and 4 on listening and reading for specific strategies for ensuring understanding during read-alouds.

- Teach new words within conceptually related sets rather than as isolated words. For example, in a lesson on animal habitats, expose children to the names of animals that live in deserts (e.g., *camels, lizards, snakes, prairie dogs*), names of plants that thrive in arid conditions (e.g., *cactus, mesquite tree, yucca*), and words that describe the climatic conditions and geology of deserts (e.g., *arid, dry, sand*). Children are more likely to remember these words and to attach meaning to them if they are exposed to the words in this contextualized way, rather than simply learning a list of animal, plant, and weather words taken out of context.

- Focus on words that are members of large morphological families (e.g., *migrant, migratory, immigrant, immigration*).

- Relate new words to words students already know. For example, to introduce the word *circumference*, begin with the word *circle* to help explain that circumference is the outer edge of a circle.

- Talk about prefixes and suffixes and relate them to root words. For example, to introduce the word *biped*, explain that *bi-* is a prefix that means "two," and give the examples of *bicycle* (two wheels) and *bilingual* (two languages).

SITUATION 1   My students have difficulty expressing themselves because they have limited vocabulary.

Targeted Strategy 1: Make picture dictionaries available.

All newcomer ELL children should have age-appropriate picture dictionaries as resources to help them communicate, as in the following scenario:

Tomás: (*looks distressed*) I can't find my . . .!

Teacher: What can't you find, Tomás?

Tomás: My . . . (*shrugs his shoulders to indicate he doesn't know the word*).

Teacher: Is it something in your desk?

Tomás: Yes.

Teacher: Let's look in your picture dictionary (*opens the picture dictionary and turns to classroom objects*). Is it something here? (*points to items on the page*)

Tomás: Yes! (*points to the picture of a ruler*)

Teacher: Oh, your ruler. Don't worry, Tomás. We'll find it. You can borrow another ruler right now (*gets a ruler and gives it to Tomás*).

As older children's English language develops, more sophisticated dictionaries that include detailed labeling of content-area subjects are available. (See Appendix K, p. 298, for a list of picture dictionaries.)

Targeted Strategy 2: Obtain bilingual dictionaries.

Some picture dictionaries are also available in bilingual editions (e.g., Spanish-English, Russian-English). Children who are literate in their home language often find these picture dictionaries comforting and helpful. Older children who are literate in their home language also find bilingual dictionaries or electronic bilingual dictionaries useful, especially to search for one or two key words that prevent them from understanding a text or to help them convey important ideas. Three precautionary notes on the use of bilingual dictionaries, paper and electronic, are necessary, however: 1) Using a dictionary is a learned skill, and teachers should not assume that all literate, bilingual children know how to use dictionaries or know how to use them effectively; 2) many words have more than one meaning and, even if examples of usage are provided, students may still not locate the correct meaning and/or use the correct word, and 3) using a bilingual dictionary for more than one or two key words is not an efficient way to learn a language. If ELL children are using their dictionaries to look up virtually every word, the text they are trying to read or the ideas they are trying to convey are disconnected from their current language stage. Teachers should encourage such students to express themselves in other ways, such as drawing or writing in their native language, and give them more time and opportunity to develop a knowledge of the words in English that they need in order to articulate more sophisticated ideas.

Targeted Strategy 3: Preview vocabulary.

As teachers begin a content unit of study, read-aloud, or literature study, they should preview the words that students will be encountering so that ELL students will be familiar with them in the context in which they are being used. ELL children need to understand these words, including their pronunciation, to fully participate in any discussion about the content. See Chapters 2 and 4 on listening and reading for strategies for previewing vocabulary.

Targeted Strategy 4: Talk about cognates, false cognates, and borrowed words.

Cognates, words in two languages that share the same root and have similar meanings, can be helpful to students learning a second language. Many cognates can be found between English and Latin-based languages, such as Spanish and French (e.g., *insist* = *insistir* in Spanish) and Germanic languages, such as German and Dutch (e.g., *active* = *aktiv* in German). In addition, languages borrow words from each other (e.g., *patio* from Spanish and *pastrami* from Romanian). An interesting collection of English words borrowed from other languages can be found at www.krysstal.com/borrow.html#s.

Nonnative speakers learn that one recourse when they are stuck for a word is simply to say the word in their native language to see if it might be recognizable in the new language. Teachers should discuss cognates with their ELL students and encourage them to take note of patterns of cognates. They should also warn their students about false cognates, sometimes known as false friends. Because they have similar pronunciations or spellings, these words are often assumed to be synonymous in English but, in fact, they have completely different meanings. A false cognate commonly encountered by English speakers learning Spanish is *embarazada* (which means "pregnant," not "embarrassed"). A list of false cognates by language can be found at home.unilang.org/wiki3/index.php/False_friends.

SITUATION 2 — My students use offensive language, but I don't think they understand the meaning of the words.

When ELL children use offensive or inappropriate words, they may not know the meaning of the words or appreciate the level of offensiveness some words convey. Also ELL children may not be attuned to the social registers incorporated in English. For example, the ELL child who learned the expression *whatever* from peers on the playground may not understand why his or her teacher responds negatively to this word in the classroom. Learning English from peers is an important part of language learning and socialization for ELL children, but teachers must ensure that students understand the social implications of offensive language or inappropriate language that other children may purposely or accidentally teach their ELL peers.

Targeted Strategy 1: Appoint cultural ambassadors.

One role that buddies can serve is that of cultural ambassadors to ELL peers. They can look out for them in the lunchroom and at recess, not only to make sure that they feel that they are part of the group, but also to protect them from peers who might attempt to take advantage of their lack of knowledge of social aspects of language by teaching ELL children to swear or make offensive hand gestures.

Targeted Strategy 2: Speak with the class about not teaching ELLs inappropriate language.

Discussions about treating all class members with respect and what forms respect can take should be a regular part of any classroom. If needed, these discussions should address the importance of not teaching ELL children inappropriate language that they do not understand. Students can be asked to imagine how they would feel if the roles were reversed and they were in a new setting in which they couldn't tell inappropriate words from appropriate words. See pp. 19–22 in Chapter 1 for further details on community-building strategies that help students empathize with and understand ELL children.

Targeted Strategy 3: Make a list of appropriate ways of expressing anger or frustration.

All students in a class will benefit from a brainstorming session on ways to appropriately express anger, including words and expressions that are unacceptable, such as *Math sucks* or *I hate Rosa*. A list of ways to express anger from a brainstorming session might include:

- <u>I'm frustrated because</u> this lesson is hard.

- <u>I can't concentrate because</u> Fran's pencil tapping is bothering me.

- <u>I'm mad at</u> Ignacio <u>because</u> he took my juice.

The brainstorming session should include ways of politely negotiating disputes or frustrations with peers, such as the following:

- Sarah, <u>please don't</u> take my scissors. I need them right now.

- Mohamed, your whistling is bothering me. <u>Could you please stop</u>?

- Wilfredo, I can't see the board. <u>Could you please</u> move your head?

Using the Native Language

Although researchers are still trying to decipher the cognitive mechanisms of bilingualism, many studies have shown its cognitive advantages. For example, bilingual speakers have been found to be superior to monolingual speakers in divergent thinking, that is, the ability to generate many different ideas about a topic in a short period of time, including brainstorming for story ideas (May, Hill, & Tiakiwai, 2004). In addition, bilingual speakers appear to have greater communicative sensitivity than monolinguals. In other words, bilingual speakers, who need to be aware of which language to speak in which situation, have an increased sensitivity to the social nature and communicative functions of language (Cummins & Mulcahy, 1978). Overall, the availability of two linguistic systems appears to give bilingual speakers enhanced cognitive flexibility and social sensitivity. Consequently, schools and teachers should do their utmost to support bilingualism among their ELL students and families by encouraging the retention of the child's native language in the home and providing bilingual support and bilingual resources in the ELL child's home language at school wherever possible. See Chapter 6 on parent communication for specific suggestions on how schools can support bilingual families.

SITUATION 1 — I don't understand why the parents speak English but the child doesn't.

It is quite possible that some parents of ELL children speak English with native or near native fluency while their children do not, since most bilingual parents prefer to speak their native language at home with their children. Research about linguistic and academic development supports this use of the native language by bilingual parents. Studies show that parents should be communicating with their children in their native language in order to support the children's cognitive and linguistic development (King & Fogle, 2006). For social and academic reasons, parents should be communicating with their children in the language in which the parents are most comfortable, no matter their level of fluency in English.

SITUATION 2 — My students switch between English and their native language, sometimes in the same sentence and sometimes across several sentences.

People used to believe that this alternating back and forth between languages, known as code-switching, indicated deficiencies in one language or the other. However, researchers in psycholinguistics now recognize that code-switching is a natural product of the interaction of bilingual speakers' two languages (Heredia & Brown, 2004). Teachers should accept that code-switching may occur and make no attempt to discourage it.

Targeted Strategy 1: Ask a question when you don't understand.

It is very rare for bilingual speakers (children or adults) to code-switch with someone who does not share their language. But if a teacher is involved in a conversation with two or more bilingual speakers and code-switching occurs, the best response is to ask questions about anything that you do not understand (e.g., *I'm sorry. I didn't follow that. Could you repeat it?* Or *I didn't understand. What color is her dress?*).

Targeted Strategy 2: Read literature in which code-switching appears.

Reading literature in which code-switching appears, such as *The House on Mango Street* by Sandra Cisneros (1984/1994), will make students feel more comfortable about their own code-switching and can open up discussions about interesting aspects of how language works for all children in the class.

CHAPTER 4

Reading Situations

I n any discussion about reading, it is important to first establish what one means by *reading*. What is reading? And what is reading for ELLs? These are especially critical questions given the current reading instruction climate in the United States, where federal mandates, such as the No Child Left Behind Act (NCLB), and state textbook adoption policies have led increasing numbers of school districts to mandate commercial scripted, prescriptive reading programs (Altwerger, Arya, Jin, Jordan, Laster, Martens, Wilson, & Wiltz, 2004). For example, Open Court is a program that has been mandated in many school districts across the nation, including in California, where approximately 33 percent of all elementary students are ELLs (Moustafa & Land, 2002; Achinstein, Ogawa, & Speiglman, 2005), yet Open Court was developed for monolingual English-speaking students, not ELLs (Rumberger & Gandara, 2004).

An additional concern about these one-size-fits-all reading programs centers on how the teacher-centered instructional practices embodied in them influence the kinds of reading-related school experiences that are available to ELLs. For example, Pease-Alvarez, Samway, Almanzo, and Cifka (2007) found that most instruction in Open Court classrooms was whole class, with very little attention to the individual reading needs of students. Also, the largest amount of time during the two- to two-and-a-half-hour reading/language arts block was devoted to teaching and practicing reading skills, with little or no time spent actually reading. In addition, teachers dominated classroom talk. All of these findings are very troubling when one considers how ELLs (like all children) need instruction geared to their needs, many opportunities to read for authentic purposes, and lots of opportunities to interact meaningfully with others.

With the current heavy emphasis on the (often decontexualized) teaching of phonemic awareness and phonics (a consequence of NCLB), one might conclude that reading is simply decoding (or making letter-sound correspondences). In fact, reading is a much more complex process, one that is grounded in making meaning from symbols. The degree to which readers are able to make sense of a text or written message is very much affected by their prior experiences, that is, their schema. As an example, take a minute to read the following text, and then paraphrase what it says.

Today's Cricket

The batsmen were merciless against the bowlers. The bowlers placed their men in slips and covers. But to no avail. The batsmen hit one four after another with an occasional six. Not once did a ball look like it would hit their stumps or be caught.   (Source: Tierney & Pearson, 1981)

Perhaps this was gobbledygook to you, even though you could decode it easily. What reading textbooks typically do in these kinds of circumstances is to reduce the readability of the text by simplifying the vocabulary and sentence structure, which is what Tierney and Pearson did in the following rewrite of the text. Again, take a minute to read it and paraphrase what it says.

(Lower readability version)

The men were at bat against the bowlers. They did not show any pity. The bowlers placed their men in slips. They placed their men in covers. It did not help. The batsmen hit a lot of fours. They hit some sixes. No ball hit the stumps. No ball was caught.   (Source: Tierney & Pearson, 1981)

Unless you know something about cricket, the chances are that this simplified text is still incomprehensible. That is, you may not have the schema to know that the *slips and covers* are positions that fielders take in cricket (and where they're located on the field), and that *fours* and *sixes* are the number of runs scored off a single bowl (ball)—a six being when the ball passes over the outer limits of the field without hitting the ground first (like a baseball home run), and a four being a ball that bounces on the ground before passing over the outer limits of the cricket field. So, simplifying the language and sentence structure to make it easier to decode probably wasn't much help to you in understanding the text. This difficulty is what ELLs who can decode reasonably well in English encounter when they read about events and experiences that are unfamiliar to them. The necessity of a schema for understanding text has implications for what we need to focus on when teaching reading.

A key factor in ELLs' reading success and development is the understanding of vocabulary, yet very little attention is paid in school to vocabulary and word consciousness development. Even when ELLs can decode words in English, they may not know what the terms mean. This is compounded for ELLs who may not understand the concept in any language, including their own. For example, Inuits, who live in the Arctic, have many words to signify the subtleties of snow; if either of us were to learn Inuit, we would struggle enormously when confronted by the multiple words for *snow* because we do not have the schema (background knowledge or experiences), even though we have spent many years living in western New York, where there is plenty of snow.

Recent national reports (e.g., RAND Reading Study Group, 2002; National Institute of Child Health and Human Development [NICHD] 2000, *Report of the National Reading Panel*; August & Shanahan, 2006, *Developing Literacy in Second-Language Learners: Report of the National Literacy Panel on Language-Minority Children and Youth*) have identified vocabulary knowledge as a key element in successful reading comprehension. Vocabulary knowledge is also known to be a key element in a language development program for ELL students (Nation, 2001), and integral to academic success (Cummins, 2000; Scarcella, 2002).

There are still other issues to take into consideration when teaching ELLs to read, such as their possible lack of familiarity with grammatical structures that assist native speakers of English in making sense of a text. For example, when native English speakers see the following sentence fragment, *When I went to the park, I . . .* , they intuitively know that what follows will often be a verb or verb phrase (e.g., *played, played croquet, fed the ducks, had a picnic*). ELLs may not have internalized that grammatical understanding. In addition, even if the ELL knows that what follows is probably a verb, the actual words that follow it may not be familiar (e.g., *croquet*).

There are also other realities that need to be taken into consideration when teaching English reading to ELLs, particularly for students who already read in their L1. For example, not all written languages are alphabetic (e.g., Chinese) and some languages, although alphabetic, do not have the same written script as English (e.g., Arabic, Greek, Hebrew, Russian). This means that students who read and write in these languages have to learn a different orthography (the written symbols used to represent the sounds of a language). However, because they already have a schema for reading, it is usually easier for older ELLs who are literate in their L1 to move into literacy in English than it is for their ELL peers who are not literate in their L1.

Another consideration to be aware of is unfamiliar teaching/learning practices that ELLs may encounter in North American classrooms. For example, if they have been taught to read in a language other than English, they may have been taught with a very heavy emphasis on decoding (common in Spanish-speaking countries due to the regularity of the letter-sound correspondences in Spanish). Also, some countries take a more didactic approach to teaching reading; for example, ELL students may not be accustomed to being asked to make inferences or evaluate texts and may react with frustration when asked to do so. If students have been taught to focus on extracting literal information from a text, rather than inferring meaning, they may view a request to infer as invalid (e.g., *But it's not in the text, so why are you asking me to do this?*). Even when ELLs intuitively and successfully infer in non-school contexts, they may still react this way in an academic setting.

Some learners excel in the print form of a nonnative language, whereas others are more developed orally. For example, Katharine was working with a teacher in a school for newcomer ELLs and observed that Chinese-speaking students from China, Hong Kong, and Taiwan, who had been schooled in their native lands and had some exposure to English instruction (typically a grammar-translation approach), were more comfortable writing English than speaking it. In contrast, she observed that Spanish-speaking students from Mexico and Central America, who had often had limited schooling in their L1, tended to be more comfortable with and confident about speaking English than reading and writing it. Similarly, Saville-Troike, (1984) observed marked differences in the language modality preferences and levels of English proficiency of middle-class ELLs in grades 2–6.

Regardless of variations in children's preferred language modalities, research shows that ELLs do not have to be fluent in English before they can read and write English (e.g., Edelsky, 1982; Han & Ernst-Slavit, 1999;

Hudelson, 1984, 1986, 1989; Retish, 2000; Reyes, 1991; Samway, 1987a, 1987b, 1993, 2006; Samway & Taylor, 1993a, 1993b; Taylor, 1990, 2000; Urzúa, 1986, 1987). In fact, reading can support auditory and oral language development by offering ELLs exposure to more standardized and sophisticated forms of English than they are able to produce at that time (Samway & Taylor, 1993a, 1993b; Taylor, 1990).

When discussing reading, it is very common to begin with decoding and then progress to comprehension. Decoding is certainly a part of the reading process, but it is by no means the most important part, as the earlier activity involving the passages about cricket reveals. Although reading in English usually requires some knowledge of phonics, ELLs often have trouble hearing certain sounds, particularly some vowel sounds, so decontextualized phonics and phonemic awareness instruction and practice can be very difficult for them. (See Chapters 2 and 3 on listening and speaking for more about this). In this chapter, we focus on comprehension, including vocabulary development, and do not pay as much attention to decoding. This is a decision we made very consciously for the following reasons:

- Comprehension, and vocabulary development, in particular, are at the heart of successful reading—one can decode lots and lots of words and still have absolutely no idea what one has decoded. For example, when Katharine was in Poland for a few days, by the end of the visit she was able to decode signs that had totally stumped her on her first day in Krakow, but she still didn't know what the signs meant (except in the case of a name she knew from living in upstate New York). Essentially, Katharine was beginning to decode, but she wasn't truly reading. If she had stayed in Poland, she would have had to build her repertoire of Polish vocabulary in order to be able to read Polish.

- North American schools pay considerable attention to decoding, beginning with students' earliest years of school (as well as preschool). So long as teachers take into account the special circumstance of ELLs (e.g., that they may not hear certain sounds in English or distinguish between some similar-sounding words), they can avail themselves of the many useful decoding teaching resources in professional books, and at workshops and conferences.

In the pages that follow, we share some general strategies for enhancing ELLs' reading, as well as several targeted strategies aligned with specific reading-related situations that teachers often comment on.

General Strategies

ELL children need to experience success with English texts, and in this section, we focus on some strategies that foster a love of books and provide scaffolded experiences for them.

General Strategy 1: Read aloud to ELL students.

Through read-alouds, teachers can extend their students' knowledge of the world, vocabulary, and grammatical structures, as well as introduce them to authors, genres, and content that they might not otherwise read. One of the goals of good reading instruction is to turn children into avid readers, and reading aloud to ELLs is one way to accomplish this. But simply reading aloud is generally not sufficient. Read-alouds need scaffolding, such as the following:

- Select books that include cultural information familiar to ELL children. (See Appendix C, pp. 273–283 for a list of suggested books.)

- Do a book talk prior to actually reading aloud, thereby activating students' background knowledge.

- Provide lots of support to ELLs so that the read-aloud isn't a cognitive overload for them. This type of scaffolding can include the following strategies:
  - Refer to pictures, sketches, and objects (realia) to make meaning more clear.
  - Use lots of gestures and dramatic displays to make meaning clear.

- Briefly discuss any concepts, terminology, and grammatical structures crucial to understanding the text that you anticipate may not be familiar to ELL students.

- Hold a quick one-minute check-in before moving on to the next part of a longer book.

- Have extra copies of the text available so ELLs can follow along, thereby having the added benefit of seeing the words on the page. This is particularly useful for novels and other longer and/or more complex texts. Often, an ELL who is literate in the L1 is able to make sense of what he or she hears being said, including in a read-aloud, from seeing words on the page. This is particularly true of students who have received some instruction in English prior to coming to North America.

- Read the same text aloud often, particularly if it is a favorite—familiarity can lead to increased understanding.

- If you have an audio version of the book, make it available to ELLs, along with a copy of the text, so they can use it in school or at home for extra listening and reading practice.

Additional issues to consider when preparing for and conducting a read-aloud include the following:

- Read from a wide range of genres, including short stories, picture books (fiction and nonfiction), poetry, and nonfiction magazine articles. For more information about conducting nonfiction read-alouds, see *Navigating Informational Texts* by Linda Hoyt (2003), and the accompanying videotapes.

- Choose texts carefully, and make sure to familiarize yourself with them. How many times have we randomly selected a book for a read-aloud, a book that even we don't know (or assigned an unfamiliar book to a student teacher or volunteer to read aloud), and the read-aloud bombed? Not all books lend themselves well to being read aloud. For example, Katharine loves Gary Paulsen's *Hatchet* (1987), but has found that some of the features that she particularly enjoys in his writing, such as the staccato-like prose, are hard for her to read aloud.

- It is generally best *not* to encourage students to do other things while listening to the read-aloud, unless they are connected very directly to the reading. Students need to concentrate—even good multitaskers can't pay full attention when engaged in more than one task. Instead, give students a text-based task. For example, when introducing a text, Katharine says something like, *I hope you'll enjoy this book as much as I do. I chose it because . . . . I'd like you to think about the following as I read it to you—What does this book remind you of?* (Or *What do you think will happen next, and why?* or *What do you think this poem is about/what's the theme of this poem?* or *What did you learn from this book about . . . ?*)

- Students need time to talk about the text, even if it's for just a minute or two. They need time to talk about what the text reminded them of, ask questions, discuss any puzzling parts or words, and explore what they learned about writing from hearing the text. The talk accompanying a read-aloud can be through pair shares or with the entire group.

- After completing the read-aloud, it can be very useful to discuss issues that the students have been exploring and charting, and add new insights to the charts. For example, some issues that teachers focus on after a read-aloud include the following:
  - ⋆ Unfamiliar words/terms
  - ⋆ Interesting use of language
  - ⋆ What we learned about writing

General Strategy 2: Incorporate shared reading/big books.

In shared reading, the teacher and students read a commercially published or teacher-made big book and/or chart featuring enlarged text that all students can see. Texts include fiction, nonfiction, poetry, rhymes, and chants that are often highly predictable and written with rhythmic language to support emergent readers. What follows is an adapted shared-reading procedure to support emergent ELL readers.

Procedure:

- When introducing a new shared reading text, the teacher briefly describes what it is about.

- Next, the teacher reads the text aloud at a normal or very slightly slowed pace, while pointing to each word with a pointer.

- The class has a brief discussion about what the text reminds them of, any unfamiliar words, and so on.

- The teacher and students read the text together, with the teacher continuing to point to the words.

- The class may reread the text again, with the teacher opting to reduce the amount of support he or she provides.

- An effective follow-up activity that uses sentence strips to support readers follows:
  - ⋆ The teacher writes a sentence from the text, along with its punctuation on a strip of paper.
  - ⋆ The words and punctuation are cut into phrases and/or individual words and punctuation marks. As the following example from a nursery rhyme shows, it can be much harder to put individual words in order than phrases.

Sentence from nursery rhyme:

If all the seas were one sea, what a great sea that would be.

Scrambled sentence (phrases with punctuation):

that would be.   were one sea,   what a great sea   If all the seas

Scrambled sentence (words with punctuation):

all   seas   one   what   great   sea   would   If   the   were   sea,

a   be.   that

- The student(s) puts the scrambled strips in order.
- The teacher and student(s) talk about any difficulties they encountered, and discuss how they knew what order to put the words in. Common answers include mechanics (e.g., a sentence begins with a capital letter and ends with a period), grammar (e.g., adjectives usually go in front of nouns, such as *great sea*), and meaning (e.g., all the seas have to come together into one sea before you can have the great sea).

General Strategy 3: *Make use of choral reading.*

In choral reading, the teacher and students recite a familiar poem, chant, or rhyme together.

Procedure:

- Select a text that:
  - Is relatively short
  - Interests students
  - Can be read by the students
  - Lends itself to oral dramatizations (e.g., a text that has interesting sounds, including alliteration and onomatopoeia; a text that lends itself to two- or three-part renditions; a text that refers to several characters and lends itself to different voices)
  - May include words in the native language of ELLs

- Make copies of the text for the students.

- Read the text to the students in an engaging, dramatic voice, while they follow along in their own copies.

- Students and the teacher then read the text aloud together—it may be necessary to do this several times, until students have memorized it (or almost memorized it).

- Students practice reading together in pairs—they can also alternate reading lines aloud.

- The whole group or class gets together to practice the performance. The goal is to present the text in a dramatically engaging way. Some performance possibilities include:

  - ⋆ Individual students, pairs of students, or small groups of students stand on either side of the room and take turns reading lines, stanzas, or sections of the text.
  - ⋆ Sound effects—such as clapping, stamping feet, making the sound of trees swaying in a storm, or animals calling out—are added at appropriate times.
  - ⋆ Key words or phrases are emphasized for effect.
  - ⋆ Soft and loud voices and high and low voices are alternated at appropriate times.

- The class or group may perform the piece for an audience.

See www.pbs.org/wnet/americanmasters/education/general.html for more information about choral reading.

General Strategy 4: Do an echo reading.

Echo reading provides ELLs with the opportunity to hear English read fluently, as well as practice reading fluently—with expression and normal pacing. The teacher, or another fluent reader, reads a phrase or sentence with expression and then the student or students repeat it. The oral reading continues in this way.

General Strategy 5: Encourage pair reading.

In pair reading, two to three students read the same book and then talk about it together. This provides a shared experience with books, peer support for readers, and also introduces students to new authors, illustrators, and genres.

Procedure:

- Select several books for which you have two to three copies. The books should be:

  - ⋆ Of interest to students
  - ⋆ Able to be read in one session in class or overnight
  - ⋆ From a variety of genres, including poetry, stories, essays, and information picture books
  - ⋆ Representative of the experiences of diverse cultures, as much as possible

- Have more titles/copies than you have students, so there is some choice.

- Do a book talk on each book.

- Students select their own books and read them—sometimes they actually read together, taking turns reading to one another.

- Students talk about their books in same-book pairs. The whole class/group gets together and discusses issues such as:

  - Successful strategies the students used when reading together
  - What students learned about the book and about reading from working with a partner
  - Difficulties they encountered when reading and how they resolved them
  - Aspects of the book they didn't understand
  - Aspects of the book that they particularly liked, and why

General Strategy 6: Use Language Experience Approach (LEA).

First developed as a means to produce reading materials that emergent readers could understand, LEA involves students dictating a text, usually based on a familiar or shared experience (Allen, 1976; Stauffer, 1970). One approach to implementing LEA with ELLs follows.

- A student or group of students dictates a text.

- The teacher writes the text exactly as each student dictates it (e.g., *We go pumpkin place Tuesday.*). If a group of students is dictating the text, the teacher writes it on chart paper so that all the students can see it.

- The teacher then goes through the text, explaining how to revise the grammar and word choices, as the following example illustrates. Note that the teacher does not change the content of the message:

  Teacher: (*repeats the first sentence that the student generated*) "We go the pumpkin place yesterday." Is that right?

  Alicia: (*nods head*) Yes.

  Teacher: Okay. And because it was yesterday, we need to write it in the past tense. "We went" instead of "We go." "We go" means we're doing it right now, and this refers to yesterday (*writes the revised text next to the original text, beginning with "We went," and says each word aloud while writing it*). And, it's "We went to." You said here (*points to the text while reading*), "pumpkin place." It's actually called a pumpkin farm. Remember?

  Alicia: (*nods head vigorously*) Yes, pumpkin farm.

  Teacher: So we'll change this to "farm" (*writes "pumpkin farm," and says the words aloud while writing them*). Now, we went to the pumpkin farm yesterday, so do you want to say, "We went to the

	pumpkin farm <u>yesterday</u>" or "We went to the pumpkin farm <u>on</u> Tuesday"? (*pauses*)
Alicia:	Tuesday. I like Tuesday.
Teacher:	Okay. In that case, we have to say "<u>on</u> Tuesday," so we add the word "on." (*writes "on Tuesday," and says the words aloud while writing them*). Okay. Let's read this together. (*points to each word while reading the revised text with the student*) We went to the pumpkin farm on Tuesday.

The teacher and student(s) continue to add sentences until there is a complete text. The students read the text many times over the course of a few days. The text is also used for language and reading practice, and may be incorporated into the following follow-up activities:

* Work with sentence strips: A sentence is written on a sentence strip and then cut apart for the student(s) to put in order and then read. Sentences from an entire short text can also be put on strips, sorted, and read.

* Generate alternate words: For a sentence such as *We went to the pumpkin farm*, the students brainstorm words that could fit in place of *went*, such as *drove, traveled, took a trip*. Then the students and teacher discuss differences in the meaning and when each word or phrase is most likely to be used. The list of alternate words and uses can be displayed for future reference and may be added to.

* Circle specific parts of speech, such as nouns, verbs, or pronouns.

* Identify and circle onsets and rimes: For example, in *went*: /w/ is the onset and /ent/ is the rime. Students can then generate other words that have the same onset (e.g., the /w/ in /<u>w</u>/ing/, /<u>w</u>/ait/, /<u>w</u>/ish) and/or rimes (e.g., the /ent/ in s/<u>ent</u>/, b/<u>ent</u>/, sp/<u>ent</u>/).

* Cloze activities: In a cloze activity, students predict which words are missing in a passage and fill in the blanks with those words. See Appendix L (p. 299) for guidelines for developing cloze activities and Appendices M and N (pp. 300–301) for two versions of a cloze text. Another procedure that can be very useful with ELLs is a selected feature cloze, which focuses on a particular linguistic feature. For example, a teacher may delete the articles, adverbs, or inflectional endings (e.g., the *–ed* in *walked*, the *–ing* in *walking* or the *–s* in *toys*) in order to give students practice using that feature in a way that fosters thoughtful reading. See Appendix O (p. 302) for an example of a selected feature cloze.

Reading Comprehension

SITUATION 1 My ELL students' limited knowledge of English words affects their reading comprehension.

Ultimately, the most important aspect of reading is to make meaning of what we read. A key factor in ELLs' reading comprehension is vocabulary knowledge (Carlo, August, McLaughlin, Snow, Dressler, Lippman, Lively, & White, 2004). In a study of elementary-aged ELL students, Saville-Troike (1984) found that knowledge of English vocabulary was the most critical factor in their literacy achievement. The following numbers show the importance of vocabulary in the academic lives of ELLs:

- English-speaking children with average and above-average verbal ability enter school with a receptive vocabulary of between 5,000 and 10,000 words (Blachowicz, Fisher, Ogle, & Watts-Taffe, 2006).

- By the time average and above average native English-speaking students leave high school, they have acquired about 40,000 receptive words; a simple calculation indicates that this is more than 3,000 new words, on average, for each year in school (Nagy & Herman, 1987).

Although ELL students often have large vocabularies in their native language, and this knowledge may transfer from their L1 to English (e.g., cognates—words that look and sound similar and have the same meaning in two languages), they still have a lot of catching up to do in the area of English vocabulary. Despite this reality, vocabulary instruction for ELLs, particularly in mainstream classrooms where reading is taught to the entire class at the same time through textbooks, is typically limited to the teaching of a few content words, some high-frequency words (many of which are very abstract, such as *their* and *of*), and affixes, which do not make words more comprehensible if students do not know the meaning of the root words (Pease-Alvarez, Samway, Almanzo, & Cifka-Herrerra, 2007).

Although reading widely is an effective strategy for building vocabulary, it has been reported that the probability of learning unknown words in this way is only about 15 percent (Swanborn & de Glopper, 1999); only avid readers seem to build vocabulary in this way. Acquiring a lot of vocabulary through reading alone is often hard for ELLs because of their lack of familiarity with the nuances of language (e.g., idioms and grammatical cues), vocabulary, and cultural knowledge. For example, there are several much-loved picture books in English that many ELLs find difficult to read because the books are grounded in well-known fairy tales and nursery rhymes in English. These include *Each Peach Pear Plum* (Ahlberg & Ahlberg, 1978, 1979), which is a rhyming picture puzzle that draws on lots of nursery rhymes; *The Jolly Postman* (Ahlberg & Ahlberg, 1986), which cleverly uses nursery rhyme and fairy tale characters who write letters to each other; and *Goodnight Moon* (Brown, 1947), which refers to the "cow jumping over the moon" from the nursery rhyme "Hey, Diddle, Diddle." When reading this kind of book to a class or group that includes ELLs, it is essential for the teacher to familiarize the ELLs with the background stories and rhymes so that they can understand the books. This background information is particularly important for both newcomers and older students who have not been schooled in an English-speaking country since kindergarten or preschool.

General Strategies

Students need to be immersed in vocabulary/concept development throughout the day. We also recommend the following general strategies.

General Strategy 1: Hold a vocabulary mini-workshop or CPR.

In many classrooms, regular times each day are devoted to reading workshop, writing workshop, and word study. We recommend scheduling 10 to 15 minutes each day for a vocabulary mini-workshop (when you can help your ELL students become more conscious of words) in addition to the vocabulary-building activities that should happen throughout the day. This vocabulary mini-workshop should occur at the same time each day (e.g., at the beginning of the day or after recess), so that children can anticipate it and come prepared with their own observations about and insights into words. The vocabulary mini-workshop is a time for students to become excited and curious about language and how it works. The teacher's role is to:

- Foster students' curiosity and excitement through sharing their own curiosity about and passion for words.

- Strategically introduce students to new concepts, terms, and relationships between words and across languages.

- Engage students in substantive and interesting vocabulary study and word-consciousness activities.

Katharine calls this type of a mini-vocabulary workshop CPR, which stands for:

C = *Curious about words and phrases and their origins*

Curious readers notice unusual or new words and intriguing uses of familiar words. They stop to think about a word they have just encountered, to figure out its meaning and maybe its origin. For example, a friend of Katharine's has the last name Toll, which he told her is found in both England and Germany, and they agreed that it was likely that his ancestors probably collected tolls on roads in Europe. Katharine wondered if the English word *toll* had its origins in German, as many English words do. The day after this conversation, she checked her copy of *Brewer's Dictionary of Phrase and Fable* (1996) (and found nothing there about *toll*, just *tollbooth*), and her copy of the *American Heritage Dictionary* (1982, 1985) (which indicated that *toll* has its origins in Old English). Still curious the next day, Katharine checked on the Internet, and came upon a brief reference on Wikipedia to *toll* meaning "great" in German. (She also saw a reference to German-English cognates—words in different languages that share the same root and meaning—and followed her curiosity about this, too.) Although she didn't get a clear answer to her original question, she had immersed herself in vocabulary and word origins and meanings. In order to foster this kind of curiosity about words in our ELL students, we need to share our own passion for words and language with them.

P = *Passionate about words*

If words are important to us, not in the sense that we get angry when others misuse them or use a nonstandard form of a word, but in the sense of appreciating their beauty and their power in conveying subtle meanings, then we are probably passionate about words. This is something we need to nurture in our students, particularly our ELLs, who often have a lot of catching up to do in English. This kind of passion can translate into an acute awareness of and curiosity about words that enhances our students' reading (as well as listening, speaking, and writing).

R = *Risk-taker*

Whether we are adults or children, we all need to feel that we can take risks and not be mocked when experimenting with language. For example, Katharine speaks Spanish and has had the good fortune to have had hundreds of conversations in Spanish with native Spanish speakers who focused on what she was trying to communicate, rather than correcting her word choice or grammar. As a result, she felt confident and willing to take risks. But, on a couple of occasions when her conversational partners insisted on sternly correcting her Spanish, she closed down and stopped talking, which is the ultimate manifestation of not being a risk-taker. As teachers, we must honor and encourage experimentation, while also teaching about words.

The following specific strategies for a vocabulary mini-workshop are designed to encourage an interest in and passion about words. Not every strategy will necessarily lead immediately to a more expansive vocabulary (e.g., word search cubes), but they can all lead to a greater appreciation for words. Some activities more directly relate to building vocabulary and word consciousness. As you will see, these activities typically encourage multiple responses, which promotes versatile, flexible thinking, an asset when learning to speak a language and becoming literate in it.

Targeted Strategy 1: Find words in names.

This activity is designed to help students notice words embedded in longer words. The process of generating words and discussing unfamiliar words can enhance vocabulary development.

Procedure:

- Demonstrate how to look for as many words possible in a name consisting of first and last names combined, without using a letter more than once in each new word (e.g., if there are two *a*'s in the name, then an *a* can be used twice in the new word but, if there is only one *a*, that letter can be used only once). For example, in Fatimah Suleyman (*fatimahsuleyman*), a very quick search reveals the following words: *fat*, *faith*, *slay*, *man*, *mean*, *time*, *timely*, *mate*, *slim*. (Teachers can select a student's name because it is his or her birthday or use the names of other people that students know, such as famous people, including authors). Give students about five minutes to find embedded words. Allow a little more time when students are new to it.

- Students can work alone or together to find as many words as they can in the designated time.

- At the end of the designated time, students take turns reading aloud their words. If someone else found the same word, it gets deleted. The winner is the person, pair, or small group with the most words that no one else found.

Variations:

- Individual students keep a record of how many words they generate each time.

- The class keeps a record of how many words they collaboratively generate.

- Once students are pretty good at locating three-letter words, they can be directed to list only words with three or more letters.

- Post a multisyllabic content-area word, such as *magnetism, photosynthesis, earthquake, denouement*.

- Post a phrase that students are familiar with, such as *once upon a time (onceuponatime)*; *I had a dream (Ihadadream)*; *westward movement (westwardmovement)*.

- Use words from different languages found in children's books. For example, the following wonderful picture books contain words in languages other than English:
  - *Only a Pigeon* (Kurtz & Kurtz, 1997) is set in Ethiopia and uses the Amharic word for wild mongoose, *shele mit-mot* (*shelemitmot*).
  - In *Nadia's Hand* (English, 1999), the author uses the Urdu word for the henna paste applied to the hands of Pakistani women, *mendhi*.
  - *Chachaji's Cup* (Krishnaswami, 2003) includes the Hindi word for spicy, sweet tea, *masala chai* (*masalachai*).
  - Pat Mora (1997) includes several Spanish words and phrases in her book about Tomás Rivera, *Tomás and the Library Lady*, including *buenas noches/goodnight* (*buenasnoches*).

Using words from the ELL students' home languages validates and shows respect for their native language.

Targeted Strategy 2: Discover words in a word search cube.

In this activity, students have a designated amount of time to find words within a word.

- Select a nine-letter word, such as a key word from a content area of study like *magnetism*. Scramble the letters and place them in a nine-box cube, as in the example at the right.

- Make copies of the cube for students.

- Students have about five to ten minutes to find as many words as they can, using the letters in the cube. Each letter can be used only once.

- Words must contain at least three letters. This can be adjusted up or down, according to the students' needs. Proper nouns, abbreviations, and non-English words do not count. (You can use your discretion about any of these stipulations.)

- Students can work alone or in pairs, and record their words on paper.

- While students are working on the cube, the teacher should check with them to clarify any confusion about the rules and to help get them started, if needed. One way to help them move on is by suggesting a strategy (if the cube contains an *e* and an *r*, words like *walk* [a verb] can be made into *walker* [a noun]).

- At the end of the designated time, the whole class comes together and generates a list of all the words they found.

- At this point, any unfamiliar words can be discussed and clarified, if it hasn't happened already.

- Discuss students' experiences. Ask open-ended questions, including the following:

  ⋆ *Was this an easy or hard search, and why?* Students might come to realize that, if there aren't many vowels in the cube, it can be hard to find English words.

  ⋆ *What strategies helped you find words/lots of word?* If there is an *s*, it's possible to make plural nouns, so *boat* can become *boats*, and to change verbs from the first- or second-person singular (I *hold*, you *run*) to the third-person singular (she *holds*, he *runs*). If there's a rime, such as *ent*, students may be able to generate lots of words, such as *sent*, *went*, *tent*.

Do not be surprised if students continue to find words long after the designated time; they may even take the cube home and return with more words that family members helped to find. Be sure to encourage and acknowledge these efforts as they demonstrate a genuine engagement with words and language.

Targeted Strategy 3: Introduce a synonym cube.

This activity may be hard for students, so it is usually best for students to work in pairs initially. They can discuss options and test and confirm or discard their selections.

Procedure:

- Select a key word, perhaps an important content word, with a familiar synonym. This synonym should be either four or nine letters long, like the following:

  - ★ Quick—<u>Fast</u> (four-letter synonym)
  - ★ Soil—<u>Dirt</u> (four-letter synonym)
  - ★ Compute—<u>Calculate</u> (nine-letter synonym)
  - ★ Colleague—<u>Associate</u> (nine-letter synonym)

- Scramble the letters in the synonym and place them in a four-box cube or a nine-box cube. (See examples below.)

- Give students the following directions:

  - ★ Think of a word meaning _____ (fill in the blank, e.g., *dread* or *inference*) that uses *all* the letters in the cube below.
  - ★ Use each letter only once.
    Here are two examples:

Example 1: Think of another word for *dread*.

(answer: FEAR)

Example 2: Think of another word for *inference*.

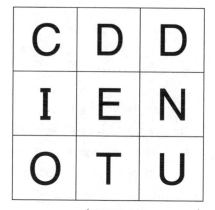

(answer: DEDUCTION)

Alternatives:

- Students generate synonym pairs for their own cubes.

- In a nine-letter cube, some squares can be shaded when there are fewer than nine letters in the synonym.

Targeted Strategy 4: Play the game, "It's a . . ."

This game, which fosters divergent thinking and the naming of words and terms, is similar to games played on the Drew Carey

TV show, *Whose Line Is It Anyway?* and in Odyssey of the Mind, a national competition for school-age children that focuses on creative problem solving and group work.[1] The competition includes spontaneous problem solving, which is sometimes called a *brain tester* or *brain builder*.

The purpose of this activity is for students to use their creative thinking to go outside the box and generate as many imagined uses possible for a simple object—e.g., a dowel, a walking stick, a large rubber ring, a plastic bowl, a sausage-shaped inflated balloon—or a drawing of an imaginary, intriguing-looking object. See Figure 4.1 below for a sample drawing.

Figure 4.1: Drawing of an imaginary object

For example, if students are given a plastic bowl, uses they generate may include: a hat, a dog-food bowl, half of a melon, a boat or dinghy, a shoulder pad, a chair. Small groups of students can compete against each other, or each group can compete against itself by aiming to better its score in each game, using different objects or drawings.

Procedure:

- ⚬ The teacher shows the class an object or a drawing of an imaginary object.

- ⚬ Groups have about five minutes to brainstorm a list of creative uses for the object.

---

[1] More information about Odyssey of the Mind (OotM) can be found at www.odysseyofthemind.com. Although OotM hosts local, regional, and national competitions, it isn't necessary to enter the competition—just working on the problems is a stimulating and authentic way for children to work together. In many schools, only children designated as gifted and talented are involved in this program, which is unfortunate as all children benefit from collaborative problem solving.

- Groups take turns demonstrating and naming the uses; members in each group also take turns sharing the information.

- Each use a group generates earns a point; only the first group to suggest the use receives the point.

- The group that generates the greatest number of original uses wins.

Alternative: Students generate props or drawings for the group or class to use.

Alternatives (adapted from Odyssey of the Mind):

  ★ **Animal Rhymes:** Students compose a rhyme that uses a name or species of animal, such as *I can see the dog in the fog* or *I'll ask the lion to iron.* (The latter rhymes when Katharine says it, but not when Dorothy does, which points to how variable pronunciation is.)

  ★ **Be a Patient:** Students pretend to be patients in an operating room, where they hear noises and conversation. They have to say what they would like to hear or *not* like to hear. Responses must begin with *I would like to hear . . .* or *I would not like to hear . . .*

  ★ **Names:** Students use common words to make up a first and last name related to an occupation. For example, *doctor* becomes Doc Tor, who is a physician; or *marker* becomes Mark Er, who is an artist; or *Bellevue* becomes Belle Vue, who is a psychiatrist.

Targeted Strategy 5: List cognates.

Cognates are words in two languages that are spelled and pronounced in similar ways and have the same meaning (e.g., in Spanish, the word for *pilot* is *piloto*.) As many as 30 percent of English words are Spanish cognates, and it is important to alert Spanish-speaking children, in particular, to this reality so they have access to another source of word knowledge.[2] Several languages share cognates with English, including Arabic, French, and German. Here are some suggestions for creating and using lists of cognates.

- The entire class and/or individual students can keep lists of cognates and their meanings, which can be generated from a variety of sources, such as their reading, the community, TV, and print media.

- Use bilingual dictionaries to verify that the words are actually cognates. Various Web sites can help with the verification process, also. See the list of Web sites in the Cognate (and False Friends) Resources on page 147.

---

[2] In a recent study of the vocabulary knowledge of fourth graders (Scott, Flinspach, & Samway, 2007), Spanish-speaking ELLs identified statistically fewer English/Spanish cognates than other ELLs.

- Students' findings can be displayed on charts and stored in three-ring binders.

- In order to enhance metalinguistic knowledge, talk with students about how they know that certain words are cognates.

- Students can talk with family members about cognates in their home language, both English cognates and cognates from other languages, and share them with the class.

Alternative Strategy 1: Read and identify.

- When reading a text with ELL students, invite them to identify words they think may be cognates.
- Ask students why they think the words are cognates. Again, this helps develop metalinguistic awareness.
- Check a bilingual dictionary or Web site to verify whether the words are cognates.
- Keep a record of the cognates.
- Use the words in reinforcement games, such as Concentration. See the guidelines for this and other games on pages 152–156.

Alternative Strategy 2: Ask, "Which words do you know, and how do you know them?"

Ask ELL students which words they know in a text, and how they know the words. Often, they will identify a cognate. Add these words to a chart of cognates, and use them for practice activities, including matching cognate pairs, and playing reinforcement games.

Alternative Strategy 3: Are words fickle friends or partial cognates?

Not all words that look alike in two languages mean the same in both languages. In Spanish, *admirar* means "to admire," but it also means "to astonish" or "to surprise." For this reason, the pairs of words are called fickle friends or partial cognates. Invite students to locate fickle friends and post them on a chart, along with their meanings. These words can be used for reinforcement games.

Alternative Strategy 4: Identify false friends.

Explain to students that some words look like they are cognates, but actually aren't, and are called false friends. The Spanish word *pie* means "foot," not a dessert made with pastry. False friends can get us into trouble. When she was still fairly new to Spanish, Katharine announced one day that she was *embarazada*, thinking she had said she was embarrassed, when in fact she had said she was pregnant! Students can search for false friends, and the teacher can share false friends with students.

Alternative Strategy 5: Find the difference.

List pairs of cognates on paper or a chart. Have students identify differences in the cognate pairs. For example, in the English-Spanish cognate *desert/desierto*, the Spanish word has two additional letters, an *i* after *des* and an *o* at the end of the word. The teacher and students can take turns circling or underlining the differences.

Cognate (and False Friends) Resources:

To find information about cognates, visit the following Web sites:

* **English-Spanish cognates and false friends:**
  Colorín Colorado at: www.colorincolorado.org/educators/background/cognates
  Jill Kerper Mora at: coe.sdsu.edu/people/jmora/MoraModules/SpEngCognates.htm
  Gerald Erichsen at: spanish.about.com/cs/vocabulary/a and spanish.about.com/cs/vocabulary/a/obviouswrong.htm
* **English-Arabic cognates** (English words borrowed from Arabic, such as *adobe*, *algebra*, *candy*, *jasmine*, *lemon*): Outreach World at: www.outreachworld.org/resource.asp?curriculumid=300
* **English-French cognates and false friends:**
  french.about.com/library/vocab/bl-vraisamis.htm
* **English-German cognates and false friends:**
  german.about.com/library/blcognates_A.htm

Targeted Strategy 6: Identify borrowed words.

Most languages borrow words from other languages. The word *coke*, for example, is used in many countries and languages for the soft drink by that name. Words in English that have been borrowed from other languages include *café au lait* (coffee with milk), which is borrowed from French, and *hummus* (a spread or dip made from ground chickpeas and tahini), which is a word borrowed from Arabic.

* The entire class and/or individual students can keep lists of borrowed words and their meanings that they find in a variety of locations (e.g., their reading, the community, TV, print media, and other sources).

- Display their findings on charts and store them in three-ring binders.

- In order to enhance their metalinguistic knowledge of features of language, talk with students about how they were able to identify the borrowed words.

- Students can talk with family members about words found in English that have been borrowed from the home language, and share their findings with the class.

ELL students benefit from seeing connections between their native language and English. Lists of words in English that have been borrowed (or loaned) from other languages can be found at www.krysstal.com/borrow.html and www.feedback.nildram.co.uk/richardebbs/essays/loanword.htm.

Targeted Strategy 7: Use word family charts.

It is particularly worthwhile to pay attention to words that are members of large morphological families—groups of words that have the same root word, such as *migrate, migrating, migrated, migrates, migrant, immigrant, immigrating, emigrant, emigrating, immigration, migratory*. Through the discussion that accompanies the development of word family charts, students will encounter many more words than if they were introduced to isolated words. These conversations can also lead to interesting discussions about parts of speech and how to recognize which part of speech a word belongs to (e.g., *migrate* is a verb, *migration* is a noun, and *migratory* is an adjective). When students are asked how they know what part of speech a word is, the ensuing discussion can enhance metalinguistic awareness and development. It is important to pay attention to word families that are connected to specific subject matter content in order to enhance ELL students' understanding of academic vocabulary.

Targeted Strategy 8: Collect words with similar meanings.

It is very useful to collect words that have similar meanings (e.g., *immigrant, refugee, migrant, settler* or *hurricane, tornado, storm, gale, cyclone*). These collections can lead to discussions about how each word in a group differs, and when each is most appropriately used. Keep lists of words with similar meanings, and use them later for reinforcement activities and as resources when students are writing. Figure 4.2 shows four groups of three words with similar meanings.

Group 1	Group 2	Group 3	Group 4
frown	tub	amble	laugh
scowl	container	stride	guffaw
grimace	pot	crawl	snicker

Figure 4.2: Words With Similar Meanings

Demonstrations can help clarify the subtle differences in meaning in Groups 1, 3, and 4. For Group 2 words, actual objects or sketches can help clarify the meaning. It is a good idea to encourage students to add to these lists whenever they encounter new words, and to point out that the lists can be useful resources when writing.

Targeted Strategy 9: Explore multiple meanings.

Many words have multiple meanings, and ELLs benefit from learning about these differences. Students can be given a target word, such as *vein*, and asked to work in groups to list as many different meanings as possible for that word. The group discussion can be a very valuable aspect to this vocabulary development/word consciousness activity. For example, *vein* has the following meanings:

* One of any of the tubes by which blood is conveyed to the heart
* A nervure (hollow tube) in an insect's wing
* A slender bundle of tissue forming a rib in the framework of a leaf
* A streak or stripe of a different color in wood, marble, cheese, and so on
* A fissure in rock filled with ore or other deposited material
* A source of a particular characteristic (e.g., *a rich vein of humor*)
* A distinctive character, tendency, disposition, mood (e.g., *spoke in a sarcastic vein*)
  (Source: *The Concise Oxford Dictionary*)

For homework, students can talk with neighbors, friends, and family members about other meanings for the target word, and share their findings with the rest of the class. These discussions can be very helpful in supporting the development of ELL students' curiosity about words and their vocabulary.

Alternative:

* Students identify words with potential multiple meanings in the text they are reading.

- In order to develop their word consciousness and metalinguistic awareness, they talk about why they think these words may have more than one meaning. For example, the student knows a meaning for a word, but it doesn't seem to fit that context, so the student wonders if the word has another meaning.

- Words with multiple meanings are displayed and stored as resources for students (e.g., on charts, in class three-ring binders, or in students' resource folders/binders).

  Other words that have multiple meanings include: *box, time, tie, drive, list, up, plant, bond, drop, dry, thing, second, seat, litter, iron, low,* and *mouth.* A quick search in a dictionary will reveal many more.

Targeted Strategy 10: Categorize words according to meaning.

An individual student can complete this open-ended activity, although the benefits of working with a partner are great.

- Words that students are familiar with through their reading and content-area studies are scrambled and listed on a sheet of paper and/or a transparency. A sample chart follows that includes terms related to housing, speaking, sports, movement, and head coverings.

baseball	cap	shout	whisper	flat
say	apartment	sing	bonnet	swing
trailer	soccer	hat	basketball	play
holler	duplex	helmet	tennis	beanie
house	slide	townhouse	run	beret

- Students are given about five minutes to sort the words into categories. They will need paper and writing utensils to do this.

- Then the whole class meets, and students share the categories they generated and explain their thinking.

Alternative:

The teacher creates a set of words and makes a copy for each student or group. Before distributing each set, he or she cuts the set up into individual words (or students can cut them up). Students then group and regroup the words into meaningful categories. These categories may range from the number of letters in the words to their beginning letters, which can be very helpful to emergent ELL readers. However, teachers may need to help their ELL students focus on connections in meaning.

Targeted Strategy 11: Identify different Englishes.

Even when countries or geographic regions share the same language, some words differ (e.g., *candy* in American English is *sweet* or *sweetie* in British English). ELLs may notice these differences in terminology when they read texts published in different countries or written by authors from different countries, and they should be encouraged to continue noticing and keeping records of these differences, as well as to investigate the origins of these differences.

- Students can begin a collection of different Englishes, a list with words from various English-speaking countries.

- In the lists below, students must match American terms with their British English counterpart terms. There is an additional word in the American English section to make it a little more difficult for students—they have to continue thinking even when there is only one word left in the British English column.

American English	British English
truck	sweets
elevator	mate
cardigan	boot
mom	holiday
friend	mum
sweater	lift
cookie	lorry
trunk	jumper
candy	biscuit
vacation	

These words can be used for reinforcement games, such as Concentration, where students try to match words with the same meaning, or Bingo, where a caller gives the word from the British English list and the players have to locate the corresponding word on the American English list.

Targeted Strategy 12: Play reinforcement games.

Children enjoy games such as Bingo, Concentration, and Jeopardy, and they can be used to great effect for reinforcing vocabulary development. These games can be played at different times in the school year, including:

- At the conclusion of a unit of study, when the game focuses on terms from that unit of study (e.g., a unit of study on magnetism).

- At intervals throughout the year, when the game focuses on terms that correspond with several units of study in one subject. For example, for a fourth-grade social studies class in California, this might include map reading, the Gold Rush, and the lives of immigrants.

- At intervals throughout the year, when the game focuses on terms from all subjects studied up to that point in the school year. For example, for a fourth-grade class, this might include the effects of the Great Depression in history, landforms in geography, electricity in science, the elements of art (e.g., color, shape/form, line, texture, space) in art, reading comprehension-related terms in reading (e.g., making text-to-self connections, predicting, inferring), writing craft moves in writing (e.g., an exploded moment, figurative language, alliteration), substance abuse in health, and algebra in mathematics.

As students become familiar with the routines surrounding these games, they can design games of their own. In these situations, the teacher acts as a resource to pairs or small groups of students as they prepare the materials. There are added linguistic and cognitive benefits to students taking on this game-designer role.

Concentration:

This game provides students with reading practice and repeated exposure to terms and definitions, while also building memory—all of which are very useful for language learners.

Procedure:

- The teacher writes terms on 3-by-5 cards of one color and succinct definitions on cards of another color. For example, in a science unit on space, terms might include *planet, sun, gravity, rotate,* and *star* written on blue cards. Definitions could be written on red cards—one definition for *planet* might be "a body in the solar system that is round and orbits the sun." The definition card can be a) just a definition, b) a sentence in which the term's meaning is available from context, or c) a combination of the definition and a sentence in which it is used. So as not to overwhelm students, we have found that it is wise to begin with about four to six pairs of words and definitions, and build up to more once students become familiar with the game.

- The cards are placed facedown so students cannot see the words and definitions. The cards are then mixed up. (The two sets of cards may be kept separate, but be sure to mix up each set.) Arranging the cards in rows and columns helps with retrieval. It is *very* important that each card remain in the same place once the game begins.

- Although students typically play for themselves, two or more students play at the same time. Each student takes it in turns to find pairs of terms and definitions. One card of each color is turned over and the player reads aloud the term and definition. If there is a match, the student keeps the pair and takes another turn. If there isn't a match, the cards are turned facedown, in the same place, and the next student takes a turn.

- The winner is the student with the most pairs.

- An alternative is for students, rather than the teacher, to select the words and write the definitions.

Modified Jeopardy:

This is a modified version of the Jeopardy game because players don't respond in the form of a question (e.g., *What is the outer layer of the Earth called?*). Instead, they provide short responses to questions. When a student is asked, *What is the outer layer of the Earth's surface called?* the student would reply *crust* or *the crust.* This game relies on listening skills, as well as knowledge of content terms, so it is often helpful to ELLs to display the questions on a transparency or on strips of paper that are then posted on the board or wall.

Procedure:

- Prepare a Jeopardy game board that can be used over and over again. Minimally, there need to be about five more terms than there are students playing the game, so that every student gets to play and every player has some choice. A sample game board designed for a class of 30 upper-grade students is shown on p. 154. There are 35 possible questions, which gives each student an opportunity to have some choice. The number of points awarded can be adjusted to correspond with students' numeric capabilities (e.g., 1, 2, 3 for kindergarten students).

Category A *Magnetism*	Category B *Landforms*	Category C *Writing Craft Moves*	Category D *Substance Abuse*	Category E *Algebra*
70 points	70 points	70 points	70 points	70 points
60 points	60 points	60 points	60 points	60 points
50 points	50 points	50 points	50 points	50 points
40 points	40 points	40 points	40 points	40 points
30 points	30 points	30 points	30 points	30 points
20 points	20 points	20 points	20 points	20 points
10 points	10 points	10 points	10 points	10 points

- Prepare a set of cards with terms from the unit(s) of study. Also prepare a set of corresponding questions, and align them with the scoring categories according to difficulty. The following samples are from a unit on landforms.

Category and Number of Points	Question	Answer
Landforms: 10 points	What is the outermost layer of the Earth's surface called?	the crust
Landforms: 20 points	What is a mountain formed by molten lava and gas called?	a volcano
Landforms: 30 points	What is the deposit left by flowing water, such as in a riverbed, called?	alluvium

- Students work in groups to help each other prepare for the game. This review may occur in short segments, such as 15–20 minutes each day. Newcomer ELLs should work with groups containing students who are more fluent in English.

- Students take turns answering a question. Each student chooses the category and the point value.

- Students are not allowed to help their team members when answering questions.

- Students are given a designated amount of time to answer (e.g., ten seconds).

- If a student does not know the answer or gives the wrong answer, the rest of the group may answer it for half the points.

- If no one in the group knows the answer, the next group can answer it for half the points.

- The game continues until all students have had a chance to answer a question—and until all groups have had the same number of turns.

- The group with the most points wins.

Bingo:

This game relies on listening and word recognition. To help newcomer ELLs, have the caller display the words as they are announced so that it is easier for students to find the words on their Bingo boards.

Procedure:

- Prepare boards with key vocabulary (words and longer terms) that corresponds with a unit of study. Each board or every four or five boards should have a different configuration of words. For example, for a unit on electricity and magnetism, the following terms may be included:

electricity	magnet	battery	magnetism
wire	magnetic field	circuit	parallel circuit
bulb	electromagnet	doorbell	repel
electric generator	attract	electric	compass
north pole	south pole	energy	convert into
heat	light	magnetic effects	motion

A Bingo board for that unit of study might look like this:

electricity		doorbell	compass
	attract	motion	
convert into	north pole		energy
	electric	electromagnet	wire
bulb		magnetic field	
heat	parallel circuit		light

Not all the words are included on any given board and, although boards have some of the same words (always in the same location), the boards are not identical.

SITUATION 2 My ELL students don't understand concepts in either the L1 or English.

Targeted Strategy 1: Use objects (realia), pictures, and demonstrations.

When teaching new concepts, it is essential to provide visual support. For example, when studying landforms, use models, videotapes and CDs, and photographs or slides.

Targeted Strategy 2: Create personal dictionaries.

It is helpful for students to create their own dictionaries of unfamiliar words/terms/concepts. The words and their definitions should be accompanied by drawings so that students can easily refresh their memories later on. Entries in these dictionaries can also be used for reinforcement games, such as Bingo, Concentration, or Jeopardy. Students can take turns generating words for these games. (See pp. 152–156 for an in-depth discussion of these games.)

SITUATION 3   My ELL students can decode words, but they don't understand what they have just read aloud.

Many ELLs, particularly young children, learn to decode well, but when they are asked to talk about what they just read, they have no idea. Being able to decode is an important step, but children need to be able to make sense of what they have just read. Developing vocabulary is an integral part of comprehension. (See the previous section for vocabulary development and word consciousness activities.) The following strategies focus explicitly on reading as a meaning-making process.

Targeted Strategy 1: Know that reading = making meaning.

Emergent or struggling readers often over-rely on one of the three major language cueing systems: the graphophonic (sound-symbol correspondence), the semantic (whether words make sense in that context), and the syntactic (whether it sounds like English, grammatically). We have observed that students often over-rely on the graphophonic cueing system and focus exclusively on decoding words, without regard to whether what they decoded made sense or sounded like English. It is important to talk with children about why we read (e.g., we read to get information or to be entertained, which means focusing on more than sound-symbol correspondences) and what reading involves (e.g., self-monitoring so that we notice if there is a breakdown in meaning and then do our best to repair the breakdown). We also need to reassure students that making miscues when reading (i.e., deviating from the text) is a normal part of reading—and that good readers correct those miscues that lead to breakdowns in meaning.

Demonstrations are a very effective way of showing the importance of reading for meaning. These can occur informally and without planning, such as when we are reading aloud. For example, when reading aloud, Katharine has read *mom* for *mother*, and pointed out to students that she did this without thinking. She went on to tell students that since it didn't change the meaning of the text, she didn't go back and repair the miscue. In contrast, on another occasion Katharine read, "she was sold to a planter in South Carolina" for "she was sold to a plantation in South Carolina." In this case, she reread that sentence fragment correctly and explained to students that she corrected it because *plantation* means something different from *planter* (even though the words have the same root and are connected).

More formal teaching demonstrations are also necessary. One that Katharine has found effective involves several demonstrations. She selects a text and then reads it while focusing on different cueing systems and reading strategies, as the following examples illustrate:

- **Demonstration 1: Sound-symbol correspondence only**

  Katharine reads the text, focusing only on graphophonic similarity, by reading words that share some of the same phonics properties as the words in the text but that lead to breakdowns in meaning, such as:

  Text: I'll taste it and see if it's sweet.

  Reading: I tastee it and see if it sw, sw, swet.

  (Neither *tastee* nor *swet* are real words in English, and the sentence does not make sense. Focusing on sound/symbol correspondence, Katharine neglected to pay attention to making meaning.)

- **Demonstration 2: Semantic/meaning making only**

  Text: She wanted to carry the groceries.

  Reading: She wanted to clean the garbage.

  (This sentence makes sense, but substituting *clean* for *carry* and *garbage* for *groceries* changes the meaning. In this case, Katharine didn't pay enough attention to graphophonics.)

- **Demonstration 3: Cueing systems working together to make meaning**

  Text: The birds flew overhead in the bright blue sky.

  Reading: The bird flows, flies over land. The bird flies overhead in the big blue, bright blue sky.

  (Using all the cueing systems, Katharine self-monitors herself. This leads her to self-correct words that change meaning, such as *flows* for *flies*, *over land* for *overhead*, and *big* for *bright*. She didn't self-correct *bird* for *birds*, however, and it could be argued that using the singular noun changes the meaning slightly.)

After each demonstration, Katharine asks students to talk about the strategies she used and how effective she was as a reader. Typically, students can see that the third demonstration is what good readers do: They pay attention to all the language cueing systems; they strive to make sense of the text; and when they make miscues, they self-correct those that change the meaning and interrupt comprehension.

Targeted Strategy 2: Use think-alouds.

A think-aloud is an instructional strategy that helps readers monitor their understanding, thereby supporting their reading comprehension. It is also a very valuable reading assessment tool as it reveals students' thinking processes and strategy use. A think-aloud occurs when readers verbalize their thinking while reading, either aloud or silently, and this makes the reading processes visible to both the reader and others (Baumann, Jones, & Seifert-Kessell, 1993; Oster, 2001). Students can either talk about their processes while reading (an oral think-aloud) or write about their processes while reading (a written think-aloud). These metacognitive conversations can involve: a) only the reader talking or writing about his or her reading processes, b) two readers taking turns thinking aloud while reading, or c) the student reading and thinking aloud with the teacher.

All readers are periodically stumped by what they read. More experienced and successful readers have access to multiple reading strategies to figure out what stumped them and repair the breakdown; in contrast, struggling and/or emergent readers typically have access to far fewer strategies. For example, successful reading taps into the following reading processes:

- Identifying a problem or difficulty (e.g., an unknown word or concept)

- Trying to solve problems by doing the following:
    - Rereading
    - Reading on
    - Identifying familiar root words
    - Identifying familiar or potential cognates

- Making predictions

- Confirming and discarding predictions

- Asking questions

- Visualizing

- Making connections (activating schema):
    - Text-to-self
    - Text-to-text
    - Text-to-world (including community)

- Making inferences

- Evaluating text

Procedure:

The teacher can work with an entire class, small groups of students with similar needs, or an individual student. It is often best to work with more than one student so they can see how other students approach texts and use reading strategies.

- Select a reading strategy that students typically do not use, which would be helpful for them to use in making sense of a text (e.g., making text-to-self connections or identifying unfamiliar words and terms).

- Select a short text that lends itself to a demonstration of the reading strategy.

- Post the text on a transparency or give each student a copy.

- Explain to students that you will be thinking aloud in order to help yourself understand the text better. Ask them to notice the strategies you use.

- Then demonstrate thinking aloud. An excerpt from a teacher's think-aloud demonstration using the opening to the picture book *Show Way* by Jacqueline Woodson (2005) follows. The book is about making quilts (show ways), which were used as maps by slaves seeking freedom. There is a picture of a little African-American girl connected to other African-American children with a loosely tied rope. The teacher's goal is to demonstrate asking oneself questions about the text. The beginning of *Show Way* is shown in the box below.

> *When Soonie's great-grandma was seven, she was sold from the Virginia land to a plantation in South Carolina without her ma or pa but with some muslin her ma had given her. And two needles she got from the big house— and thread dyed bright red with berries from a chokeberry tree.*

While reading aloud, the teacher demonstrates thinking aloud. (What she reads in the text appears in italics.)

"*Show Way.* That's the title. I wonder what this is referring to. I'll read on and maybe I'll find out. *When Soonie's great-grandma was seven, she was sold from the Virginia land to a plantation in South Carolina without her ma or pa but with some muslin her ma had given her.* Yes, this must be about slavery because it mentions a plantation and people being sold. How awful to be sold and to be separated from your parents. *Muslin.* I know that's very thin cloth. I wonder why her parents gave it to her? Maybe so she could make a dress for herself? *And two needles she got from the big house.* That must be a reference to the slave owner's house, so maybe her mom worked there. (She points to the picture of the children, who are tied together with a rope.) I wonder why the children are roped together and where they're going?"

- Have a discussion with students about the strategies you used (e.g., asking questions) but also about making text-to-self connections (e.g., how awful to be sold and to be separated from your parents), and making a prediction (maybe her mom worked there). If students don't mention the strategies you used, point them out and explain your thinking, if needed.

- Chart the think-aloud strategies that you and the children generate. Write the name of the strategy, and add an example of it so students have a clear understanding and can refer to the chart later.

- Ask pairs of student to work on a think-aloud. It's a good idea to ask them to try the strategy you focused on in the demonstration, but they don't have to be limited to it. Students should read texts that are slightly above what they can read independently with understanding, so that they are likely to have some breakdowns in meaning, but will still be able to make sense of the text. Students take turns reading a couple of lines or a paragraph, and then think aloud. When not thinking aloud, they should make notes on the strategies they observe their partner using.

- The whole group or class talks about the strategies they used or observed, and any new strategies are added to the chart.

- It is useful to provide daily think-aloud practice until students have internalized what is involved.

- Whenever introducing a new reading strategy, demonstrate how it is used through a think-aloud.

Alternatives:

- Think-alouds can be used to help make sense of the text structure of different genres (e.g., line breaks in poetry, the use of headings and subheadings in nonfiction books).

- Think-alouds can also be used to teach about literary features and how authors reveal these features (e.g., character development, setting, subplots) and craft elements (e.g., the use of rhythmic language, circular stories, the infusion of non-English words to convey cultural meanings).

Targeted Strategy 3: Do cloze activities.

A cloze activity involves students in predicting words that are missing in a passage and filling in the blanks. See Appendix L, page 299, for guidelines for developing cloze activities and Appendices M and N, pages 300–301, for two versions of a cloze text. Cloze activities support meaning-making as they require students to go beyond simply decoding.

Targeted Strategy 4: Create strip stories.

- Select a familiar text, particularly one that has clear story demarcations, like *Goldilocks*.

- Cut the story into segments, such as by page or by event, and attach the segments on strips of paper. One strip could show Goldilocks sitting on one of the bear's chairs; another could show her eating the porridge; the arrival of the bears could be on another strip.

- Scramble the strips.

- Then have students arrange the strips in order. If they are working in pairs or small groups, the conversation leading to the decisions they make can be very valuable.

Alternatives:

- Use a text generated through a language experience approach (LEA). (For more information on LEA, see Chapter 3, p. 135.)

- With students' help, rewrite a familiar text so that it has fewer words, but retains the main events.

- Students write their own stories, which are then copied, cut into segments, and put on strips of paper. Their peers have to put the story back in order.

- Write a how-to procedure (e.g., a recipe, directions for playing a game), copy the steps, cut them up, and put them on strips.

SITUATION 4 I see very irregular reading behaviors in my ELL students. Sometimes they read a text smoothly and with understanding. At other times they struggle to decode and understand a text at the same reading level.

Background knowledge and previous experience is essential in the understanding of any text, and irregular behaviors are often grounded in students' lack of familiarity with the content of the text. Some strategies that help in these circumstances include the following:

Targeted Strategy 1: Ask, "What do you know?"

Students' background knowledge can be accessed by:

- Briefly discussing what they think the text will be about, based on the front cover, the title, and quickly browsing through the text and illustrations

- Discussing what students know about the content of the text

- Providing background information about the text, especially for content that is culturally and/or academically unfamiliar

Targeted Strategy 2: Do picture walks.

Before reading aloud a new text, many teachers routinely do a picture walk in order to stimulate students' background knowledge and curiosity.

Procedure:

- Show the book's cover and read the title.

- Slowly flip through the pages of the book, asking who/what/why/where/when/how questions about the illustrations (e.g., *Who do you think this character is? What do you think will happen next? Why do you think she's crying? Where do you think he's going to take the dog? Where do you think this story is taking place? When is this story taking place? How do you think the story will end?*).

- Make sure *not* to give away the story line while doing the picture talk.

A Student Has Limited Purposes for Reading

SITUATION 1 My students think that reading is decoding, and they focus exclusively on sounding out the words.

SITUATION 2 My students read in a non-fluent, staccato way.

SITUATION 3 My students read very quickly, but without making meaning.

We have grouped these three situations together because they all reflect a limited view of why one reads. Sadly, these situations often arise because of the kinds of learning experiences that children have in school, which all too frequently are disengaged from reading for enjoyment or to gain information. When students have experienced early reading instruction as decoding—without much, if any, emphasis on authentic reading that has meaning and informs or entertains—then it may be inevitable that they do not approach reading with enthusiasm. This is particularly true if students have had few successful experiences with reading, as typically happens when they are taught to read through one-size-fits-all textbooks. If the reading program is the focus of instruction, rather than the individual learner, then many students will not receive the appropriate instruction. Katharine often asks children what reading is, and she has found that those who are being taught to read with textbooks and work sheets, with a heavy emphasis on decontextualized phonics instruction, tend to view reading as work sheets.

In addition to the strategies on pp. 157–162, the following strategies can help expand students' views of why we read and, in the process, teach them additional strategies to use in becoming accomplished readers.

Targeted Strategy 1: Use guided reading, or group strategy instruction.

Children benefit from focused instruction that is grounded in their needs, and guided reading (sometimes called group strategy instruction) provides that kind of instruction to groups of students with similar needs. See Fountas and Pinnell's *Guided Reading: Good First Teaching for All Children* (1996) for a very helpful and detailed discussion of guided reading. Two videotapes, *Guided Reading: The Essential Elements* and *Guided Reading: The Skillful Teacher* (Fountas & Pinnell, 2001), accompany the book. Figure 4.3 gives an overview of the component parts of a guided reading lesson.

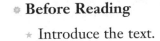

- **Before Reading**
  - ★ Introduce the text.
- **During Reading**
  - ★ Support effective reading (focus on strategies that effective readers use).
- **After Reading**
  - ★ Revisit and discuss the text.
  - ★ Teach processing strategies.
  - ★ Extend the meaning of the text.
  - ★ Introduce word work.

Figure 4.3: Components of a Guided Reading Lesson

When organizing and implementing guided reading or group strategy instruction groups, it is wise to consider the following:

- Use an assessment tool that reveals children's reading processes, such as running records[3] or miscue analysis.[4]

- Group students according to their reading skills and strategy needs. These groups should be flexible so that as children progress, they can be moved to a group where their needs can continue to be addressed. Keep in mind that these are not like traditional reading groups, so groupings need to be revisited every six weeks, if not more often.

- Select a text that fits the instructional level of the group. It can be a fiction or nonfiction book, a poem, a selection from a reading textbook, or a magazine article.

- Introduce a new text (see the picture walk strategy on p. 163), including any terms, phrases, punctuation, or text structures that may be new and/or tricky for students.

---

[3] A running record is an assessment tool that records a student's oral reading of a text, and assesses the language cueing systems and self-monitoring strategies used. It relies on the use of check marks for the correct reading of words. See Marie Clay's *Running Records for Classroom Teachers* (2000) for detailed guidance on administering and interpreting running records.

[4] A miscue analysis is an oral reading assessment tool in which the teacher records deviations from the written text on a copy of the text, and students provide a retell, which aids the teacher in determining the student's understanding of the text, and reading strategy use and needs. See Sandra Wilde's *Miscue Analysis Made Easy* (2000) for detailed guidance on administering and interpreting a miscue analysis.

- Students read the text independently, but in a low voice so the teacher can listen in and briefly intervene to help a student address any problems that arise. These interventions focus on meaning making and using multiple information sources while reading, and this underscores authentic purposes for reading.

- After reading, talk about the text with the students (e.g., what they learned, questions they now have, what they think will happen next). Also, select a teaching point you observed students struggling with (e.g., how words work; the importance of paying attention to punctuation when reading; reading fluidly by reading chunks of text rather than sounding out words, word by word).

Targeted Strategy 2: Introduce literature study circles (LSCs).

Literature study circles (LSCs) are similar to book discussions that adults often engage in. A group of students meets together or with the teacher on two or more occasions for an open-ended discussion about a book they have all read. We have found that children of all ages can have successful LSCs, and we have seen how LSCs build their enthusiasm for books and reading and help them realize that reading is much more than decoding words. See Katharine Davies Samway and Gail Whang's *Literature Study Circles in a Multicultural Classroom* (1996) for an in-depth discussion of how to establish and maintain LSCs.

Features of successful LSCs include the following:

- The teacher selects texts that are well written, likely to extend students' knowledge, and engage them. Genres that work particularly well in LSCs include picture books, novels, short stories, poetry, essays, and magazine articles.

- The teacher should have about six to ten copies of the text on hand. We have found that groups of five to seven seem to work particularly well for a literature circle.

- The teacher presents brief text talks about each selection. For example, "*Children of the River* is written by Linda Crew. It's about a Cambodian girl who flees her homeland and comes to live in the U.S. It's a wonderful story about immigrants and cross-cultural encounters," or "*Too Many Tamales* by Gary Soto is about a young girl at a Christmas get-together. She tries on her mother's ring while helping to make tamales . . . and loses it!"

- Students select the text they want to read.

- If the text is long, such as a novel, each group meets with the teacher to establish a date by which they will finish it (usually no more than seven to ten days). The group also discusses how many pages they will need to read each day and each student records this on a reading contract.

- Students read the text during independent reading time and for homework. They should come to the LSC prepared to discuss issues, such as their reactions to the book, questions the book raised for them, and writing techniques they noticed and appreciated.

- The first discussion is totally open-ended. The teacher follows the lead of the students and is a co-discussant. Rather than plying the students with questions, the teacher begins the conversation with an open-ended question, such as, *So, what do you think of this book?*

- Based on the first discussion, the teacher assigns a follow-up activity that leads to a deeper exploration of the text. For example, after talking with a group of fourth graders about *Hatchet* by Gary Paulsen, a teacher said, "You were mentioning how you felt nervous for Brian—would he survive or would he die? You really noticed the tension in the book, which isn't the easiest thing for writers to show. So, I'd like us to go back to the book and figure out what Gary Paulsen does as a writer to build this tension. Is it through dialogue? Is it through descriptions of the setting? Is it through the length of his sentences? How does he build tension?"

- Students work either independently or with partners to explore the issues raised in the assignment and identify examples from the text to support their thinking.

- The group returns on a subsequent day for a second discussion, which focuses on what they found in their deeper examination of the text.

- At the end of each discussion, the group evaluates the meeting. They might ask questions like these: *How do you think this discussion went? What did you learn from this discussion? What did you learn about writing from this book and the discussion?*

Adaptations for newcomers, very young ELLs, and struggling ELL readers:

- Read picture books or magazine articles or other short texts to the students, while they follow along in their own copies.

- Use texts that are grounded in the cultures of the ELLs.

- Pair more fluent readers with emerging readers, or let students pair themselves.

- Hold the first discussion right after reading the short text.

- Expect that the discussion may focus on the illustrations, but this often leads to insights that more text-oriented people, such as teachers, often miss.

Targeted Strategy 3: Encourage pair or partner reading.
See pair reading on pp. 134–135.

Difficulty Decoding in English

SITUATION 1   ELLs get confused by similar sounds and letters, such as *n/m, b/p, b/d, ch/sh.*

SITUATION 2   ELLs have difficulty with phonemic awareness and phonics activities. They don't seem to hear certain sounds.

SITUATION 3   ELLs have a hard time with long and short vowels.

We have put these situations together because they are all connected to phonemic awareness and phonics, and we thought it best to address them as a group. Any difficulties related to the sounds of English that ELLs have are often connected to how sounds work (and how they work differently across languages). For example, an *aspirated* sound involves expelling a puff of air when producing the sound (e.g., in English /p/, /t/, /k/, and /ch/ are all aspirated sounds). English has more aspirated sounds than many other languages, and it is often hard for nonnative speakers to hear and form aspirated sounds in English. For example, the initial sounds of the aspirated /p/ and unaspirated /b/ often confuse ELLs. There are also *voiced* and *unvoiced* sounds, which affect pronunciation and discrimination between sounds. For example, in English, /g/ is a voiced sound, whereas /k/ is not a voiced sound. To understand the difference, touch your throat while saying each of the sounds to see how voiced sounds make the throat vibrate.

In addition, the placement and movement of the tongue and lips affect sounds. For teachers interested in knowing more about phonology, David and Yvonne Freeman's *Essential Linguistics: What You Need to Know to Teach Reading, ESL, Spelling, Phonics, Grammar* (2004) is an excellent resource.

ELL children who arrive in North America early in their lives usually speak like natives, whereas older children may continue to speak with an accent even when they have become accomplished readers and writers. Rather than exposing young ELLs to decontextualized phonemic awareness activities and pronunciation practice, they should be exposed to sound play activities, such as the following:

- Rhymes

- Poems

- Alliterative word play (e.g., *the silly snake slithered sideways*.)

- Jazz chants (See Chapter 3, Oral Situations, pp. 74–75, for information about jazz chants.)

- Nursery rhymes

Older children may need to be taught about the differences in sounds and how to hear and produce unfamiliar sounds. In both cases, developing vocabulary is of critical importance to the academic success of ELLs. Reading instruction should not overemphasize phonemic awareness or phonics instruction.

Does My ELL Student Have a Learning Disability?

Being a newcomer to English and not being able to speak the language fluently is not the same as having a handicapping condition or a learning disability. In the past, ELLs were sometimes automatically placed in classes for children with handicapping conditions. Beginning in 1991, the Office of Civil Rights (OCR) in the U.S. Department of Education started to look more closely at whether ELLs were being placed inappropriately in programs for children with special needs. OCR began to examine several issues, including whether ELL students were being placed in special education programs because of their lack of proficiency in English, and if disabled ELL students were being excluded from programs for children with special needs because of their ELL status (Stewart, 1993).

Even today, a disproportionate number of ELLs have been classified as having a handicapping condition, and a major contributing factor is that they are assessed in English before they are fluent in it, even though Public Law 94–142 (amendments of Part B of the Education of the Handicapped Act), passed by Congress in 1975, requires that ELL students be assessed in their native language (Fradd & Wilen, 1990). The opposite situation also occurs all too frequently—children do not make progress in either English and/or academic subjects over several years, yet they are not referred for assessment of a potentially handicapping condition, in large part because it is assumed that their ELL status is causing this lack of progress.

Some districts use speech and language teachers to work with ELL students, which may seem like the proper placement for them, given the teachers' knowledge of language development. However, unless the speech and language teacher is also knowledgeable about second-language acquisition and learning, this is generally *not* the best placement for the ELL child. Native speakers of English who receive language development support from a speech and language teacher typically experience a language delay, whereas ELLs already have control of their native language and are simply learning a new language. Also, any speech "deficiencies" that ELLs manifest are usually associated with acquiring a new sound system (e.g., saying *dem* for *them*).

SITUATION 1 — My school wants to test our ELLs for special needs.

Unless there are other reasons for suspecting that ELLs have special needs, testing for such a condition is not appropriate (just as placing them in classes for children with special needs is not the appropriate placement for them).

SITUATION 2 — How can I tell if my ELL student has a learning disability?

According to Ortiz (1997), for schools to determine that an ELL has a learning disability, the following conditions should be met:

- The student is in a positive school environment.
- The teacher has used instructional strategies that are known to be appropriate for and successful with ELLs.
- Appropriate interventions have been unsuccessful.

Ortiz concludes that, if an ELL student continues to struggle despite these efforts to provide appropriate, individualized instruction, then he or she may well have a learning disability, and should be assessed in the native language. Morrison (undated) also points out that it is very important to take the following into account when trying to determine if an ELL has a learning disability:

- Native language and literacy development/progress—some children have been schooled in a nonnative language, even in their home country, such as Mon-speaking Mexicans and Guatemalans.

- Previous schooling—many ELLs have had interrupted schooling due to conflicts in their home countries, and this can affect their levels of literacy. It is essential that someone who is fluent in their native language and familiar with the schooling circumstances of their native land assess their previous schooling.

The resource guide, *English Language Learners With Special Needs* (Morrison undated), can be accessed at www.cal.org/resources/archive/rgos/special.html. This Web site is very useful as it includes links to articles about ELLs and various learning disabilities.

Some behaviors that suggest a child might have a learning disability, and should be carefully monitored, include the following:

- An inability to remember nonlinguistic routines from day to day (e.g., where to put backpacks)

- Difficulty following a series of nonverbal instructions that have been reviewed on a regular basis (e.g., *Hold the book in your hand, put the book on your chair, pick up the book*)

- Has problems identifying common objects, even after several weeks' exposure to them (e.g., not being able to identify pictures of classroom objects often referred to, such as rug, chair, table, book)

- Routinely loses homework and/or schoolwork

- Expresses frustration

It should be remembered that traumas of various kinds—war, separation from close family members, and lack of previous exposure to a school environment—can also lead to these behaviors.

Targeted Strategy 1: Wait and watch carefully.

It is usually too early to tell if an ELL student has a handicapping condition, unless the student has been in a North American school for at least a year and has not made much progress in English language and literacy. However, it is essential to monitor ELLs' development carefully and be ready to seek professional help, if it is required.

Some nonlinguistic behaviors that suggest a child may have a possible handicapping condition include the following:

- The child walks with an extremely awkward gait.

- The child exhibits difficulty hearing, in one or both ears.

- The child has difficulty reading from close up and/or far away.

If you encounter any of these behaviors, immediately refer the child for further assessment.

Targeted Strategy 2: Seek professional guidance.

If you are unsure about whether a student may have a handicapping condition, it is wise to seek professional help, either from a school district employee, such as a bilingual home-school liaison or psychologist, or from community resources, such as local mental health clinics and not-for-profit organizations.

SITUATION 3 My ELL student has been with us for seven months, and despite the efforts of classmates to befriend her, she remains socially isolated and sometimes appears hostile. Is this indicative of a learning disability?

Social isolation, acting out, clinging to the teacher or instructional aide, crying more easily and more excessively than other children, unfocused staring into space, and drawings that depict physically violent or sexually explicit situations may be signs of serious emotional problems that are unrelated to cultural assimilation or language confusion.

Targeted Strategy 1: Seek professional help from mental health workers.

In these situations, it is crucial to immediately contact your school psychologist and/or mental health worker for assistance.

Targeted Strategy 2: Seek professional help from immigration/refugee specialists.

In the case of refugee children, the school should also contact the appropriate refugee resettlement agency for a referral to mental health workers who work with victims of trauma. As so many children come from war-torn countries, where they have seen atrocities that no one—let alone a child—should have seen, it is not uncommon for immigrant/refugee children to exhibit behaviors associated with trauma. (See pp. 34–35 in Chapter 1 on sociocultural issues for additional information.)

Targeted Strategy 3: Seek professional help from L1 and bilingual resources and services.

It is essential for ELL children and families to receive mental health services in their native language. (See pp. 34-35 in Chapter 1 for additional information.) Trauma and other serious emotional illnesses do not generally heal themselves, but skilled intervention can help children enormously in returning to a normal emotional state. It is imperative for teachers and other school professionals to seek help for their emotionally disturbed ELL students immediately, rather than waiting until their language develops.

SITUATION 4

Initially, my student made steady progress, but he hasn't made much or any progress in the last six months. Should I refer this child for special needs testing?

No. Development isn't linear and regular. Peaks and valleys are common. However, a child who is not making progress needs to be monitored carefully. Also, it is important to ask oneself if the child is being challenged academically and linguistically. Is the lack of progress a result of the child being asked to do superficial things, such as drawing and cutting out pictures, rather than asking him or her to engage in academically and linguistically challenging activities? If the former is true, then an institutionally induced learning lag may be occurring.

When ELLs reach a learning plateau, it may also be connected to moving from beginning ELL activities to more challenging mainstream activities, without transitional or intermediary learning experiences. This lack of progress may also be related to how progress is measured. For example, if the teacher has used ongoing assessments, such as running records and observational records, to gauge the student's strengths and needs and has observed progress, and suddenly the student is assessed on a high-stakes normed test and scores in the bottom percentile, then it may appear that the student hasn't made any progress. However, the high-stakes test may not be a valid measure of what the child has learned and the progress he or she has made.

Another factor affecting an ELL's progress may relate to the child's prior experiences with schooling. For example, if ELLs enter North American schools with little or no prior schooling, they may make a lot of progress very quickly (e.g., in oral, interpersonal language skills). However, their progress may slow down as they begin to tackle the much harder task of academic learning and procedures (e.g., how to organize their papers, how to label papers, how to make an oral academic presentation, how to prepare a science fair poster, and how to write notes).

SITUATION 5 A family is resistant to the child being assessed and possibly classified as having special learning needs.

Families of ELLs have good reason to be leery of their children being identified as having a handicapping condition. First, in most cultures, including in North America, there is a stigma attached to having family members with special needs. Second, parents may be concerned that their children won't learn much in a non-mainstream classroom, based on the quality of care that they are familiar with elsewhere. We need to acknowledge parents' fears and be sensitive to their apprehensions. Also, great care must be taken in selecting who will speak with them about such a potentially difficult subject as special needs. We have found it best if a known and respected person talks with the parent.

Targeted Strategy 1: Ask parents to visit the class with a mediator.

It is essential to acknowledge the legitimate fears of parents. One way to do this is to invite them to visit the classrooms and programs for children with special needs. It is also helpful for a mediator who is familiar with both the school and home cultures to be present to act as a go-between, so that parents' questions can be answered.

Targeted Strategy 2: Set up meetings with community agencies.

Inviting speakers from local community agencies who work with and on behalf of children with special needs can go a long way toward diminishing the pressures that parents often feel when their children are regarded as having special needs. It is usually best if the speaker(s) are members of the parents' culture and speak the home language. When this is not possible, then it is crucial to have translators available at these meetings.

Targeted Strategy 3: Make a home visit.

Home visits can be extremely valuable in building bridges between the school and home. (See Chapter 6, particularly p. 238, for more discussion about home visits). Be prepared to share the strengths of the child, as well as specific examples of behaviors that concern you. For example, a teacher we know had a 6-year-old ELL child in class who couldn't retain information from day to day, giggled inappropriately, drooled, couldn't manipulate blocks, and walked with an awkward, out-of-balance gait. The teacher suspected a neurological problem, so she visited the parents to explain her concerns and elicit their support in making a referral. The parents thought their daughter's difficulty was due to dealing with multiple languages, and the teacher respectfully and kindly explained that she was not aware of any research that indicated that the symptoms were caused by learning multiple languages. The parents agreed to have their daughter assessed, and the assessment was conducted in the child's native language. She was subsequently diagnosed as having special needs, and began to receive physical therapy and occupational therapy, which helped her enormously.

CHAPTER 5

Writing Situations

As ELL students gain more experience with print and with expressing themselves through writing, their texts become more sophisticated and can be read more easily. Writing is a developmental process, just as reading and spoken language are developmental processes, and development for ELLs varies from learner to learner (Heald-Taylor, 1986; Hudelson, 1989; Samway, 2006; Urzúa, 1987). For example, although we know nonnative English-speaking children who made rapid progress over a relatively short period of time, we also know many ELLs who took much longer to approximate the abilities of native-speaking writers. Also, it is very common to find that the writing of even very fluent ELLs is marked by characteristics that are not typically found in the writing of non-ELLs (e.g., mixing up *she/he* pronouns or omitting the article *a* or *the*).

Even teachers who understand that writing is a developmental process for ELLs can feel overwhelmed when newcomers to English enter their classrooms. Some of these students may not be able to write anything or very little in English. Some may not be able to write much or anything in any language due to interrupted schooling. Other students may be able to write, but their writing may not be on a par with their English-speaking peers. Still others may know how to write in English, but are overly concerned about accuracy, and self-monitor themselves so rigorously that they are reluctant to write anything that they suspect may not be correct. All of these situations are normal and occur frequently. And, for each of these situations, there are strategies that a teacher can draw upon to support ELL writers.

Students Are Reluctant Writers or Don't Write Much

When ELLs can write little or nothing in English, it may be related to one or more of the following factors:

- If they can write in their L1 or another language that is not English, they may be acutely aware that they are not skillful writers in English and are afraid to make mistakes.

- ELLs who can write in a language other than English may come to our schools having had very different writing experiences. For example, some children whose prior, school-based writing experiences involved copying words may have difficulty when asked to write on self-selected topics. Their reluctance to write in English may result from being asked to do something very different from what was valued in previous school-based writing.

- If ELLs' native language orthography is very different from English (e.g., Chinese, Japanese, Arabic, Urdu), they may have difficulty forming letters and words in English.

- If ELLs are unable to write in any language, their reluctance or unwillingness to write is likely to be connected to a lack of experience with writing (and possibly reading).

Writing is a developmental process for all writers, and for English learners there is an added developmental element. Even if ELL children are developmentally accomplished writers in their native language, when they begin writing in English, they are likely to go through the following stages until they have become immersed in English print and oral language, and have gained confidence:

- Not draw or write anything

- Draw only

- Copy words, phrases, or longer texts

- Label drawings

- Write simple sentences

- Write longer and more complex texts

Children do not usually progress through these stages in a linear fashion, so it isn't uncommon to encounter what seems to be a regression. For example, a student may have moved from labeling drawings to writing simple sentences, and then suddenly revert back to labeling drawings. This seemingly backward step is often related to the student encountering new challenges as a writer (e.g., writing about less familiar content or writing in a new genre). What may seem like a regression is, in fact, usually reflective of the nonlinear, often messy nature of writing development.

ELLs who appear to be reluctant writers often manifest a variety of behaviors, including the following:

- They don't write anything.

- They don't know what to write about.

- They don't write anything original—they just copy.

- They only list words.

- They don't do anything during writing time.

In the rest of this chapter, we offer some general strategies that can be helpful in addressing these phenomena. We will then follow with strategies that are geared to specific situations.

General Strategies

General Strategy 1: Draw first.

Drawing is a universal experience, and it is something that most children are able to do, and do willingly. Reluctant and inexperienced ELL writers often respond very positively to invitations to draw first (Barbieri, 2002; Fu, 1995; Hoyt, 1993; Samway, 2006). Children can then be shown how to label their pictures or write short captions to accompany them. This reduces the writing demands placed on students and allows them to express more complex thoughts than they are able to produce orally or in writing in English. For example, when fourth-grade ELLs in Dorothy's pullout ESL class were writing about their science experiments, they were able to express more complex thoughts in their native languages than in English, orally, or in writing. However, they were able to use labels and drawings to convey more complex thoughts than they were able to do at that time in English, as the following example from Paulo, a native Portuguese speaker, illustrates.

Figure 5.1: Paulo's Text and Drawing

It is interesting to observe how Paulo uses humor, one of the hardest language functions to convey in a nonnative language, to indicate how he feels about the progress of his pea plant (through *Grrrrrau* and the use of exclamation points). He did this using just a few words that are not particularly sophisticated and some simple labeled sketches.

General Strategy 2: Read student-authored texts to ELL students.

It is very important for teachers to read student-authored texts to ELLs, particularly those written by other ELLs, so that reluctant writers can see how accessible writing can be and gain inspiration and encouragement from their peers (Taylor, 1990). (It is also a way to celebrate the achievements of students.)

- These pieces of writing should be illustrated for greater comprehensibility, and may include memoirs/personal narratives, information books, cartoons, poems, letters, labeled pictures, and book reviews.

- When reading aloud to ELLs, the text should be visible so students can follow along. If the read-aloud is with a large group of children, this can be accomplished by having copies available, using an enlarged or big book version, or projecting the text and illustrations on a screen (e.g., via an LCD projector, overhead projector, or opaque projector).

- Read aloud texts written by newcomers, as well as more sophisticated texts written by more experienced and fluent writers. For example, from

Figure 5.2: Maya's Book

her earliest days in the U.S., Maya, a Russian-born sixth grader, was adept at writing simple books about her life and family that inspired many other ELLs to write their own books. One of Maya's books, called *About My Family*, was six pages long and consisted of the text and illustrations shown in Figure 5.2:

Ultimately, 17 books about students' families sat on a library bookshelf.

* After a read-aloud and the accompanying discussion, talk with students about what they can borrow for their own writing. For example, after an ESOL teacher read a piece written by a student about the death of a favorite pet that included the refrain, *I am sad*, she asked the other students what ideas for their own writing they got from the piece. One student said, "I go write my snake. It new." Another student said, "My grandpa die. I'm write that." Another student said, "I like *I am sad. I am sad. I am sad.* That strong." In her own piece about the recent birth of her brother, she included the refrain *I am happy*. In each case, these students borrowed features of the original text read to them by their ESOL teacher (i.e., an animal, a death, and a refrain).

* Texts may be written in English, the native language, or they can be bilingual (written in the L1 and English—two or more students may collaborate on these bilingual texts).

* Texts may be saved as books with simple or elaborate bindings, or as anthologies stored in photo albums or three-ring binders.

General Strategy 3: Have students read student-authored texts.

Students need time to read the texts that their peers and other students write, such as during independent reading time (Atwell, 1998; Calkins, 1986, 1994; Graves, 1983). Although many writing workshops integrate the sharing of texts in both informal and formal ways (e.g., through conferring, author's chair, and publishing parties), in some classrooms, including in some writing workshops, there are actually few opportunities for students to read the writing of their peers. For example, if children *only* listen to what their peers have written (e.g., in a writing conference or in a whole-group share), they have not experienced the piece as a reader; instead, they have experienced it as a listener. This is regrettable, as students need to actually read the texts that their peers write to make the act of writing more tangible.

- Student-authored texts need to be stored in easily accessible locations in order to validate the students' writing. Ways to store these texts include the following:

  - Cardboard, wooden, or plastic containers placed in the classroom library or on tables around the room, including students' tables—books may be stored according to genre (e.g., poetry, information books, stories) or theme (e.g., books about animals, our families, immigration stories). Although copies of student-authored books should be mixed in with professionally published books, it is also a good idea to store copies more visibly.

  - Displays on the walls of the classroom—some teachers allocate a space (e.g., 15 by 18 inches) for each child to post his or her work, and to change it on a regular basis.

  - Walls and bulletin boards outside classrooms and in school corridors—some teachers use these spaces to display student work.

  - Class and school newsletters that are published on a regular basis.

  - Electronic newsletters or class Web sites.

  - A mobile library of student-authored texts that moves from classroom to classroom.

- If texts are widely accessible, be sure to make backup copies so that, if any get lost, there is a mechanism in place for replacing them.

General Strategy 4: Write in the native language.

While students are still adjusting to their new language and not yet writing in English, it is a good idea to encourage them to write in their native language (Freeman & Freeman, 2006), even if one cannot read it (Taylor, 1990). It is important for ELLs to know that the goal is for them to write and that, while they are becoming familiar with their new language, they should be a writer in a language that they know. Ask other students or adults to translate these texts into English as bilingual versions make texts written by these ELLs more accessible to more readers. Another benefit of encouraging students to write in their L1 is that it often leads to a greater respect for and recognition of the ELLs by classmates who don't speak or write their language. This is one occasion when ELLs are the experts, something that is so hard to come by when one is a newcomer to a language and culture.

General Strategy 5: Use Language Experience Approach (LEA).

First developed as a means to produce reading materials that emergent readers could understand, LEA involves students dictating a text, usually based on a familiar or shared experience (Allen, 1976; Stauffer, 1970). It has proven to be a useful early writing strategy for ELLs (Rigg, 1989). One approach to implementing LEA with ELLs follows:

- A student or group of students dictates a text.

- The teacher writes the text exactly as each student dictates it. If a group of students is dictating the text, the teacher writes it on chart paper so that all the students can see it.

- The teacher then goes through the text, explaining how to revise the grammar and word choices, as the following example illustrates. Note that the teacher does not change the content of the message:

Teacher: (*repeats the first sentence that the student generated*) "We go the pumpkin place yesterday." Is this right?

Alicia: (*nods head*) Yes.

Teacher: Okay. And because it was yesterday, we need to write it in the past tense. "We <u>went</u>" instead of "We <u>go</u>." "We go" means we're doing it right now, and this refers to yesterday (*writes the revised text next to the original text, beginning with "We went," and says each word aloud while writing it*). And, it's "We went <u>to</u>." You said here (*points to the text while reading*), "pumpkin <u>place</u>." It's actually called a pumpkin <u>farm</u>. Remember?

Alicia: (*nods head vigorously*) Yes, pumpkin farm.

Teacher: So we'll change this to "farm" (*writes "pumpkin farm," and says the words aloud while writing them*). Now, we went to the pumpkin farm yesterday, so do you want to say, "We went to the pumpkin farm <u>yesterday</u>" or "We went to the pumpkin farm <u>on</u> Tuesday"? (*pauses*)

Alicia: Tuesday. I like Tuesday.

Teacher: Okay. In that case, we have to say "<u>on</u> Tuesday," so we add the word on. (*writes on Tuesday, and says the words aloud while writing them*). Okay. Let's read this together (*points to each word while reading the revised text with the student*). We went to the pumpkin farm on Tuesday.

The teacher and student(s) continue to add sentences until there is a complete text. The students read the text many times over the course of a few days. The text is also used for language and reading practice, and may be incorporated into the following follow-up activities:

* Work with sentence strips: A sentence is written on a sentence strip and then cut apart for the student(s) to put in order and then read. Sentences from an entire short text can also be put on strips, sorted, and read.

* Generate alternate words: For a sentence such as *We went to the pumpkin farm*, the students brainstorm words that could fit in place of *went*, such as *drove, traveled, took a trip*. Then the students and teacher discuss differences in the meaning and when each word or phrase is most likely to be used. The list of alternate words and uses can be displayed for future reference and may be added to.

* Circle specific parts of speech, such as nouns, verbs, pronouns, or articles.

* Identify and circle onsets and rimes: Students identify the onset and rime in a word, such as *went*: /w/ is the onset and /ent/ is the rime. Then they generate other words that have the same onset (e.g., the /w/ in /w/ing/, /w/ait/, /w/ish) and/or rimes (e.g., the /ent/ in s/ent/, b/ent/, sp/ent/).

* Cloze activities: In a cloze activity, students predict which words are missing in a passage and fill in the blanks with those words. See Appendix L for guidelines for developing cloze activities and Appendices M and N for two versions of a cloze text. Another procedure that can be very useful with ELLs is a selected feature cloze, which focuses on a particular linguistic feature. For example, a teacher may delete the articles, adverbs, or inflectional endings (e.g., the *–ed* in *walked*, the *–ing* in *walking* or the *–s* in *toys*) in order to give students practice using that feature in a way that fosters thoughtful reading. See Appendix O for an example of a selected feature cloze.

General Strategy 6: Focus on collaborative writing.

Under authentic writing conditions in which ELL students are encouraged to share their writing processes and confer about their writing, collaboration naturally occurs (e.g., Hudelson, 1994; Samway, 1987a; Serna & Hudelson, 1993; Urzúa, 1987). This is one of the characteristics of a writing workshop approach to writing (e.g., Anderson, 2000; Atwell, 1998; Calkins, 1986, 1994; Graves, 1983, 1994; Ray, 2001).

Even when a collaborative, authentic writing experience is available to ELLs, it can still be rather daunting for some students. In these cases, pairing an ELL writer with a more experienced writing partner as a mentor is one way to jump-start them. Inexperienced writers do not always realize that they can approach other students for help with their writing, so in order to facilitate collaboration, teachers may want to partner students. We have learned that pairing writers should be done very carefully because not all partnerships work well. Consider the following when pairing students:

- The partnered students must want to work together. A willingness and a desire to work together should be high on the list of selection criteria.

- Each student must have a valued role. The less experienced writer should have an important role in the process, such as generating text ideas and content or illustrating the text.

- Students should work side by side most of the time so the ELL student can learn from the more experienced student.

- The respective roles of the students may not be identical. One student may be primarily responsible for encoding the text that was generated collaboratively, whereas the other student (usually the ELL) may be primarily responsible for the illustrations.

- The teacher needs to be alert to students becoming over-reliant on always writing with a partner.

General Strategy 7: Practice shared writing with students.

Shared writing is a scaffolded approach to emergent writing. The teacher and student(s) share the pen while writing a text (unlike LEA, in which the teacher encodes the text generated by a student or a group). The content of the text is agreed upon collaboratively (e.g., about a time when a student won a prize in a town footrace, an invitation to a local zoo employee to talk to the class about reptiles), and it may be revised in the process of writing. Initially, the teacher takes the lead in physically writing the text (encoding it), with the student(s) contributing what they are able to write, which might be a letter, a word, or a phrase. With experience and growing familiarity with English, students can take on more responsibility for encoding the text themselves. There should be considerable talk while the text is being written, as the following excerpt of a group-generated shared writing activity illustrates:

Teacher: So, we're going to write to Ms. Pamela Argüeda to invite her to share her collection of musical instruments from around the world (*writes the visitor's name on the board*). How do we begin a letter like this? (*pauses*) If you're not sure, remember, there are charts on the wall to help us (*pauses*).

Flora: With the date?

Teacher: Okay. We do need the date, but there is something that we need to put first.

(*The group discusses the component parts of a letter.*)

Daniel: The address.

Teacher: Right. Our address comes first. We'll use the school address because we're writing from the school (*writes the first part of the school address on chart paper hanging on an easel, talking through what she is writing and asking for input on how to spell words*). Okay, so I've just written our room number, the name of our school, and the street address. Now, what do we need to complete the address?

Marita: The town.

Teacher: Right. The town and zip code (*writes the zip code on the board, speaking the numbers as she writes them*). The post office will know where to deliver the letter when Ms. Argüeda writes back to us. I think most people know how to write San José and the zip code (*points to the zip code on the board*), so who would like to write it?

(*Several children raise their hands. Angelina comes to the easel and writes the town and zip code. The teacher asks her to stay and write a little more.*)

Teacher: How do we start the letter?

Augusto: Dear Pamela Argüeda.

Teacher: Right, we start with "Dear," but we should probably make it a bit more formal since we don't know her. How about "Dear Ms. Argüeda"?

(*After a brief discussion about the differences between Ms., Miss, and Mrs., Angelina writes the salutation. Then she returns to her seat on the rug.*)

Teacher: Now we get into the main part of the letter, where we invite her to come to our class.

(*The group discusses the best way to invite the speaker, and they decide on the following text: "We love music in our class, and we play lots of instruments. We hope that you can come to our class to share your instruments and play for us. We come from lots of countries, and we would like to see instruments from all around the world. Please come and visit us."*)

Teacher: Now, let's take turns writing the letter. And we can all help each other. Tito, can you start it, please?

(Tito takes the pen and writes the first part of the first sentence, checking for words on the word wall and charts displayed around the room, and occasionally accepting the suggestions offered by the rest of the students. He writes, "We love music in or clas and we play lots of," then stops and says he doesn't know how to write the word "instruments." Alex offers to take over and writes "instriments," and he continues writing: "We hop you can com to our clas to sher yor instriments and play for us.")

Because the focus of the activity is on helping the students generate a written message, the teacher doesn't address their nonstandard spelling or correct what Tito and Alex have written. She also knows that she may use this text for some interactive writing practice later in the week (see pp. 209–211).

The teacher then repeats the third sentence that the group has collaboratively generated, *We come from lots of countries and we would like to see instruments from all around the world*, and invites Flora to write that sentence. With help from the rest of the group and what her peers have already written, Flora writes, *We com from lot of countrys and we wood like to see instriments from all arund the world*. In this way, the group collaboratively writes the entire text of the letter.

General Strategy 8: Have a range of writing materials available.

Having a preference for a particular writing implement isn't unusual among writers. For example, some writers prefer to write with a well-sharpened #4 pencil. Others have a favorite ballpoint pen, while some do almost all their composing on a computer keyboard. It can be quite extraordinary to observe how having access to a range of writing implements can free up some reluctant writers. For example, we know students who suddenly began writing when they were offered the option of using colored markers or pens. Other students, who struggled to form English letters, responded well to being able to compose on a computer.

General Strategy 9: Publish students' writing.

Young writers learn a lot from each other, and one way to encourage this learning is by publishing their writing, no matter how simple or underdeveloped it is. Seeing their writing published validates young writers. And having access to other students' writing helps ELL students see what is possible.

Not everything needs to be published. In fact, with very young children who tend to write many pieces in a week, publishing everything would be unrealistic and unnecessary. Also, students benefit from analyzing their own writing and selecting pieces that merit being published. The criteria for publication vary, but may include the following:

- *This is the best piece of writing I've done* (e.g., *this year, ever, this month*).

- *This piece stretched me the most.*

- *I am most proud of this piece because . . .*

There are many ways to publish students' work, including the following:

- Books: These can range from simple booklets written in the student's hand with construction-paper covers to more elaborate books with hard covers and typed text (word-processed or typed by the students or adults). The books need to be easily available to students, so store them on a bookrack or shelf in the class library or in bins on tables.[1]

- Bulletin board displays: Single pieces of writing can be displayed, along with artwork. The copies can be hand written or typed. One bulletin board can be designated for displaying students' work. For example, a 14- by 18-inch or a 16- by 20-inch space can be allocated to each student. Students are responsible for posting their work on an ongoing basis. This can occur on a weekly or biweekly basis during class time so the whole class can discuss the criteria for selecting a piece to display.

- Publish students' writing on class, school, district, state, and other Web sites.

- Publish their writing in class, school, district, local and not-so-local newspapers, and children's magazines.

SITUATION 1 Students don't know what to write about.

If students have had few, if any, experiences writing for authentic purposes and have become accustomed to writing on assigned topics or genres, or in response to sentence starters and patterned forms, or they equate writing with copying someone else's message, it can be hard for them to exhibit much initiative as writers. For ELLs, this reality is often compounded by the

---

[1] For book publishing ideas, see Paul Johnson (1997), *Pictures and Words Together: Children Illustrating and Writing Their Own Books*. Portsmouth, NH: Heinemann.

expectation that they write in a language over which they may not have much control. When teachers encounter students who say that they do not know what to write about, we are often tempted to allocate topics or sentence starters, in the belief that this will lead students to writing independently and/or writing more. However, it is important to recognize that, if we want students to become enthusiastic, independent, and successful writers who understand that writers compose texts for multiple authentic purposes, we must provide them with real opportunities to write, along with the support that acknowledges their strengths and needs as writers. If students don't know what to write about, it is helpful to encourage them to focus on topics that are familiar to them (e.g., their families, favorite pastimes or interests, and early impressions of life in their new country, school, and community). In addition to the strategies identified earlier, we recommend the following strategies to help students find their writing topics.

Targeted Strategy 1: Read and connect.

Published authors frequently comment on how much they are influenced by what they read, and young writers can be mentored in similar ways. After students have read or been read to, it is a good idea to ask them what the piece reminded them of. Often, students make text-to-self connections, which they can then translate into their own pieces of writing. For example, after having heard Patricia Polacco's *The Keeping Quilt* (1998), a group of ELL students recounted their own family stories describing objects that were very significant in their families' lives. One child told of how the only object that his family had brought from their homeland was a key, which his grandparents had brought with them when their family had been forced to leave their home during a war. When the story of their survival was recounted at family events, the key was taken out. Another child brought a cloth to school that was embroidered with brightly colored yarn. The cloth was a gift from her godmother, who had received it from her own godmother many years before, and it was like a memory cloth, a way for the child to remember a special person in her life. In both cases, the students later wrote about these special objects.

Procedure 1:

- Select a book that you think will spark your students' memories. (See a list of recommended picture books in Appendix Q, pp. 304–306.)

- Before reading to the students, explain that you are going to read a book that you think they will like and that may help them think of their own stories.

- Read the book.

- After reading the book, have a conversation with the students. You might ask, *What did this story remind you of?* or *While I was reading this book, what did it make you think about?* or *What memories did this book encourage?*

- Allow students some time to think, but if after 10–15 seconds they remain silent, briefly share some connections you made from the book to your own memories.

- List the connections on chart paper and post the chart. Alternatively, students can write their individual connections on sticky notes, which they then post on the chart paper.

- If the connections students make can be categorized, do so with their input, and post the connections on a chart. Alternatively, if students write their connections on sticky notes, they can categorize their connections.

- Remind students that the charts are a resource to help them think about writing topics.

Procedure 2:

- Read the memoirs or personal narratives written by other students.

- Follow the steps listed in Procedure 1.

Targeted Strategy 2: Generate topics.

If students have few experiences in generating their own writing topics, it is important to teach them how to do so. One way to do this is through demonstrations; the following basic procedure has worked well for us.

- Before meeting with the students, the teacher generates a list of topics that he or she is knowledgeable about and would like to write about. It is important to list topics that are small in scope (e.g., a series of incidents involving one's mother as opposed to *my mother*) and likely to be of interest to students. Also, it is important to include both personal experiences and memories along with nonfiction topics you are familiar with. For example, Katharine's list might include the following:

  ★ When she lost two of her teeth playing field hockey
  ★ When her family got gerbils . . . and the gerbils reproduced and reproduced and reproduced
  ★ How to take care of gerbils
  ★ Getting stuck near the top of a cold mountain when the clouds descended and the path disappeared
  ★ Her first visit to the U.S. and the agony of not being understood in restaurants (even though her native language is English)

★ Visiting the house where she grew up and being presented with her bracelet from childhood that the current owner had found during a remodeling project

● The teacher shares the list of potential topics with the students, talking about each one briefly. The topics are accompanied by drawings, artifacts (e.g., photos and objects), and gestures, as needed. (This may be a mini-lesson with the entire class, done with a group of students, or one-on-one.)

● Ask students to generate their own lists, which can be written and/or drawn. For example, Ali wrote the following on his list of topics:

  ★ Wen I win gol (*When I win goal/When I scored the winning goal*)
  ★ Mi (*my*) dog hav babe (*baby*)
  ★ I fall of (*off*) tree
  ★ I lose mi jaket (*jacket*)
  ★ We go NY siti (*city*) with unkl (*uncle*)

● Students share their lists with each other and then revise them. (Hearing what others listed often jogs students' memories; it is also a means to underscore how writers frequently borrow ideas from each other.)

● It is a good idea to paste these lists inside students' writing notebooks so that topic ideas are always accessible—and it is also a good idea to encourage students to add to their lists on an ongoing basis.

● Students select one of the topics to write about.

● Whenever students talk about an idea or experience that you think could be a good writing topic, mention this and encourage the students to add them to their lists (or to a class-generated list of potential topics posted in the classroom).

Alternatives to this topic-generation strategy:

1. Good things/not so good things that have happened to me[2]:

● Divide a sheet of paper into two columns, and label the columns: "Good things that have happened to me" and "Not so good things that have happened to me."

● Number each column 1–5.

● Demonstrate how to fill in the spaces. (A completed example is shown on the next page. The grammar, spelling, and punctuation have been standardized.)

---

[2] Linda Rief (1992) describes a similar process using a "Significant Positives and Negatives" graph in which students list the best and worst things that ever happened to them. See *Seeking Diversity: Language Arts with Adolescents*. Portsmouth, NH: Heinemann.

- Ask students to generate their own lists, using words and/or drawings.
- After generating their lists, students share their potential writing topics.

Good things that have happened to me	Not so good things that have happened to me
1. When I saw my baby brother for the first time	1. When I got lost in Sears
2. When I made a puppet show for my mom's birthday	2. Falling through the ice in the canal
3. Getting chosen for the soccer team	3. When my grandpa didn't come home from the hospital
4. Finding two dollars under my pillow when I lost a tooth	4. When I broke my Christmas toy before we'd opened all the presents
5. When I won a prize for summer reading	5. When my best friend moved to a different state

2. Brainstorm topics:

- The entire class or a group generates a list of possible topics. This list can refer to shared experiences as well as individual experiences.
- The list is posted so that students have easy access to it.
- An example of a group-generated list appears below.

Example of a group-generated list of topics

Going to the science museum	Pets	The first time
★ Angel almost missed the bus ★ Getting to touch live animals, like a starfish ★ Having a talent show on the bus ★ The bus breaking down	★ Getting a pet for the first time ★ Meeting a pet for the first time ★ Losing a pet	★ Riding a bike without the training wheels ★ Going to school—the first day ★ Going to the snow/mountains/ocean/city for the first time ★ Meeting a baby brother or sister ★ Being in a wedding party as a flower girl or ring bearer

3. Brainstorm genres:

* The entire class or a group generates a list of possible genres.

* Part of the brainstorming may include a discussion of how different genres may coincide with different purposes for writing. For example, when writing a letter to a family member, it is often necessary to inform them of one's activities and development and to express love, whereas an obituary is written to honor a deceased person.

* The list is posted so that students have easy access to it. An example of a group-generated list of genres follows:

What to Write When You're Not Sure What to Write About	
* Lists	* Letters
* Birthday cards	* Magazine articles
* Invitations	* Newspaper articles
* Directions for games	* Jokes
* Recipes	* Cartoons
* Plays	* Advertisements
* Poems	* Obituaries
* Song lyrics	* Lab reports

4. Brainstorm letter-writing options:

Letter writing is one of the most common and authentic writing experiences (as long as the letters are written for a real audience and sent), and reluctant writers often respond very favorably to having opportunities to correspond with others. Many different types of letters can be written, and we have found that the following approach works well:

* Begin by discussing with students why people write letters (e.g., to inform, make requests, complain, express love and gratitude, entertain, remind, confirm).

* Using a two-column format, students (the whole class, a group, or an individual student, depending on the instructional format) generate a list of the different kinds of letters they have written and/or might write. These are listed in the left column.

* Then the students generate a list of people to whom they might write each of these different types of letters. These are listed in the right column.

An example of this type of letter-writing chart follows.

Type of Letter	Potential Audience
Catching up with someone	Grandma, friend from home, last year's teacher
Invitation	Parents (about conferences, Back to School Night)
Thank you	Museum guide, speaker to class, janitor/secretary/librarian/principal, volunteers, specials teachers
Request for information or free items	Magazines, newspapers, community organizations, government organizations
Complaint	School employees (e.g., the cafeteria is dirty, art class has been cut), local authorities (e.g., library hours have been cut), businesses (e.g., a new skateboard wheel has fallen off, a magazine you paid for didn't arrive)
Pen pal	Introducing yourself, subsequent letters
Community activism	Local, state, and national authorities (e.g., requesting a soccer field, requesting more stop signs around the school, requesting more policing in the neighborhood, requesting more time for learning and less time on testing)

Targeted Strategy 3: Create family photo books.

All students are experts on family, and writing family books can be very successful with reluctant writers. It is helpful if the teacher has his or her own family book to share with students—not only does this help build classroom community, but also it can be a very powerful means of demonstrating the project. Taking photographs adds a dimension that can support reluctant writers. The following procedure can be helpful:

- The teacher and students discuss:
  - The purpose of the family books project.
  - When the students might take pictures (e.g., during the week and on weekends; early morning, afternoon and evening).

- ★ What students might photograph (e.g., when family members are doing ordinary everyday tasks, such as cooking, fixing a car, and reading the newspaper; when family members are engaged in special events, such as celebrations).
  - ★ The importance of explaining the project to family members and getting their permission to take pictures.

- ⚘ The students learn how to use inexpensive, disposable, or Polaroid cameras to take pictures of their family members engaged in different activities (e.g., Grandma Ji-Mei taking care of her flowers; Uncle Ahmed reading the newspaper).

- ⚘ After the photographs are developed, the students write books about their family members. The photos serve as the illustrations for the books.

- ⚘ The books are stored in the classroom and/or school library, so they can be read widely.

- ⚘ We recommend making extra copies—we have found that family books are often very popular with ELL students.

SITUATION 2 — Students copy everything instead of producing original work.

Copying is a stage that ELL students often go through as they become increasingly more skillful and confident writers (e.g., Heald-Taylor, 1986; Hoyt, 1993). Also, in many cultures, copying is a respected aspect of learning to become a writer, as it is thought that studying (and copying) the style of more accomplished writers helps one become a better writer. In this context, students aren't encouraged to be creative and generate original messages; instead, they copy the writing of respected, revered writers. However, it can be disconcerting for teachers in North America, where original writing is more respected and where native English-speaking students pass through a copying stage when they are much younger.

Although copying is a natural part of an ELL student's writing development, there are occasions when copying becomes a crutch. In such cases, it is prudent to encourage ELLs to become more independent writers. Sometimes all it takes is simply showing students alternatives, whereas at other times, they may need more explicit instruction in how to use other writing strategies. For example, some students are stalled by their inability to spell English words and rely on copying to produce "correct" writing.

In such cases, spending a few minutes on a regular basis teaching spelling strategies (which is *not* the same as giving them lists of words) can accelerate their willingness and ability to write more freely.[3]

Some strategies that can assist students move beyond copying include the following:

Targeted Strategy 1: Draw and label.

Invite students to write labels and captions to accompany their drawings. Demonstrate how to do this and share examples of students' labeled and captioned writing. Figure 5.3 shows a labeled picture of the Titanic, indicating the main parts of the ship and equipment.

Figure 5.3: Student Drawing of *Titanic* With Captions: *crow's nest, passengers, crew, captain, stern, hull, cabin, anchors, lifeboats, bow, deck*

This picture was part of a culminating project for a combined social studies and science unit on learning about discovery and exploration. Dorothy's intermediate-grade ESOL class had read about the discovery and exploration of the sunken *Titanic*.

Targeted Strategy 2: Use sentence starters.

Sentence starters provide a bridge to original writing for reluctant writers. They also offer an opportunity for teachers and students to get to know each

---

[3] There are several excellent resources available for teaching spelling strategies, including the following:
F. Bolton & D. Snowball 1993, *Ideas for spelling*, Portsmouth, NH: Heinemann;
C. Marten 2003, *Word crafting: Teaching spelling, grades K–6*, Portsmouth, NH: Heinemann;
D. R. Bear, M. Invernizzi, S. Templeton, & F. Johnston 2004, *Words their way: Word study for phonics, vocabulary, and spelling instruction* (3rd ed.), Upper Saddle River, NJ: Prentice Hall.

other better. If students have a writing journal, they can write sentence starters there, accompanied by drawings. It can also be very helpful to have picture dictionaries available, including bilingual picture dictionaries, to help students in locating words and/or activities. (See Appendix K, p. 298, for a list of picture dictionaries.) Some sentence starters that we have used with success are shown below.

My favorite games are . . .

In the morning, I . . .

After school, I . . .

In school, I like . . .

In school, I don't like . . .

My favorite foods are . . .

My favorite TV shows are . . .

On the weekend, I like/don't like . . .

My favorite book/authors are . . .

My family is made up of . . .

My favorite time of the day is . . .

My favorite time of the year is . . .

My favorite place is . . .

My favorite music is . . .

What I like best about living in (name the country)

What I like least about living in (name the country)

I am good at . . .

My earliest memory is . . .

What I'd like to do better in (name a subject) is . . .

Procedure:

- Demonstrate to students what they need to do. For example, Katharine might say, *My favorite sports are soccer, tennis, and hiking* or *My earliest memory is of riding a donkey on a beach in Wales* and then talk about any unfamiliar words.

- If students aren't familiar with the picture dictionary, show them how it is organized.

- Give students about five to ten minutes to write their sentences.

- Students share what they have generated, in pairs, small groups, or the entire class, depending on the size of the group, the sentence starter, and what you hope to accomplish. For example, if you are doing a unit on family and you want students to know a little more about each other, you might ask the whole class to sit in a circle and take turns sharing who is in their family. On the other hand, you may decide to have students do a pair share about favorite movies and then have the class generate a graph of favorite movies.

Alternative Sentence Starter 1: I like . . . because

Many basic sentence starters can be extended by adding *because*, such as, *In school, I like/don't like to . . . because . . . .* This also provides more insight into the student.

Alternative Sentence Starter 2: Days of the Week: What I Like to Do

⚬ Each line starts with *On*, followed by a day of the week and the phrase, *I like to*, and a blank for students to fill in. An example is shown below.

On Monday, I like to <u>go to my uncle's restaurant after school and do my homework there.</u>
On Tuesday, I like to <u>go to art class and make pictures and mobiles.</u>
On Wednesday, I like to <u>help in the library at lunchtime and read new books.</u>
On Thursday, I like to <u>go to dance class with my sisters and cousins.</u>
On Friday, I like to <u>help my mom with her hair and nails.</u>
On Saturday, I like to <u>go to language class and hear stories. I'm bilingual.</u>
On Sunday, I like to <u>go to the park with my family for a picnic and ice cream.</u>

Targeted Strategy 3: Spin off patterned writing books.

As a bridging writing activity to independent writing, many teachers of ELLs have found success in writing class books modeled after a favorite book. For example, after reading aloud Bill Martin's *A Ghost Story*, students have been invited to replace the repeated adjective *dark* with another adjective, such as *big*, *noisy*, or *scary*, and then make appropriate substitutions as they complete their stories.

The discussions that occur in the brainstorming component of this kind of collaborative writing can be very valuable to ELLs, particularly if the discussion includes pictures, sketches, and gestures to demonstrate vocabulary and to ensure meaning. See Appendix I, p. 295, for a list of patterned books to use for this kind of spin-off book writing.

Students can either contribute to a single page or to every page of a class book. In the latter case, do not spend too much time making the book as students may lose interest if the process is too prolonged. Also, in order to retain their interest, students may need to write this book in short segments of not more than 20 minutes each day. The same is true for the writing of individual books (although we have known students who were so invested in writing their book that they wrote it in one long session, and then illustrated it in another session).

Patterned writing can become a crutch to students, however, so it should be approached with care, and students should continue to be encouraged to write on self-selected topics. A range of patterned-writing possibilities exists, including the following options:

Months of the Year Book:

In elementary schools, students often become familiar with Maurice Sendak's books, including *Chicken Soup With Rice: A Book of Months* (1962). This book can be used as the inspiration for students' own books or a class book about what they like to do in each month of the year.

Procedure:

- Read and discuss *Chicken Soup with Rice: A Book of Months.*

- Explain to the students that they will be writing their own book about months of the year. (Individual students can write their own books, small groups can write books collaboratively, or the entire class can write a class book.) An excerpt from a class book follows:

> ### In January,
> *I like to visit my grandma in the city. (Amelia)*
> *I like to play soccer when it's not snowing. (Franco)*
> *I like to go sledding in the park. (Augustina)*

- Brainstorm with students what they like to do in a given month. List these ideas on a chart or on the whiteboard/chalkboard. Do this month by month.

- Students draft their sentences for a given month.

- After editing, students copy their sentences onto sentence strips (or directly onto the pages of the book, if it is an individual student's book).

- Attach the sentence strips to the book's pages.

- Students make illustrations for each page of the book, which are also attached to the book (or are drawn directly onto the page, if it is an individual student's book).

- Attach a cover.

- Students read the book together, if it is a class book, or individually and in pairs, if books are written by individual students. Also, these books can become part of the teacher's repertoire of read-aloud books.

- Store the books in a prominent place so students have easy access to them throughout the school year.

Alternative 1: Months Spent in Two Locations Books

- If children have lived in or visited two distinct locations, they can write a book in which they compare what they like to do at the same time of the year in the two locations.

- First, brainstorm activities in a given month in a range of locations. Chart the activities and name the locations. (See Figure 5.4 on p. 200 for an example.) This can lead to interesting conversations about the globe, weather, seasons, and the northern and southern hemispheres.

- Demonstrate how to compare activities. For example, Katharine might write:

  In January, I like to hike in the snow in Scotland,
  but I like to visit the beach in California.

- Students write their comparative sentences. Here is an example of a child's sentence:

  In January, I like to play with my cousins and run in the sunshine in El Salvador, but I like to go to a café for hot chocolate with my dad in New York. (Juan Andrés)

- Students can write the text for just one month or for each month of the year. For the latter situation, it can help to provide a sheet for completing the sentences. (See Appendix R, p. 307, for a sample sheet for all 12 months.)

- After the editing phase, students copy their sentences onto sentence strips, along with a small illustration.

- Attach a cover.

- Students read their book together, if it is a class book, or individually and in pairs, if books are written by individual students. Also, these books can become part of the teacher's repertoire of read-aloud books.

- Store books in a prominent place so students have easy access to them throughout the school year.

In February, I like to . . .	Location
Run in the sunshine	San Salvador, El Salvador
Go to the beach and swim in the ocean	Durban, South Africa
Wear new clothes because it's the beginning of the school year	Lima, Peru
Go to a café for hot chocolate with my dad	New York, NY
Go sledding in the park and make snow angels	Chicago, IL
Go to the circus and watch the animals and acrobats	Kansas City, MO

Figure 5.4: Examples of Months Spent in Two Locations Chart

Alternative 2: What We Like to Do Book:

- Students brainstorm their favorite activities in a given month.

  In January, <u>Anton</u> likes to <u>play in the gym in the school</u>, <u>Angelica</u> likes to <u>visit her grandma and hear stories</u>, <u>Roberta</u> likes to <u>play with her cats</u>, and <u>Kim</u> likes to <u>watch cartoons when it's raining</u>.

- Students write sentences for the designated month.

- After the editing phase, students copy their sentences onto sentence strips, along with a small illustration.

- Students write their names in the designated spot, and then attach their sentence strips.

- Attach a cover.

- Students read the book together, if it is a class book, or individually and in pairs, if books are written by individual students. Also, these books can become part of the teacher's repertoire of read-aloud books.

- Store the book in a prominent place so students have easy access to it throughout the school year.

Targeted Strategy 4: Write in dialogue journals.

Journals and logs give students the opportunity to reflect upon their lives and their learning. One form of reflective writing that is often very successful with ELLs, including reluctant writers, is dialogue journals (e.g., Peyton & Reed, 1990; Peyton & Seyoum, 1989; Reyes, 1991; Rous, 1993; Samway & Taylor, 1993a, 1993b; Taylor, 1990; Urzúa, 1987).[4] In dialogue journals (DJs), students correspond with their teacher or another person. Topics may be entirely open-ended, or there may be content guidelines. For example, Dorothy's ELL students corresponded with her about books they had been reading (Samway & Taylor, 1993a, 1993b; Taylor, 1990); they also corresponded with Katharine about their reading and writing processes in letters (Samway & Taylor, 1993a, 1993b).

Some useful maxims for successful dialogue journal writing that we have learned to respect over the years include the following:

- Avoid cheerleading comments in the margins (e.g., *Interesting! Nice job! Too bad!*). Instead, respond authentically to what students write (e.g., *I'm so sorry to hear about your dog being sick. If it were my dog, I'd be as upset as you. How is she now?*).

- Be prepared to read your entry aloud to the student . . . and then allow him or her to respond.

- Monitor how long your entries are. When we are interested in a topic, it can be particularly tempting to write very long entries, which can overwhelm students. It's generally a good idea to write an entry that's similar in length to that of your correspondents.

- Do not correct students' writing. A dialogue journal is a form of communication, and the teacher's writing should be in response to the student's entry. Also, keep in mind that a DJ is almost always a first-draft type of writing.

- Although it is important to demonstrate standardized language (spelling, grammatical structures, and punctuation) and correct use of vocabulary in your entries, be prepared to teach to these items at another time, such as in a writing workshop mini-lesson or during word study time. Sometimes, students pick up on our correct usage, but not always.

- If you are corresponding with a whole class, stagger how many DJs you respond to on a given day, so you don't become overwhelmed.

---

[4] Dialogue journal writing is sometimes referred to as *interactive writing*, but should not be confused with another form of interactive writing that is used with emergent readers and writers (e.g., McCarrier, Pinnell, & Fountas 2000). This other form of interactive writing focuses on the teacher and students sharing the writing utensil and producing a text that is completely standardized. This form of interactive writing will be discussed later in the chapter.

- Other DJ configurations that we have seen work well include the following:
  - ★ Students writing to other students (in the same class or another class)
  - ★ Students writing to student teachers
  - ★ Students writing to volunteers

- DJs can be written by hand or typed on a computer and sent via the Internet.

SITUATION 3   My student just lists words.

A developmental stage in writing that many ELL students go through when they are new to English writing is listing isolated words or phrases, much like labeling (e.g., *dog*, *mom*, *my house*), instead of placing words in sentences (see Hoyt, 1993; Taylor, 1990). The strategies listed earlier under patterned writing, language experience approach (LEA), and reading beginning ELL students' texts can all be very helpful in this situation. The following additional strategies can help move ELLs into writing more complete texts:

Targeted Strategy 1: Incorporate Read Aloud Plus.

Reading aloud to ELL students (along with discussions about the text) is an invaluable activity as it builds vocabulary and awareness of the rhythms of the language. However, for read-alouds to really support ELL writers, it is a good idea to give students copies of the text being read aloud so they can follow along. We call this "Read Aloud Plus." This form of read-aloud allows students to see how spoken English corresponds with written words and conventions, such as punctuation, capitalization, spelling, and text organization. This strategy can also show ELLs who simply list words when writing how to structure longer sentences and texts.

Targeted Strategy 2: Make use of shared reading.

In shared reading, the teacher and students read an enlarged text that all students can see—commercially published or teacher-made big books and/or charts. Texts, which include fiction, nonfiction, poetry, rhymes, and chants, are often highly predictable and written with rhythmic language, features that support emergent ELL writers. The procedure that follows is an adapted shared reading procedure to support emergent ELL writers.

Procedure:

- When introducing a new shared reading text, the teacher does a short introduction, mentioning what the text is about.

- The teacher reads the text aloud at a normal to very slightly slowed pace, pointing to each word with a pointer while reading.

- The class briefly discusses the text (e.g., what it reminded them of and any unfamiliar words).

- Students are then invited to join in, and the teacher and students read the text together, with the teacher continuing to point to the words.

- The class may reread the text again, and the teacher may reduce the amount of support that he or she provides.

- One follow-up activity that supports writers who just list words is sentence strips, the procedure for which follows:

  - The teacher writes a sentence and its punctuation on a strip of paper.
  - The words and punctuation are cut up into phrases and/or individual words and punctuation marks, such as the following example of a sentence from the nursery rhyme "If All the Seas Were One Sea" shows. As ELL students are likely to find it harder to put individual words in order than phrases, it is usually best to start with phrases.

  Sentence from nursery rhyme:
  If all the seas were one sea, what a great sea that would be.

  Scrambled sentence (phrases with punctuation):
  that would be.   were one sea,   what a great sea   If all the seas

  Scrambled sentence (words with punctuation):
  all seas one what great sea would If the were sea, a be. that

- The student puts the scrambled strips in order.

- The teacher and students talk about any difficulties they encountered.

Targeted Strategy 3: Tape-record, and then write.

If ELLs speak in extended sentences, they can often be supported in moving from listing words to writing sentences by listening to themselves speak and then writing down what they said.

Procedure:

- The student tape-records himself or herself while orally narrating a text, such as a story, memoir, how-to directions, or book review.

- While listening to the recording, the student writes down sentences.

- The student may have to listen to the tape several times to capture the text.

- The student can work with another student to capture the text.

Alternative Procedure:

- The student tape-records himself or herself narrating several examples of a particular genre (e.g., several stories, memoirs, poems, how-to directions, book reviews).

- The student selects one example to write down.

- While listening to the recording, the student writes down sentences.

- The student may have to listen to the tape several times to capture the text.

- The student can work with another student to capture the text.

Targeted Strategy 4: *Introduce collaborative dictation.*

Instead of speaking into a tape recorder, another useful strategy is to have one student dictate to another student. So long as the ELL student can speak in more complete sentences, it isn't usually necessary to partner him or her with a student who writes more complex sentences. In fact, by taking dictation, the student who is only listing words gets practice in writing more complete texts.

Procedure:

- Explain the task and its purpose to the students—to record well-developed texts in writing.

- Demonstrate unsuccessful and successful collaborative dictation. For example, unsuccessful collaboration might include the person taking dictation using put-downs and taking over the composing of the text. In a successful collaboration, the person taking dictation asks for clarification, both students work together to figure out how to spell words, and the person taking dictation shows appreciation for the content of the text.

- Two students work together to take turns dictating their texts to each another.

SITUATION 4 — During independent writing time, my ELL student doesn't do anything.

Several factors may influence how ELLs use their time in independent writing, and it is essential to assess whether they know how they should spend their time and whether the environment is conducive to writing. For example, do they know what they need to do? Do they know what to do when they get stuck? Are they allowed to talk with other students while writing?

Having opportunities to talk while writing is essential for ELLs, as it is through talk that learning is often mediated (e.g., Ammon, 1985; Urzúa, 1986, 1987). Through talk, ELLs can often figure out what they want to write and how they want to write it. The prohibition of productive, focused talk can impede learning. For example, in some writing classrooms, independent writing time is viewed as a silent writing time, and newcomer students or struggling writers may spend the entire period not doing anything. In fact, we have visited classrooms where students write alone and in silence, and we have observed ELLs starting off the independent writing period with enthusiasm and confidence. However, within a short time, they get stuck and often remain stuck for the entire period, unless the teacher happens to come by for a conference. On occasion, students have told us that they don't know what to do, and when we have asked if they could get help from another student at their table, they have indicated that they aren't supposed to talk during independent writing time.

The need for an environment that values talk has to be balanced, however, with an environment that has high expectations for how students use their independent writing time. That is why we advocate talk that is focused and productive. We have visited classrooms in which students are free to talk during independent writing time, and we have seen students not writing, but visiting with each other for up to 30 minutes. Clearly, this can be very problematic.

In order to support ELL students who don't seem to use their time productively during independent writing time, we suggest the following:

- Make sure all students know what they are going to do during independent writing time (e.g., after a mini-lesson, send students to their tables or desks once they have indicated that they know what they are going to do next).

- Make sure that all students are actively engaged in their writing before beginning to confer with them—that is, move around the room quickly, checking in.

- Make sure that students have topics on which to write (see strategies listed earlier in the section on topic generation that begins on page 189).

- Make sure that students know their options during independent writing time (e.g., write; do research, such as through reading; confer; edit). Post a chart of options as a reminder.

- Have students set goals for themselves each writing session (e.g., *Today, I'm going to finish this draft*; or *Today, I'm going to try different leads* or, in the case of a student who spends all of his or her time drawing, *Today, I'm going to draw for ten minutes and then write words to go with the drawing*).

- If students distract other writers when they talk, allocate areas in the classroom where students can confer and/or write collaboratively—and monitor that they use these spaces productively.

- If newcomer ELLs are literate in their L1, encourage them to write in their L1, even if you cannot read it. They can later translate it. Sharing examples of bilingual texts and texts written in the L1 is one way to encourage ELLs to write in their L1.

- Make sure that students have opportunities to read other students' writing on a regular basis. In some classrooms, student rarely, if ever, read each other's texts. They write in silence, don't confer, and when their pieces are published, they read them to their peers, rather than having their classmates actually read them. Writers need to talk about their writing, but they also need to read what their peers write.

My ELL Students Don't Seem to Be Improving as Writers

As we mentioned in the beginning of this chapter, writing is developmental, and development is often very irregular. Sometimes, students may seem to have plateaued or even regressed, which can be very discouraging to teachers. However, it is not uncommon to encounter these realities, and they appear to be grounded in the brain's being able to cope with only so much new information at a time; that is, students may be encountering linguistic overload. For example, after an intense period of language input through what has been explicitly or implicitly taught, learners often need time to process and experiment with the new information, which can lead to phenomena that appear to be plateaus or regressions. Other contributing factors to what appears to be a learning slowdown may be related to issues surrounding cultural assimilation and little or no previous exposure to a school environment.[5]

SITUATION 1 — I correct my students' writing, but they continue to make the same mistakes.

There is no evidence that correcting students' writing actually leads to improvement. However, targeted instruction that focuses on one or two of the most crucial items (e.g., those that impede meaning) can be useful to learners. The following strategies can also help ELL writers.

Targeted Strategy 1: Introduce a Teaching Points Checklist.

In order to have a record of what one has taught and to hold students accountable for what you have taught, have students keep a record of what you have taught them on a Teaching Points Checklist.

Procedure:

- After teaching about a particular writing skill, strategy, or feature, ask students to briefly share what they learned—with you, if it was an individual conference, or in a pair share, if you taught more than one student. For example, after being taught about the need to label illustrations, the ELL student may say, *I learn how use label here with the picture* while pointing to a picture in his/her brochure about his/her native land.

- If there are more than two students, ask the students to orally explain in their own words what they learned.

---

[5] A lack of development over an extended period of time, such as a year, may also be an indication of a learning disability, and teachers should follow up, if they suspect one. However, when assessed for a potential learning disability, ELLs should be assessed in their L1. See Chapter 4 for additional information and strategies relating to ELLs with learning disabilities.

- Place a three-column Teaching Points Checklist on an overhead, and then write the date, the teaching point, and a succinct explanation, comment, and/or example. Figure 5.5 shows an excerpt from a completed Teaching Points Checklist.

Date	Teaching Point	Comments
11/3	Question mark (?)	Use at the end of a question. *Do you like pizza?*
11/6	Past tense of *go* is *went* (not *goed*)	*We went to the fair this weekend.*
11/9	Read my writing aloud	This helps catch mistakes and anything that's missing.
11/9	Adjectives go before nouns	*I love sweet strawberries.*
11/10	Words to use instead of *said*	*shouted, called, announced, whispered*

Figure 5.5: Sample Teaching Points Checklist

- Student(s) record the teaching point on their own Teaching Points Checklist. This checklist may include points taught to the whole class, small groups, or in one-on-one conferences.
- Encourage students to refer to this checklist whenever they are writing, not just when they are editing.
- The checklist is stored in students' writing folders, in a place where students can easily locate it, such as inside the front or back cover.
- When a piece of writing is handed in, a student can attach the checklist to it.
- If you read a student's piece that does not incorporate the features you taught, check to see if he or she has referred to the list. If not, then ask him/her to do so. Note that there are times when a student *has* used the checklist but needs additional teaching, which should be provided— this is particularly true of points taught to a whole class or large group.
- The list is individualized and should be updated on a regular basis.

Alternative:

If the student is very young or new to writing, you may decide to record points on the checklist, either in addition to or in place of the student's notations.

Targeted Strategy 2: Utilize modified interactive writing.

Interactive writing is typically used with young children who are emergent readers (McCarrier et al., 2000).[6] It involves the teacher and students sharing the pen while writing a text (e.g., a thank-you letter or a list of procedures for looking after a classroom pet). By the end of the interactive writing session, which may last from a few minutes to about 20 minutes, a text has been written conventionally, with standardized spelling, punctuation, word choice, capitalization, and paragraphing. It may take several days to write a longer text. For an interactive writing session, you will need chart paper, markers, and correction/cover-up tape.

Interactive writing can be a very effective strategy because it can help ELLs focus on two aspects of language that often distinguish them from their native English-speaking peers—grammar and word choice. However, interactive writing should not replace authentic writing opportunities. A short interactive writing session of about 10–15 minutes can be very effective. The teacher and student(s) collaboratively generate the text, but in contrast to collaborative writing, this text is completely standardized. Hence, if words are misspelled or there are nonstandardized grammatical structures, the teacher points them out, invites corrections, and supplies the standardized form, if the students are unable to do so.

Procedure:

* The teacher and students collaboratively generate the text, such as a letter of thanks or a record of a shared experience; the teacher records a standardized version on a piece of paper, which he or she can use for reference.

* The writing of the text on chart paper begins. The text for a sample interactive session is shown below.

When we select a pet for our classroom:

* It should be big enough for us to see.
* It should move a lot so we can see it.
* It shouldn't cost a lot of money to feed.
* It should be easy to take care of.
* It should be easy to take home on the weekend and on vacations.

---

[6] The following joint NCTE/IRA/Verizon Foundation Web site for teachers provides information on interactive writing: www.readwritethink.org/lessons/lesson_view.asp?id=242.

An excerpt from an interactive writing session related to this sample text follows:

Teacher: So, we have our text. (*She reads to the students what they had collaboratively generated.*) Let's begin with the first line, "When we select a pet for our classroom." (*The teacher writes the introductory eight words, talking through what she's doing.*) W-h-e-n, when. Do you remember that "when" has a silent "h" in it, like "where" and "what"?

Now, I'm going to put a colon here at the end because we're going to list five points, right? The first point is "It should be big enough for us to see." We need a bullet first. (*She puts a bullet on the second line and writes "It."*) I'm using a capital "I" because the first word in each line in this list needs to be capitalized.

Okay. Now for "should." Who knows how to spell "should"? Here you go, Javier. (*She passes the marker to Javier, and he writes "shoud," looks back at the word wall, takes a small piece of correction tape to delete the "d," and then writes "ld."*) Great, Javier. Why don't you go ahead and write "should be"? (*Javier continues writing.*)

Let's read what we have so far. (*The students and teacher read, "When we select a pet for our classroom, it should be."*) Now we need "big." Who can write "big"? Okay, Matilda, come on up and write "big." (*Matilda writes the word without looking around, then looks up inquiringly at the teacher, who smiles.*) That's it. You've got it! Let's all read it together. (*The teacher and students read, "When we select a pet for our classroom, it should be big."*)

Now we need to write "enough." This is a tricky word. How do you think it's spelled? (*Students look at the word wall, but the word is not there. The teacher asks what sounds they hear, and students say /i/, /f/, and /n/.*) You've got good ears. Like I said, it's a tricky word. It's spelled like this: e-n-o-u-g-h. (*Javier hands her the marker, and she writes "enough" next to "be."*) The e-n makes the /in/ sound and the o-u-g-h- makes the /uff/ sound. Enough. Okay? (*Students nod.*)

Let's read what we have so far. (*The students and teacher read, "When we select a pet for our classroom, it should be big enough."*) Let's finish off this bulleted point, shall we? "It should be big enough for us to see" (*stressing "for us to see"*).

Ana how about you? Can you come and write that last bit, please? "For us to see." (*Ana takes the marker and finishes the sentence.*) Good job.

- The writing of the text continues in this way, with frequent stops to reread what has been written.

- The text is posted in the classroom to be used for reading practice and reference purposes when talking about writing (e.g., when to use bullets, how to use bullets, how to punctuate, word choice, spelling).

Alternative:

The teacher may decide to use a text written by a student or students for an interactive writing session (See the letter of invitation to a potential speaker that a group wrote collaboratively, on p. 185.)

Targeted Strategy 3: Use a modified cloze.

After teaching a surface feature item (e.g., a grammatical point or a punctuation mark), a useful follow-up practice activity is a modified cloze. In a regular cloze activity, words in a passage are deleted at regular intervals, such as every five, seven, or ten words, but in a modified cloze, the teacher selects which words, phrases, or punctuation marks to delete. For example, after teaching about how to use articles (*a, an, the*), the teacher would selectively delete them from a passage. The short passage below shows the complete text, followed by three modified cloze passages that focus respectively on 1) the past tense marker *–ed*, 2) nouns of location or place, and 3) punctuation. Note that the length of the blanks for the punctuation modified cloze requires less space than the blanks for words and phrases.

Text

I had such a good weekend. My auntie visited us for three days. We shopped at the mall, walked in the hills, and cooked a barbecue in the backyard. It was one of the best weekends I've had.

---

1. Modified cloze focused on the past tense marker *–ed*

I had such a good weekend. My auntie _____ us for three days. We _____ at the mall, _____ in the hills, and _____ a barbecue in the backyard. It was one of the best weekends I've had.

2. Modified cloze focused on nouns of location or place

I had such a good weekend. My auntie visited us for three days. We shopped at the _____, walked in the _____, and cooked a barbecue in the _____. It was one of the best weekends I've had.

3. Modified cloze focused on punctuation

I had such a good weekend. My auntie visited us for three days__ We shopped at the mall__ walked in the hills__ and cooked a barbecue in the backyard__ It was one of the best weekends I've had.

Procedure:[7]

- Select or write a passage that includes several instances of the targeted teaching point. (When using a cloze for reinforcement rather than assessment purposes, this point should be one that has been taught.)

- Make a copy of the text and delete the words or punctuation marks you want your students to practice using—but remember to keep the first and last sentences intact.

- Students can work alone or in pairs to generate words or punctuation marks to fit the spaces.

- Discuss with students what they generated. Be alert to the possibility that they may have written perfectly acceptable alternatives that fit the context of the passage as opposed to what was in the original passage, and be sure to acknowledge this. The discussions that accompany these cloze activities are very valuable and shouldn't be overlooked.

Alternative Modified Cloze: Scaffolded Modified Cloze

To provide more scaffolding, you can have students select words from a list that you provide. In this case, it is advisable to have more words on the list than there are blanks so students aren't simply going through an exercise of elimination or guessing. An example follows.

A more scaffolded modified cloze focused on the past tense marker *–ed*

Select from these words: *washed   cleaned   asked   rained   rushed.*
I spent the long weekend helping my grandparents. We
_____ the house from top to bottom. First, we _____
all the curtains. We hung them outside to dry, but it _____. So,
my grandma and I _____ outside and brought them back in.
After we finished all the work, my grandma treated me to my
favorite dinner.

The complete text

I spent the long weekend helping my grandparents. We cleaned
the house from top to bottom. First, we washed all the curtains.
We hung them outside to dry, but it rained. So, my grandma
and I rushed outside and brought them back in. After we finished
all the work, my grandma treated me to my favorite dinner.

---

[7] See Appendix L, p. 299, for more detailed guidelines on how to prepare a cloze passage.

Targeted Strategy 4: Observe and record.

Procedure:

- Students leave the classroom to observe what is happening around the school and playground. Allocate up to about ten minutes for this.

- When they return to the classroom, students take turns writing sentences on an overhead, chart paper, or plasma screen.

- After each student writes a sentence, the group corrects it collaboratively. (See interactive writing, described on pp. 209–211, for a similar activity.)

Targeted Strategy 5: Do focused editing.

Procedure:

- Students create a piece of writing (e.g., in a writing journal).

- The teacher holds an editing conference, focusing on a point that has been taught, but which the student or students have not internalized or used correctly in their writing (e.g., mixed-up verb tenses, lack of punctuation marks, absence of articles, misuse of terms).

- During the conference, the teacher talks with the student(s) about the teaching point; it may be necessary to reteach the point.

- Students edit their writing, keeping in mind the teaching point that was discussed.

- These conferences should be short and focused. They may be held with individuals or small groups.

Targeted Strategy 6: Read to the wall (or a puppet).

A strategy that we have found to work well in supporting student self-editing is reading to the wall, which allows for a more private self-editing experience than typically occurs when students peer edit and read to each other. We have noticed that when children read their writing aloud, they often catch errors that they don't catch when they read their work silently.

Procedure

- The student reads his or her writing aloud to the wall to help catch any missing ideas or words, or grammatical errors.

- This strategy can be modified slightly for younger children by putting one or two life-size cutout figures on the wall, which class members can name.

- Students read their writing aloud to the wall or to the figure(s) on the wall before the teacher reads it.

Alternative: Read to a puppet.

We have found that a puppet can be a very liberating artifact for some ELL students, particularly the more reticent the child. Hand puppets, finger puppets, and puppets on popsicle sticks can all work well, but it is often best to let the student select his or her puppet. The student then reads his or her text aloud to the puppet before the teacher reads it.

SITUATION 2 My students' writing isn't very sophisticated and seems to have been that way for a long time.

It is not uncommon to find that older ELL students' writing isn't very well developed and may resemble this kind of writing: *This is boy. This the house. The big dog.* Sometimes this is due to developmental issues. For example, the ELL student may be a relative newcomer to writing, may be processing a lot of new information about English and writing, and needs time to progress to more complex writing. However, lack of sophisticated writing may be due to other factors, such as a lack of confidence, real audiences, or authentic purposes for writing. Also, overly simple writing may be influenced by the type of texts that ELL students are reading—some instructional reading materials are overly simplified, and provide poor writing models.

The following strategies can help writers develop into increasingly more sophisticated writers:

Targeted Strategy 1: Model.

- In a writing conference or mini-lesson, share a piece of writing that resembles the underdeveloped writing of the student(s).

- Explain that writers need to write in a way that captures the interest of their readers. Then, briefly talk about two or three ways that writers do this, including adding important details, using intriguing words, having a captivating lead, using dialogue, and using rhythmic language. When talking about a particular strategy, display an example illustrating the point—the examples can be those of adults as well as young writers.

- Then revise the underdeveloped piece, keeping in mind the strategies discussed—the teacher may do this alone or with input from students.

- Ask students to revisit a piece of their writing and revise it, trying one or more of the strategies.

Targeted Strategy 2: Compare two versions of a written piece.

- Put together two versions of a piece of writing, one that is written very simply and one that is more sophisticated in its development. The two versions can be written by the teacher, if versions written by another student aren't available.

- Make copies for the students or put them on chart paper so everyone can read them.

- Read the two pieces aloud, and ask students to compare them: *Why is one better than the other? Why is one more interesting to read than the other?*

- Ask students to revisit a piece of their own writing and revise it, trying one or more of the strategies identified in the discussion.

Targeted Strategy 3: Try an inquiry approach.

- Put together a packet of two to four excerpts from pieces of writing that students are familiar with and that are good examples of more sophisticated writing (e.g., from read-alouds or from touchstone texts in writing workshop[8]).

- Display an example of one of these excerpts and explain why you think it is a well developed piece. You might say, *I like the way the author began with dialogue*, or *I like the descriptive language here because I can really feel how excited this character is*, or *These details help me to understand why it can be dangerous to live close to an active volcano.*

- Ask the student(s) to read the rest of the pieces, paying attention to what the author does to make the writing interesting.

- Discuss what students noticed, and chart the features.

- Ask students to revisit a piece of their own writing and revise it, trying one or more of the features identified in the discussion.

Targeted Strategy 4: Employ reading/writing connections dialogue journals.

Reading/writing connections dialogue journals (DJs), in which the teacher and a student correspond about books they are reading, offer an opportunity for more complex writing. It's also possible to include three people in the

---

[8] Touchstone texts are texts that are rich in writing craft elements (e.g., rhythmic language, strong leads, powerful dialogue, captivating headings and subheadings) and that a teacher refers to often when teaching about writing. These include picture books (nonfiction and fiction), poetry, book reviews, short stories, novels, and magazine articles. See Appendix V, pp. 311–315, for an annotated list of touchstone texts that we have found work well with ELLs.

written dialogue. In this case, each person writes in his or her own journal and then hands it off on a rotating basis. For example, in week 1, Student A responds to Student B, who responds to the teacher, who responds to Student A; in week 2, Student A responds to the teacher, Student B responds to Student A, and the teacher responds to Student B. One advantage to this procedure is that students read each other's entries.

Procedure:

- Provide written guidelines for the dialogue journal, and have students attach them to the inside cover of the journal. An example follows.

Dear Student,
We're going to have a written conversation about books in this dialogue journal. You can use the journal to write about your thoughts about the books. Some things you may want to write about include:

  - ★ What you think about the book.
  - ★ Why the characters (the people in the book) are interesting or not interesting to you.
  - ★ What this book reminds you of. It could be a personal experience, other books you've read, or anything else.
  - ★ What you are learning about writing from reading this book.
  - ★ Questions that the book raises for you.

Please write in your dialogue journal at least three times a week. You will hand it in on _____ (*day of week*). I'm looking forward to "talking" with you about books in this dialogue journal.
     (Signed by the teacher)

- Go over the guidelines and explain what each point refers to by displaying an example and discussing it.

- If needed, provide additional scaffolding by collaboratively generating an entry for a text that all students are familiar with, such as a book that was read aloud that day.

- Ask students to write an entry about a book they are reading.

- Respond to students' entries. Although it's a good idea to respond to all entries the first time students write in their DJs, teachers typically stagger the times when students hand in their DJs, to make the process more manageable.

Targeted Strategy 5: Make use of a reading/writing log.

In a reading/writing log, students comment on what they have learned about writing from their own reading.

Procedure:

- Select a short text to read aloud to students, and explain that you are going to demonstrate the process to follow when writing in their reading/writing logs.

- Display the text so everyone can follow along.

- Read the text aloud and discuss with students what they learned about writing from it. Be prepared to share your own insights. For example, in *Nadia's Hands*, Karen English (1999) uses rhythmic language, such as repetition of a phrase (e.g., "She <u>sat watching</u> the door . . . She <u>sat watching</u> out the window . . . Finally, she <u>sat watching</u> the big kitchen clock over the stove").

- Demonstrate writing a reading/writing log entry on an overhead, chart paper, opaque projector, or plasma screen.

- Ask students to read their independent reading book for about 10–15 minutes, and then write their own entries.

- Invite students to share their entries. Praise students who are reading like writers.

Grammar and Mechanics

It must be remembered that the acquisition of grammatical structures for ELLs is a developmental process found in both oral and written language (Dulay et al., 1982; Ellis, 1994; Wells, 1986). That is, some grammatical structures in the L2 tend to appear before others, as in stages. For example, the present progressive (e.g., she *is talking*) tends to appear before the past participle (e.g., he *has taken* the ball). Also, there is a big difference between being taught grammatical structures and being able to use them. And, because of the complexities of language, linguists haven't been able to generate an order of acquisition that teachers can use; students are often taught structures and are able to demonstrate the ability to apply them in practice exercises, but then fail to apply them in spontaneous uses of language. Another aspect of second-language development is the tendency to overgeneralize after beginning to internalize a feature of language. That is,

ELLs may apply a rule where it doesn't belong, such as using the regular past tense marker *–ed* when the verb is irregular (e.g., *putted* instead of *put* or *goed* instead of *went*). This is true in both grammar and spelling.

Our best advice to teachers is not to worry, but to allow plenty of time and opportunities for ELLs to write for authentic purposes and to read English texts that are comprehensible to them. If the absence or misuse of a grammatical structure leads to a reduction in meaning in an ELL's writing, then this is the most appropriate context in which to teach to that point (e.g., in a writing conference, or in a mini-lesson, if several students manifest the same need). However, it is important to limit one's teaching to one or two points at a time, as students can become cognitively and linguistically overloaded very quickly.

In this section, we suggest some strategies that can be used for teaching to a number of common grammatical and punctuation errors that frequently appear in ELLs' writing, including the following:

- Mixes up pronouns (e.g., uses *he* instead of *she* or uses *him* instead of *her*)

- Omits articles (*a*, *an*, and *the*)

- Omits word endings/inflections (*-ing*, *-s*, *-es*, *-ly*)

- Mixes up word order (e.g., *The hamster brown is in cage*)

- Mixes up negation (e.g., *My dog no like run*)

- Plural nouns, both regular forms (e.g., *ball/balls*, *house/houses*) and irregular forms (e.g., *foot/feet*, *child/children*)

- Superlatives (e.g., *fast<u>est</u>*, *silli<u>est</u>*)

- Contractions (e.g., *I am/I'm*, *let us/let's*, *cannot/can't*)

- Asking questions (e.g., *Is this right? Will we go tomorrow?*)

- Mixes up or omits punctuation marks

When teaching grammatical and punctuation points, be prepared to discuss differences across languages (e.g., word order varies across languages, some languages do not use articles, and not all languages use the same punctuation marks or use them in the same ways).

Targeted Strategy 1: Conduct interactive writing activities.

Do an interactive writing activity in which the text focuses on the targeted grammatical or punctuation feature. (See pp. 209–211 in this chapter for a discussion of interactive writing.) For example, if students are learning about subject/verb agreement with *have* and *has*, the text for an interactive writing session might be the following:

> *Mary has a dog. It has black spots on its back. Her friend has two*
> *dogs. When they go for a walk together, they have a very good time.*
> *But, they have to be careful that their dogs are on their leashes.*
> *If not, they have a very difficult time because Mary's dog has lots*
> *of energy and wants to run free.*

As the teacher and students recreate the text, the teacher explains why *has* and *have* is used in each case, and the use of the subject/verb agreement is reinforced as students reread the passage.

Targeted Strategy 2: Introduce patterned books.

Select books that contain the targeted feature for shared reading sessions. (See pp. 202–203 earlier in this chapter for a discussion of shared reading.) After reading the book together, there are several activities that can be done relatively quickly to reinforce the role and function of the feature, including the following:

- Locate each occurrence of the targeted feature.

- Collaboratively figure out its function and discuss its use.

- Cover up the feature with sticky tape, reread the text with the students, and ask them to figure out what goes in the covered-up spaces. The conversations that stem from this activity can be very useful for both students—they can gain a greater understanding of the feature—and the teacher—who can gain insight into students' understanding and can plan instruction accordingly from this observational assessment data.

- Write sentences from the text on sentence strips, scrambling them so they are out of order, and then asking students to put them back in order. Students read the sentences aloud, which gives them practice in using the targeted feature.

- Cut up sentences into words and phrases, scrambling them, and asking students to put them back in order. Reading their reordered sentences aloud gives students practice in using the targeted feature.

- Ask students to revisit their own writing and revise it, focusing on the targeted feature.

Targeted Strategy 3: Use jazz chants.

Carolyn Graham, an ESL teacher and jazz pianist, integrated her love of jazz and teaching ELLs to create jazz chants (1992, 2001). These chants use jazz rhythms to illustrate and provide practice in grammatical structures and the normal rhythms of spoken English. We have found that students enjoy jazz chants; the lively, brief chanting sessions often lead naturally into conversations about when and how to use the targeted structure. Teachers can also write their own jazz chants targeted to a particular structure. (See Chapter 3, p. 75, for an example of a jazz chant.) Students can then be encouraged to use these chants as grammar resources.

Targeted Strategy 4: Incorporate modified cloze activities.

Modified cloze activities can provide valuable practice with a targeted grammatical structure or punctuation mark. (See pp. 211–212 earlier in the chapter for a description of how to design cloze exercises.) Students can work alone or in pairs to figure out which words are missing in a passage. The conversation that occurs when pairs work together is often very valuable, particularly if partnerships and expectations are carefully established.

Targeted Strategy 5: Make use of sentence strips.

Practice in targeted grammatical features and punctuation can be provided through sentence strips:

- Write sentences containing the targeted feature on strips of paper. For practice with pronouns, you might write, "I live with my father." "He speaks Spanish." "My friend is Fatimah." "She speaks Arabic."

- Cut up the sentences into single words and/or phrases.

- Have students put the words and phrases back in order. Students can work individually or in groups.

- As a whole group, discuss whether students' contributions are right or wrong.

- Ask students to revisit their own writing and revise it with the targeted feature in mind.

Incomprehensible Writing

The writing of some ELLs can be hard to read, and this may be related to several factors, including the following:

- The students may have had little or no formal schooling in the past and are only now learning how to write.

- The students can write in their native language, but it has a very different writing system from English (e.g., Arabic, Chinese, Japanese, or Urdu).

The writing of ELLs is also sometimes hard to read as a consequence of grammatical, spelling, and/or word choice issues. We have found the following general strategies to be helpful in addressing these issues of legibility. After the general strategies, we provide some additional strategies and recommended resources for specific situations.

General Strategies

General Strategy 1: Students read their writing aloud.

- So that you know what the student has written, have him or her read the piece aloud.

- Keep a written record of what the student says, so you can analyze what he or she knows about writing in English, and decide the area of instruction to focus on next.

General Strategy 2: Read text aloud while writing.

By frequently reading aloud what they have written, emergent writers learn to monitor what they have written. This practice can also help them remember what their intention for writing was. If the students are older—and/or are embarrassed about reading their writing aloud—teach them how to subvocalize, or speak very softly, under their breath. However, as subvocalizing and frequently reading aloud slow down writers (and readers), students should not become too reliant on these strategies. Once students are writing legible texts that they can read back, they should be encouraged to use these strategies only in specific circumstances, such as when they are confused or they want to hear how their writing sounds.

General Strategy 3: Read text to a partner.

Knowing that they are going to be reading their writing to another student can sometimes help students pay more attention to the legibility of their writing, as they need to be able to read aloud as fluently as possible. Teach students how to practice reading aloud so their reading is smooth and engaging.

General Strategy 4: Use the print resources in the room.

Make and display posters of the features of writing that you have taught for students to use as reference (e.g., how to form letters and numbers; when and how to use punctuation marks; spelling families and spelling patterns). Post information that you have recently taught most prominently (e.g., one poster can be hung on top of another on an easel, so that all the posters are accessible and at a height suitable for children). If there isn't room for posters on the walls, then store smaller versions in photo albums and binders, with labeled dividers. Also, students can keep their own copies in binders. We have found that simply making these resources available to students doesn't mean that they necessarily use the material or know how to use it, so it is important to periodically remind students of the information's value.

General Strategy 5: Ask students to rewrite the work more legibly.

Teachers who know their students can tell when children have become stalled and need to be nudged. For example, in a first-grade class that we know that has an experienced teacher, an ELL child asked the teacher to read her journal entry, which consisted of a picture and random letters. With her hand around the child's shoulder, the teacher looked at the page. After a few moments, she said, "Anita, I'd really like to be able to read this, but, you know what? I can't, because I don't know what these letters mean. So, can you rewrite it so I can read it, please?" Anita nodded eagerly. About 15 minutes later, she returned with a new version, which was written using some sound-symbol correspondences in the form of beginning and ending consonants. The teacher clearly knew what Anita was capable of and didn't hastily or randomly ask her to do more than she could handle independently.

In another classroom, a second-grade boy and his teacher had great difficulty reading his writing, in part because the student didn't space his words and often didn't pay attention to letter-sound correspondences. In this situation, the teacher taught the boy how to segment words and the importance of listening to the sounds in words when encoding them. During subsequent independent writing periods, the teacher reminded the student of these two points until he began to self-monitor.

SITUATION 1   The handwriting of my ELL student is very hard to decipher.

As the years pass, more and more children around the world have some exposure to schooling and writing. Nevertheless, many children continue to have little or no formal schooling, or even access to writing implements, which are too expensive for families living on about one dollar a day. In North America, we often take paper and pencils for granted, but these materials aren't easily available for low-income families in developing countries, where children are often required to purchase all of their own school supplies. Consequently, children (even older students) may not form letters with ease.

A lack of developed letter formation in older students should not be immediately equated with a learning disability. ELL children in the primary grades can usually be taught letter formation skills alongside their English-speaking peers, but older students may need to learn letter formation separately. Some strategies for helping ELLs develop legible handwriting include the following:

Targeted Strategy 1: Teach students how to form letters.

* Select letters and numbers with which the individual student has the greatest difficulty (e.g., the letters *q, Q, j, J, t, T*; the numbers 1 and 7, which are often confused because in many countries the number 1 has a downward left slanted line from the top: 1. This makes it resemble the number 7.

* If you have a lot of students who need help with letter formation, group them according to need.

* Explain why it is important to have clear handwriting. Show two examples of a text, one that is easy to decipher and one that is difficult to read. Do a think-aloud. That is, talk through your thinking processes while reading the texts, as in the following excerpt:

Teacher: It's important to form letters and words clearly so other people can understand what we've written. (*He demonstrates letter and word formation in a slightly exaggerated way on an overhead.*) Here's an example. (*He shows an example of a student's writing that is hard to read because of the handwriting. He points to a part that is legible.*) Now, I can read this part, but I don't know what this says. (*He scratches his head and verbally demonstrates how hard it is to decode another part of the text.*) Is this a *t*, an *i*, or an *l*? I really want to understand what this student has written. (*The teacher displays another piece of writing by the same student.*) Now here is something written by the same person, but it's written more clearly so we can understand it. (*He shows the same text with more legible letter formation. The teacher reads the text easily and paraphrases what he has read.*)

- Demonstrate how to form the target letter or number on lined paper, explaining any special features it has (e.g., the top of the *l* goes higher than the top of the *i*) and ways in which it may differ from how it is formed in the L1 (e.g., in many parts of the world, the number 7 has a line through the middle to differentiate it from the number 1). Point out that some letters, such as *a* and *g*, are different in their typographic form than their handwritten form. This is of particular importance for students who have taught themselves to write by copying from published texts.

- Have students practice forming the letter or number on lined paper.

- Combine letters, including letters the student can already form, such as *o*, to form words (e.g., *to*, *on*, *top*), and follow the same procedure.

- Introduce another letter or number, and use the same procedure.

Targeted Strategy 2: Discuss uppercase and lowercase letters and their usage.

Teach students about the differences in forming uppercase letters (capitals) and lowercase letters. Also, teach them about the differences in the usage of uppercase and lowercase letters.

- Capital letters are used at the beginning of sentences, at the beginning of proper nouns, and for emphasis (e.g., titles and headings; to highlight a word or phrase).

- Lowercase letters are used in almost all other situations.

Targeted Strategy 3: Teach printing before cursive.

Printing is usually much easier to read than cursive, in part because the letters aren't connected, but also because printing more closely resembles published print found in books, newspapers, and magazines.

Targeted Strategy 4: Teach word processing.

If students continue to have difficulty forming letters, it may be helpful to introduce them to a word processing program on the computer so they can write texts that others can read. After all, some native speakers, including published writers, have handwriting that is virtually impossible to read. The most important point is that student writers need to be understood, and we need to use all resources available to make that possible.

SITUATION 2   I can't understand what my ELL student has written because of the spelling.

Research shows that ELL children's invented spellings aren't random, but are evidence of hypothesis generating and hypothesis testing (e.g., Edelsky, 1986; Edelsky & Jilbert, 1985). Even in languages that have a lot in common, such as English and Spanish (both are alphabetic, Latin-based languages), letter-sound correspondences in the L1 and L2 are sometimes markedly different. Since ELL children who are moving into English tend to use their knowledge of the orthography of their native language when writing in English, it is inevitable that their early messages reflect their knowledge of their L1. For example, this message was written in English by a native Spanish-speaking child: *ai joup llu gou agien/I hope you go again* (Edelsky & Jilbert, 1985). It reflects knowledge of Spanish spelling (e.g., ai for the /i/ sound in ai/I, and the double ll for the /y/ sound in llu/you). As children become increasingly knowledgeable about English orthography, English phonics generalizations tend to inform their invented spellings in English. General strategies that help ELLs become familiar with and internalize English spelling patterns include the following, which have been discussed earlier in this chapter:

- Shared reading (see pp. 202–203)
- Interactive writing (see pp. 209–211)

Instead of giving students lists of spelling words to memorize (and to be tested on), it is much more effective to teach them spelling strategies. Like native English-speaking children, ELLs benefit from being taught specific spelling strategies that are grounded in and informed by their own writing. That is, rather than randomly choosing a spelling strategy to teach, it is best to analyze a student's spelling needs and then select a focus for instruction.[9]

---

[9] There are many excellent resources available that focus explicitly on teaching spelling strategies, including the following:

Bear, D. R., Invernizzi, M., Templeton, S., & Johnston, F. (2004). *Words their way: Word study for phonics, vocabulary, and spelling instruction* (3rd ed.). Upper Saddle River, NJ: Prentice Hall.

Bolton, F., & Snowball, D. (1993). *Ideas for spelling*. Portsmouth, NH: Heinemann.

Marten, C. (2003). *Word crafting. Teaching spelling, grades K–6*. Portsmouth, NH: Heinemann.

CHAPTER 6

Communication With Parents

Parents of ELL students care deeply about their children's education, well-being, and future (see, for example, Huss-Keeler, 1997; Samway & McKeon, 2007). In fact, many immigrant and refugee parents say they know their lives in their new country will always be difficult, but they have come to give their children a better future. The parents quoted below touch on some of the issues that schools and parents of ELL children must deal with together: meeting the challenge of a new language, dealing with past traumas, struggling to survive in a new culture, adjusting to new standards of education and behavior, and supporting the home language of the child.

> *My daughter for years old I like to play wiss she talking play wiss the toy talk a out family totd she color the paper my daughter she is my live.*
>
> My daughter is four years old. I like to play with her, talking play with the toy talk about family. Today she colored the paper. My daughter she is my life.
>
> (from a Laotian mother's journal, when asked to write about herself)

- *My name is ___. I form Liberia. I like to pelay wst my kis I isae two kids one is ___ and ___ they and I fmli. And my Love kids.*

  My name is ___. I am from Liberia. I like to play with my kids. I have two kids, one is (<u>name</u>) and (<u>name</u>). They and I are family. And I love my kids.

  (from a Liberian mother's journal when asked to write about herself)

- *When my wife leaving Sudan, she must walk many miles. Our two youngest girls, they didn't make it. They were too small. Now my wife and me, we have twin daughters. God gave us two healthy girls. I am so happy to be in this country.*

  (told by a Sudanese father to his ESL teacher)

- *Teachers should pay careful attention to our children. Our children do not understand when children tell them bad words. They do not have words when other children push them. Teachers should explain these things to all children.*

  (told by a Russian mother to her ESL teacher)

- *Communication is important. Schools should communicate with parents. They should ask parents what they need. Do they need knives and forks? Do they need coats?*

  (told by a Somali father to his ESL teacher)

- *My daughter like school. Her teacher send home books every week and she reads for 20 minutes. One week the books are in English, one week the books are in Spanish. Once a week he take one hour with her. He explains words to her.*

  (told by a Puerto Rican mother to her ESL teacher)

Difficulty Communicating With Parents

Communicating with parents of ELL children can be challenging. The lack of a shared language is one of the challenges faced by schools and parents, but it isn't the only one. Finding the time to interact with school personnel is difficult for many parents, who work long hours, sometimes at more than one job, go to school themselves, deal with social services agencies and medical appointments, and take care of younger children. Cultural expectations around parent/school interactions may be different as well. In some countries, school and family life are separate. Parents are not expected to take an active role in their children's educational experiences, or the role the parents take is very different from the role expected from them in North America.

Some families, particularly refugees, may be dealing with the aftermath of traumatic events or current issues of domestic violence or substance abuse. Bad experiences with government officials in their home countries or current undocumented status in this, their adopted country, may lead family members to fear anyone with official status, including school authorities. In addition, lack of transportation and child care, illness or disabilities, and limited language skills may leave many families socially isolated and reluctant or unable to leave the safety of their homes or ethnic communities to venture out into the schools or community at large. Despite these difficulties, parents of ELL students are eager for their children to be successful in school, and often value contact with the school. Parents of ELL students also welcome opportunities to share information about their native country and culture. We have found that they appreciate home visits by teachers and other school staff, and generally have tremendous respect for their children's teachers.

General Strategies

Visiting families in their homes, providing parents with a welcoming school environment, and making sure that oral and written communications, including school or district Web sites, are translated into their home languages are the keys to good communication with parents of ELL children.

Schools can address the language needs of parents by offering or working with community-based organizations to offer adult ESL and literacy classes along with homework help for children (Adger, 2000). Parents should also feel that the school supports their children's home language and culture by including bilingual books in school and classroom libraries and holding school-wide cultural events, such as international food festivals, dances, talent shows, plays, or fashion shows. In this way, ELL families have opportunities to be experts in the school environment, one in which they are typically not viewed as experts.

Parents will be most likely to attend parent-teacher conferences if teachers accommodate work schedules and schools make child care available by having older students watch younger children and providing appropriate activities for them in the same or a nearby classroom.

SITUATION 1 The parents of my ELLs don't speak English and I don't speak their languages, so we can't communicate.

Targeted Strategy 1: Arrange for translators.

Many school districts have a central office that arranges for translators for written and phone communications and for parent-teacher conferences. These translators are often the best option since they have usually been carefully screened for language ability and professionalism.[1] If this type of service is not available, or if the language of the ELL child is one for which a translator is not available, other translators can often be found within the community from organizations or groups such as the following:

- Refugee resettlement agencies and agencies that deal with immigrants

- Specific ethnic or language community groups or organizations

- Former Peace Corps volunteers

- College or high school foreign language departments or organizations

ELL children themselves should not be asked to translate for their parents or other adults. It is embarrassing for the parents, and neither the teacher nor the parent will feel free to discuss sensitive issues.

Targeted Strategy 2: Have parents bring a trusted friend or family member.

If an official translator is not available, or if the parents are not comfortable with a school-assigned translator, invite them to bring a trusted family member or friend to translate.

Targeted Strategy 3: Schedule same-language families together.

When scheduling parent conferences, cluster families that speak the same language together. During orientation, invite families to sign up for conferences in ways that will accommodate language support, transportation needs, and babysitting help.

---

[1] For guidelines on how to successfully interact with parents and translators, see www.thecenterlibrary.org/cwis/cwisdocs/translate.html.

Targeted Strategy 4: Send personalized invitations.

Ask the children to create invitations in class for back-to-school nights or parent conferences. ELL students can write in English and their native language, if they are able to, and include drawings, photos, and/or personal messages.

Targeted Strategy 5: Send positive notes home.

Make it a habit to write to families about positive features of their children's school life. Rotate the writing of these notes so every child's family receives a note once or twice in the school year. Make sure the children know what the notes say so they will not be afraid to take them home.

Targeted Strategy 6: Send newsletters home.

Newsletters are a good means of communication. Students can create a newsletter in class as part of a communications genre study. The teacher and students can keep a running record of what was accomplished in class to include in the newsletter, and also include class and school activities and upcoming events. Students who are literate in their home languages can provide brief translations. Teachers should ensure that all children are able to read and understand the contents of the finished product so they can share this information with parents who might have difficulty reading it themselves.

SITUATION 2   How do I communicate with parents who are illiterate?

Targeted Strategy 1: Assess the degree and nature of illiteracy.

Find out if the parents are illiterate only in English or in their native language as well. If they are literate in their native language, arrange to have letters or notes translated. (See the strategies on p. 229 and pp. 231–233 for locating and using translators.) Even if a teacher knows that parents are illiterate, all written communication should be sent home, as a friend or family member may be able to read or translate the material for them.

Targeted Strategy 2: Offer telephone support.

Offer telephone translations for important documents sent home from schools. Put a graphic of a telephone and a phone number to call at the top of the document, so parents can call to hear a recorded message in their native language of the document's essential information. For low-incidence languages or languages for which a translator is not available, the message can be left in English for parents who are able to understand spoken English, but are not very literate.

Targeted Strategy 3: Use a rebus or graphics.

You can supplement notes going home with a rebus or graphics to give parents a general idea of the message. (See Appendix T, p. 309, for an example.) Keep in mind that some symbols may be culturally specific. For example, ELL parents might recognize a picture of a heart, but not understand that it is a symbol for Valentine's Day if it is not celebrated in their native country.

Targeted Strategy 4: Have students create calendars.

At the beginning of each month, students can create calendars with pictures and a few words for important events happening in that month. Encourage them to take the calendars home to display in a prominent place, such as on the refrigerator.

SITUATION 3 The parents of my ELL students decline a translator, but we have a hard time communicating.

There are many reasons why parents might choose to decline a translator. Some may involve the parents' feelings about language translation in general; they may be embarrassed that they are not fluent speakers of English and feel that using a translator would make them less highly regarded. Other reasons might have to do with the particular translator. For example, ethnic communities can be close-knit, and parents may be sensitive about others in their community being privy to personal issues. Sometimes, translators share the same language as the parents but come from conflicting tribes or ethnic groups in the home country, or from different social classes. Parents should never feel forced to accept a translator with whom they do not feel comfortable. Their decision to decline the services of a translator should be respected and, at the same time, every effort should be made to ensure that parents and teachers are able to understand each other.

Targeted Strategy 1: Ask about acceptable translators.

If parents decline the use of an official school translator, teachers can ask if they know of someone else who could translate for them at meetings and/or conferences.

Targeted Strategy 2: Communicate effectively.

If parents prefer to meet without a translator, keep these points in mind during meetings or conferences:

- Smile.

- Express regret that you don't speak their language.

- Speak slowly and clearly, but not loudly or in an exaggerated way.

- Avoid complex sentences (e.g., *This is the book that Suma is reading* vs. *Suma is making tremendous progress and I think it's partly related to her liking to read, including rather complex texts like this one, which is part of a series that has won lots of awards.*).

- Use more common language (e.g., use *talk* instead of *communicate*).

- Use gestures.

- Pause frequently to give parents time for processing, and ask if they have questions.

- Show samples of their child's work.

- If parents are literate, keep a bilingual dictionary handy to use for key words.

- Draw sketches of important content words or concepts.

- Make a list of talking points that parents can take with them so someone can explain them later.

SITUATION 4 Parents don't respond to permission slips and notes sent home, or telephone calls I make.

Parents may not understand what they're being asked to do in a permission slip or in a note. Making phone calls in a nonnative language is one of the most stressful experiences for a nonnative speaker because all of the visual cues that we rely on in interpersonal communication are absent. Because of busy work schedules, parents and children may not see each other for several days, so parents may not be up to date about their children's school experiences—for example, this may happen if another family member takes care of the children after school and the children are asleep when the parents come home from work. For these and other reasons, a lack of response should not be construed as a lack of interest.

Targeted Strategy 1: Talk to the child.

Ask the child why the parents have not responded. It is possible the permission slips or notes are still in the child's backpack or have been lost. Make sure the child understands what the communication is about and what kind of response is expected from the parent. For newcomers, have a peer explain in the native language, wherever possible, or use volunteers.

Targeted Strategy 2: Translate into the parents' native language.

Whenever possible, permission slips and other notes sent home should be translated into the parents' native language. Schools or school districts can develop a collection of standard communications, such as field trip permission forms, translated into the most common languages, with blanks for teachers to fill in essential information. These forms should include the same information in English as well, in case parents are not literate in their native language, but want to ask an English-speaking friend for help.

Targeted Strategy 3: Differentiate types of communication.

Simple graphics placed at the top of a page, such as a picture of a school bus for field trips or a camera for school photos, can clarify the main focus of the communication. Also, using different colored paper for different kinds of communication can help (e.g., permissions slips in blue, parent conference letters in pink). It is important to explain what these colors represent to parents at orientations, as well as to the children.

Targeted Strategy 4: Make phone calls.

Call the parents or ask a parent liaison to call. Many parents of ELL students work second or third shifts, so try calling at different times of the day.

Targeted Strategy 5: Establish a phone tree.

Establish a phone tree in which parents who speak the native or home language of ELL students contact the parents of newcomer ELLs or parents who haven't responded. These phone trees can be set up at the beginning of the year, possibly at orientation, and updated as needed.

Targeted Strategy 6: Pair families with mentors.

At the beginning of the year, invite parents to mentor newcomer ELL families. Mentor families don't have to speak the same language as the ELL families, but should be committed to making regular contact with the ELL families. Mentors can advise families about school- and community-related events and issues; they can do this directly or through a translator.

Targeted Strategy 7: Offer incentives.

Build in incentives, such as pencils or points, for returned papers, notes, and permission slips. Points can be collected for special activities or privileges, such as movies and popcorn.

SITUATION 5

The parents of my ELL students don't oversee homework and don't sign off on homework.

In many cultures, parents are not involved in school activities, including overseeing homework, so the idea of signing off on homework may be unfamiliar to ELL parents. In addition, many immigrant parents are working several jobs to clothe, feed, and house their families and may not be available when children are completing homework. Homework can put a great deal of stress on many ELL families (as well as non-ELL families). Parents who have few English skills or who are illiterate in English and/or their native language are often embarrassed that they cannot help their children with schoolwork. Also, older children are often called upon to help younger siblings, which takes time away from their own studies. Teachers should be mindful of these issues when assigning homework to ELL children.

Strategy 1: Assign independent homework carefully.

Homework should be carefully selected so that children can complete the work independently. If a child does not understand the concept, homework is not appropriate or helpful and often puts a strain on family members who may not know how to teach their children (Samway, 1986). Some homework assignments that are supportive of ELL students and can be completed independently include the following:

- Designated time to read (e.g., 20–30 minutes)
- Writing journal entries

- Reading to younger siblings

- Drawing pictures of family members, rooms and/or household objects, to be labeled later in class

Strategy 2: Set up family projects.

Some projects that students can do in collaboration with family members include the following:

- **Interview a family member:** Students can ask about a family treasure, a special family celebration, how they got their name, or a story around their name.

- **Observational logs:** Children can write entries on topics ranging from such simple tasks as counting the number of windows or doors in their house, to recording the amount of food their family consumes for later classification in a discussion about the food pyramid.

- **Book bag projects:** Students fill book bags with a book, a CD or cassette tape, if available, and objects or activities centered around the book for families to read and enjoy. A journal for parents, older siblings, and the child to write observations about the book may also be included in the bag. Encourage parents to write in English, their native language, or both, or to draw pictures. The books in the bag should be in English and the home language, whenever possible, and should include themes related to the lives of the children (DiMarzio & Coustan, 1996).

- **Family inquiry projects:** Parents can keep records of content-area questions their children ask at home. For example, Callanan, Alba-Speyer, and Tenenbaum (2000) reported on a successful family science workshop program that asked parents to keep records of the science-related questions that children asked in the home; these questions then informed the content of science workshops that were offered to families. This project could be extended to focus on questions centering on other subject areas, such as history or language.

- **Home object show-and-tell:** Ask students to bring in an object from home that a family member made or uses, and describe the object, its use, and how it was made. Objects might include embroidered cloth, carved wood, cooking utensils, or auto repair tools.

Strategy 3: Distribute homework journals with easy symbols.

ELL students whose parents find complex directions difficult to read or understand can be given a homework journal with easy-to-understand graphics for different content areas (e.g., the number symbol for math, a book for reading), followed by the number of pages or papers to be completed. Parents can check off whether the child has completed the work, and teachers can follow up with symbols such as smiling or frowning faces to indicate whether homework was successfully or unsuccessfully completed. (See Appendix U, p. 310, for an example.) More elaborate explanations or communications should be discussed on the phone or at parent-teacher conferences, with the aid of translators.

Strategy 4: Provide additional ways for parents to support children's learning.

Teachers should point out to parents that there are many ways, in addition to helping with homework, for them to support their children's learning, including the following:

- Taking them to the library to check out books and/or to listen to story hour
- Allowing their children to participate in an after-school homework club
- Reading to them in the native language
- Telling them stories
- Singing to and with them
- Attending cultural and children's sports events
- Playing family games, such as charades, Pictionary, or card games
- Developing quizzes on familiar topics, such as sports or the history of their native land

SITUATION 6 — The parents of my ELL students don't come in for parent conferences.

There are many reasons why parents may not come in for parent conferences, many of which have been mentioned previously. The first step in encouraging parents to come to school for conferences is to find out what is affecting their attendance. Is it because of their work schedules? Do they lack child care for younger children? Do they feel uncomfortable or unwelcome in the school? Are translators available? Are parents comfortable working with the translators? The answers could vary as widely as the number of parents in the school, but knowing the reasons will help teachers and schools address these issues in some of the following ways.

Targeted Strategy 1: Create a welcoming environment.

Schools and teachers can make the parents of their ELL students feel more comfortable by relieving some of their concerns or fears, such as their lack of English-language skills, unfamiliarity with the school system, or lack of day care. Following are some ways to make parents feel welcome and comfortable at parent conferences or meetings:

- Have translators available.

- Offer an orientation specifically for ELL parents.

- Show a welcome video.

- Offer bilingual handbooks.

- Serve refreshments.

- Offer free books through programs such as Reading Is Fundamental (RIF).

- Offer child care or make it clear that young children are welcome.

- Offer different times to meet for parents who have complicated work schedules.

- Don't just talk at parents; instead, provide ample time for their questions.

- Ask parents to tell you about their children such as, what they are good at, when they read, when they write, and what their talents are.

- Show samples of children's accomplishments (e.g., artwork, published books, completed projects).

- Ask parents for recommendations of children's books in their home language or to evaluate books for the school and classroom libraries.

Targeted Strategy 2: Send out personal invitations.

Send out a personal bilingual invitation (in the parent's native language and English) or ask children to create an invitation for their parents.

Targeted Strategy 3: Provide helpful information.

Offer meetings for parents of ELL students focusing on topics of interest to them, such as family literacy, family math, how to buy a computer, or everyday science. Invite community services experts, such as health care workers, housing officials, or banking and mortgage representatives, to present information, or have bilingual brochures about these areas available for parents during open-house events and parent conferences. Parents can be asked to generate ideas for speakers and topics at orientation or at the first meeting.

SITUATION 7 — I don't know the families of my ELLs as well as the families of my non-ELLs.

Targeted Strategy 1: Schedule home visits.

Parents of ELL children have told us how much they appreciate home visits from teachers and other school members. In a recent study on refugee children's needs, one mother commented that she could not persuade her 10-year-old son to go to school until his ESL teacher visited him in their home (Szente, Hoot, & Taylor, 2006). He and his mother were not only pleased that the teacher showed concern for the boy, but were also pleased to share food from their culture and show the teacher objects and pictures from their lives in their native land. During home visits, parents are often more willing to talk about sensitive issues, such as traumatic events they have experienced or concerns about aspects of their children's school lives.

Targeted Strategy 2: Attend events from students' cultures.

Many communities hold special events for holidays or other special occasions that are open to the public or to which school members would be warmly welcomed. Attending sports events, dance performances, or music recitals in which ELL students are involved, can provide insights into the children's lives outside of the classroom.

Targeted Strategy 3: Read books or articles about students' native cultures.

Ask parents for recommendations of reading material and movies about their country or ethnic group. Refugee resettlement groups and other cultural organizations in the community are other good sources for information. Showing interest in and appreciation for another culture goes a long way in building strong bonds between the home and school.

Targeted Strategy 4: Invite parents to share their cultures.

Most parents of ELL children welcome the chance to share information about their language and culture. Invite them to make presentations to the class or hold international festivals during the day, in the evening, or on weekends. Also, it can be very informative and helpful to invite parents to make presentations at faculty meetings about their cultures and the educational systems in their home countries.

Targeted Strategy 5: Offer two-way language classes.

Schools that have a large number of ELL students who speak the same language can offer two-way language classes one or two nights a week. Half of the class would be devoted to parents learning English, and the other half to teachers learning the parents' language. Older siblings or volunteers can serve as babysitters and/or offer homework help.

What Schools Expect as Opposed to What Parents Expect

In addition to speaking languages other than English, ELL children and their parents have had different experiences with school systems outside of North America. Parents and children from war-torn countries may have had access to little or no formal education for several years. In addition, parents from rural areas may not have attended school at all. Often, refugee families travel to more than one country, living in camps before settling in other countries. English may be the third or fourth language in which these children have been taught. For example, a Somali mother explained to a teacher we know that her son had spent time in Kenya after leaving Somalia. He began his schooling in Somali, then it switched to Kiswahili, and now it was in English. She said, "My son was confused when he arrived because he spent some time in Kenya. When he was here, he stopped talking. The teachers thought he was not normal. They say he needed Speech (therapy). Now he is talking. He is okay. He was just confused."

Of course, not all parents of ELL children have had little or no formal education. Some parents come from countries with sophisticated, but different approaches to learning. School systems in some countries place a great deal of emphasis on memorization and rote learning. Whole-class lectures are the norm in many countries, and collaborative or learner-centered activities are seldom, if ever, practiced.

The role the school plays in family life also differs from country to country. In some countries, school is sacrosanct; children must never be absent, and the school acts as a kind of guardian for them. As the parent of an ELL child told a teacher we know, "While my child is at school, you are his mother." In other cases, school personnel sometimes become frustrated as parents seem to be placing the needs of the family above the educational needs of the children (e.g., when they pull children out of school to babysit for younger siblings, to translate at medical appointments, or to return to their home countries for extended visits).

General Strategies

Teachers can learn a great deal about their ELL students by talking to parents about their own and their children's past educational experiences. Keep in mind that parents may be sensitive about discussing their lack of education. However, asking the following questions of a parent can reveal important information without being intrusive:

- Did the children go to school in their home country?

- Did they spend time in a refugee camp?

- What languages do they speak at home?

- What languages have they used in previous schools?

- What were their favorite subjects?

- What did they like/not like about school in the past?

Be aware that language is not the only adjustment ELL children and their parents have to make. Parent orientations and parent-teacher conferences can be used to explain to parents how learner-centered or collaborative activities help children learn—often, actually engaging parents in an activity that reflects the kinds of activities that children engage in can help parents better understand the teacher's goals. Also, teachers can encourage parents to visit the classroom to see these activities in action. Teachers should listen carefully to issues raised by parents, try to understand concerns from the parents' perspective, and work with them to resolve concerns in a manner that is respectful of their point of view.

SITUATION 1 — The parents of my ELL students lack schooling and don't know how to help their children.

Often, parents of ELL students come from situations in which they did not have the opportunity to go to school. Some parents may come from rural communities where schools were not available, or as children, they were expected to work in the fields or perform other household roles, such as taking care of younger children. Also, parents and their children may have had their schooling interrupted by war or political unrest. Parents are often embarrassed by their lack of formal education, and feel inadequately prepared to help their children with homework or other school projects. Teachers can help parents and their children by stressing the positive contributions that parents make to their children's social and academic development, and by guiding them in finding resources to help them and their children.

Targeted Strategy 1: Tell stories.

Many nonliterate societies have a rich tradition of storytelling and oral narratives. Without a base of printed material for their culture, these communities pass down their history and traditions orally. Parents should be encouraged to continue this tradition with bedtime or regular storytelling sessions; parents can also come into the classroom to tell their traditional stories, perhaps bringing in artifacts that are referred to in the story.

Since many folktales, fairy tales, and myths we read today have their origins in oral traditions, it is valuable to include international versions of them, such as Ananse the Spider tales and Baba Yaga, in the language arts curriculum. Also, many fairy tales, such as the Cinderella story[2], have distinct versions found in many parts of the world, and it can be very powerful to study fairy tales around the world. Folktales, fairy tales, and myths should be readily available in the classroom and school library, and teachers may also want to include them in book bag programs. Parents may recognize the stories that their children bring home, which can lead to valuable conversations both at home and in the classroom.

Targeted Strategy 2: Encourage library visits.

Parents should be encouraged to regularly take their children to the public library. For example, a refugee father in Buffalo, New York, whom Dorothy

---

[2] A list of Cinderella stories around the world can be found online at www.ucalgary.ca/~dkbrown/cinderella.html.

works with, had no schooling in his home country. Nevertheless, he takes his school-age children to the library for two hours every Saturday morning, where they browse through the books, the children work on homework and other school projects, and the father works with a librarian to develop computer skills.

Targeted Strategy 3: Suggest resources for educational activities.

Parents of ELL children may not be aware of educational programming on television or good Web sites for their children to explore on the Internet. Teachers can provide lists of good age-appropriate television programs, movies, and educational Web sites. Some time during open house or PTO meetings can be devoted to presentations and demonstrations of these media items.

SITUATION 2 My students' parents say they've been told not to speak their native languages at home so their children can learn English, but they can't communicate with their children in English.

SITUATION 3 The parents of my ELL students don't speak English at home, and I wish they would so the children can learn English more quickly.

Although these two situations may seem totally different, they are, in fact, two sides of the same coin, so we are addressing them together.

Sometimes well-meaning school staff or community members think they are helping parents of ELL students by advising them to speak English with their children, instead of their home language. Their thinking is that the more English the children are exposed to, the more quickly their English will develop. However, this advice runs contrary to all research about linguistic and academic development. Parents should be communicating with their children in their native language in order to support the children's cognitive and linguistic development (King & Fogle, 2006). These cognitive and linguistic skills transfer from one language to another, so to deny this cognitive and linguistic scaffolding is potentially harmful to children. Also, it is harmful to children *not* to be able to communicate fully with their parents.

Sometimes parents of ELL students express the belief that they are helping their children by speaking only English in the home. However, teachers should urge all parents of ELL students to use their native or home language to support the retention and use of the native language

Targeted Strategy 1: Educate parents and school personnel.

Provide parents and school personnel with literature about the benefits of bilingualism and the transfer of skills from one language to another.

Targeted Strategy 2: Support native language use at home.

Encourage parents to support their native language at home in the following ways:

- Talk a lot with children in the home language—about what they are doing when they are cooking, writing, shopping, and so on.
- Teach nursery rhymes and songs in the home language.
- Tell stories in the home language, and encourage children to join in with the storytelling.
- Talk to children about what they did at school or after school. If children use English words, repeat what they have said using the home language.
- Take children to concerts, plays, poetry readings, films, etc., where they will hear people using the native language.
- Try to make sure that children play with other children who speak the same home language.
- Find out if there is a community language school where the native language is taught, so that children can benefit from attending classes there.
- Find children's books written in the home language. If there aren't any, children (and family members) can make their own.
- Help children feel proud of their native language.
- Don't laugh at or tease children because of their accents or when they make mistakes.

Targeted Strategy 3: Support native languages at school.

Teachers and schools should support the native languages of their ELL students by including books in the native language in classroom and school libraries, participating in book clubs that offer bilingual books, inviting bilingual guest speakers into the classroom, and holding international language weeks or international festivals. In addition, teachers should speak regularly about the advantages of being bilingual and include readings about bilingual people in their curriculum.

SITUATION 4   The parents of my ELL students don't advocate for their children's needs.

As we have discussed previously, parents of ELL children typically lead very busy lives, leaving little time for advocacy, despite the fact that they recognize the importance and value of such activities. In some cases, the process of advocating for one's children may be a new and fearful concept to parents coming from political regimes where such actions could put their lives or the lives of their families in jeopardy. It is also possible that parents are advocating for their children in ways that might not be recognized as such by schools. For example, a migrant father who shows his children the hard life of physical labor and urges them to work hard in school is advocating for his children by teaching them the value of hard work and by showing them the reality of the life they might lead if they don't work hard in school (López, 2001).

Targeted Strategy 1: Use schools as advocates.

Teachers, support specialists, parent liaisons, and school administrators should be mindful of the fact that parents of ELL children, newcomers in particular, are facing incredible linguistic and social challenges. They should serve as surrogate advocates for ELL children whenever possible. In addition, schools and teachers can seek ways to help parents advocate for their children by working with other schools and community agencies with a vested interest in ELL families. Some forms of support may include:

- Visiting legislators

- Hosting breakfasts or luncheons for legislators and their staffs, community agency workers, and local and state officials

- Inviting legislators, community agency personnel, and local officials to cultural events and festivals

- Offering citizenship classes or tutoring for the citizenship exam

- Providing voter information and voter registration forms

- Hosting Kids Vote (www.kidsvotingusa.org) in the school

- Organizing rallies in support of proposed beneficial legislation or in opposition to legislation that is potentially harmful to ELL families

Targeted Strategy 2: Establish international parent groups.

Encourage and support international parent groups by offering time during PTO meetings or parent conferences for organizational meetings. Provide office and clerical services for printing, mailing, or translating services.

Targeted Strategy 3: Talk about advocacy at orientation meetings.

Include information about advocacy during parent orientation meetings. Be specific about how and when to advocate. Many examples for advocating for ELL families are listed on p. 244. In addition, schools or parent groups can alert ELL families (via phone calls, e-mail, or regular mail) to proposed legislative bills or potential policy changes affecting them or their children. It is also helpful to provide parents with sample form letters or e-mail messages, detailing the specific concerns or desired result, which they can then send to legislators. Include names and contact information for local, state, and federal legislators, particularly those who have been supportive of ELL students and families in the past. Also provide information about past advocacy successes.

Targeted Strategy 4: Attend events or meetings of cultural groups.

Teachers and other school staff members can discuss the needs of ELL students at meetings of neighborhood groups or cultural events and suggest ways that these groups can work to support their ELL children.

SITUATION 5 Parents pull their children out of school to take them out of town for family visits, and ask for makeup work.

Teachers often find it frustrating and disruptive to children's academic development when ELL children or their parents suddenly announce that they are returning to their homelands for a long period of time. There is no question that long absences result in missed schoolwork and can lead to setbacks in English language development. However, in cases of illness or a death in the family, these trips cannot be delayed or prevented. Some families may have saved for years to fund a return visit, and thus have decided that an extended visit warrants the loss of schooling. Teachers should encourage parents of ELL students to plan out-of-town trips around school vacations, but when parents have made the decision to take their children out of school for an extended period at other times, teachers should offer educational support to ELL children and their parents during the absence.

Targeted Strategy 1: Put together a class packet.

Offer parents a packet of materials that includes the kinds of work that will be done in the classroom while the children are gone. Include a timetable for working on the materials. Teachers sometimes express concern that putting together such packets will be a waste of time since the children are unlikely to complete them; however, parents of ELL children have told us how grateful they are when teachers have supported their children in this way. The packets have offered their children a structured time to devote to their studies and provided ways in which family members, including siblings, aunts, and cousins, have benefited from working together on these packets.

Targeted Strategy 2: Ask students to keep journals.

Students can keep many different kinds of journals:

- **Daily diary:** Ask the child to write about what he or she does each day, where, and with whom.

- **Reading response journal:** Provide the child with a variety of materials to read every day and respond to in a journal (e.g., fiction and nonfiction books, magazines) or ask his or her parents to provide them.

- **Math journal:** Have children keep a math journal or ledger, in which to record and comment on changes in time and currency, distances traveled, cost of fuel and meals, and other real-life experiences involving numbers.

- **Travel journal:** The child keeps a scrapbook or travel journal of special places the family visits. The scrapbook can include postcards, pamphlets, drawings, and so on. Maps with routes marked on them and short paragraphs about the historical significance of certain landmarks are useful additions.

- **Observational journal:** The child can write about the similarities and differences between the area just left and the area they are visiting, noting the similarities and differences in climate, geography, flora and fauna, language, culture (e.g., art, music, performing arts, and customs), and food.

Targeted Strategy 3: Assign photojournalism projects.

Ask the student to take pictures and interview family members and friends about aspects of the area they are visiting. Visits to family members who are infrequently seen, such as grandparents, aunts, and uncles, often provide a good opportunity for the children to interview relatives about their family history or their home country's history. Or, they can select one friend or relative on which to base a "day in the life" photo story. Children visiting a rural area could focus on animals, while a child visiting an urban area could concentrate on architecture. Invite children to share these projects with the class when they return from their trips.

Targeted Strategy 4: Make use of e-mail.

As computers and Internet access become more readily available around the world, children can be encouraged to stay in touch with the teacher and their class through e-mail. Communication could be as sophisticated as Webcams and real-time chats to less complicated weekly or occasional e-mail reports.

SITUATION 6 — Some parents won't let their children go on field trips.

Parents of ELL children may not allow their children to go on field trips because they cannot afford the expense involved. Also, parents may not be accustomed to the idea of field trips and may view them as a frivolous waste of a school day instead of a valuable educational experience. In addition, some parents may object for cultural or religious reasons. Dealing with parents who choose not to allow their children to go on field trips must be handled sensitively and respectfully, and in a way that does not cause stress for the child.

Targeted Strategy 1: Discreetly find out the reasons for objections.

Teachers should try as discreetly as possible to find out why the parents have refused to allow their children to participate in a field trip. The children themselves may be forthcoming about the reason, but if they don't volunteer a reason, do not press them to provide one. A phone call or a visit to the parents should be made by someone the parents trust, such as the teacher, parent liaison, or a translator. Parents may be embarrassed to admit that they cannot afford to pay for the field trip, and schools should establish ways to help pay for trips in such situations.

Targeted Strategy 2: Support ways for students to pay for trips.

It is important for schools to seek ways to make funds available for low-income families who cannot afford to pay for field trips. The best approaches allow for students or parents to contribute to the fund-raising process in order to save them from feeling that they are accepting charity. Some fund-raising activities in which parents and/or children can participate include:

- Bake sales

- Car washes

- International buffets

- International cookbook sales

- Auctions of children's art

- Craft and plant sales

In addition to fund-raising activities, teachers can help children anticipate and save for field trips. For example, knowing that many of their students would find the field trips planned in the spring a financial hardship, teachers at a school in Rochester, New York, instituted a "savings bank." Each student was given a savings passbook and encouraged to bring in 50 cents to deposit in their account every Monday. Teachers recorded the deposit and stamped the date in their passbook. At the end of the year, the students had saved enough money for their field trip, and often had saved a little extra, which the teachers returned to them as spending money for souvenirs or snacks on the trip. Parents were delighted with this system, which helped children fund their trips without taking a large chunk out of the family budget at one time, and it also instilled in the children the importance of saving (Zimmer, 1992).

Targeted Strategy 3: Have a translator explain a trip's educational purpose.

Translators or parent liaisons can be very helpful in explaining to parents the educational purpose of the field trip and how it is connected to the curriculum. If parents still decline for personal reasons, teachers should indicate that they respect the parents' decision.

Targeted Strategy 4: Provide educational activities for students left behind.

Teachers should plan carefully to provide meaningful educational activities for children who do not go on field trips, and parents should be encouraged to send their children to school, rather than keeping them at home on these days. For example, children can spend the day researching information on the content of the field trip or other class subjects, taking virtual field trips on computers, or producing a hands-on project.[3] For example, when fourth-grade classes in Virginia went on a field trip to Jamestown and Williamsburg, the ELL support specialist worked with the students who remained behind to build a model of the Jamestown settlement. The children used books and computer resources to research their project. When the students returned from their field trip eager to talk about their experiences, the ELL children who remained behind were equally eager to show and explain the model they had created.

SITUATION 7 Some parents of ELL students are upset because we're asking students to do family trees.

Parents of ELL students may be confused or disturbed by a family tree assignment. They may be dealing with many difficult situations that a family tree may bring up, including the traumatic loss of family members through war, issues of illegitimacy, parents or siblings left behind in their home countries, children who are the result of rape, and families separated as a result of domestic violence. Parents and ELL children may also be perplexed when asked to represent their family as the typical American nuclear family. For example, in some families around the world, the children of certain aunts and uncles are viewed as brothers and sisters, rather than cousins. Children could be confused about how to represent the closer relationship they have with their mother's sister than their father's sister, or vice versa. Some of these dilemmas are not limited to ELL families, of course. Both traditional and nontraditional families often appreciate a more flexible classroom approach to studying families, including the following strategies.

Targeted Strategy 1: Undertake a Tree of Life project.

Second- and third-grade teacher JoAnna Lovato adapted a middle school Tree of Life Project (Freeman, Freeman, & Mercuri, 2002; Northwest Regional

---

[3] See www.tramline.com/trips.htm for links to many virtual field trips appropriate for children in the elementary grades.

Educational Laboratory, 2001–2004) for her bilingual students. The children read autobiographies by authors with multicultural backgrounds and then created a colorful paper "wheel" that carried stories and images of their lives to show how life is like a tree from which encounters and experiences yield fruit. The wheel included a three-stanza autobiographical poem, stories of significant events in their lives, and four artifacts from their lives.

Targeted Strategy 2: Assign a My Home project.

Children draw and name the people they live with inside a simple house frame.

Targeted Strategy 3: Initiate the Caring Tree project.

Children draw themselves on a tree trunk and then put the faces and names of the people they love or care about on the branches. Then they briefly tell how each person cares for them.

Targeted Strategy 4: Read about different kinds of families.

Family studies should include readings about many different kinds of families. UNICEF puts out a series of beautifully illustrated books about children around the world, including *Children Just Like Me* (A. Kindersley & B. Kindersley, 1995) and *A Life Like Mine* (D. Kindersley, 2002).

SITUATION 8 My ELL students' parents are critical of my learner-centered teaching approach. They want me to use textbooks and give work sheets instead of reading and writing workshops and projects.

Like all parents, the beliefs about school that parents of ELLs hold are often influenced by their own school experiences. Some ELL parents and children may not be familiar with learner-centered or collaborative activities in school. In many countries, students are not expected to participate actively in the learning process; instead, instruction is provided by lecture or through rote learning. And in some countries, students complete class work silently and independently. Hence, many families may be more accustomed to recitation, memorization, and copying of material than the learner-centered approaches in many North American classrooms.

Targeted Strategy 1: Vary instructional methods.

In order to accommodate different learning preferences, it is advisable to provide different kinds of instruction in a single instructional block (including mathematics, language arts, or science) via individualized instruction, pair work, small-group work, and whole-class instruction. When parents visit, they will see that their children have an opportunity to learn in the kind of context in which they are most comfortable, while they are becoming familiar with other ways of learning.

Targeted Strategy 2: Share end results.

It is important to share with students and parents the end result of process-oriented learning experiences (e.g., how teachers learn from the developmental errors that students make and how they use these data to help them decide what to teach). For example, a teacher could highlight the child's development as a writer through sharing and talking about several drafts of a piece written by the child.

Teacher: Let's look at these three pieces of Omar's writing. In his first draft on butterflies, he used the same pattern in his sentences and included a few details. I could tell that he knew how to write many consonant sounds, such as *b, t, f, w, n, g, s*. Also, he knows some important words, such as *butterfly* and *wings*.

> **Omar's first draft**
> A btfi have wngs. A btfi can fli. A Btfi is butful.
> (A butterfly has wings. A butterfly can fly. A butterfly is beautiful.)

Teacher: After we talked about his writing, Omar used a picture dictionary to help him with his spelling. And he read some books about butterflies. We also talked about including vowel sounds in words. As you can see, his second draft shows what he learned.

> **Omar's second draft**
> Butterflys com from catepilars. Dey mak a crysalis. A butterfly stay in a crysalis for mane days. Dey com out and dey can fly becaus dey hav wings. Butterflys is butiful.

Teacher: In this second draft, he included more information and words about butterflies that he got from reading. He also included more vowels in his words. We then talked about the silent *e* on the end of "come" and "make." And, we talked about the *th* sound in "they." Omar was ready to finish and publish his piece, so we fixed all of the spelling and grammar. Also, he did some more research to find that butterflies stay in their chrysalis for ten days.

> **Omar's published work**
> Butterflies come from caterpillars. They make a chrysalis. A butterfly stays in the chrysalis for ten days. They come out and they can fly because they have wings. Butterflies are beautiful.

Teacher: Omar learned a lot about butterflies and about writing by working on several drafts. I think he'll remember this information because he worked hard on it and didn't just copy it from a book. Also, in the future, Omar will be able to use the information that he learned about spelling and grammar and how to do research for his next piece.

Targeted Strategy 3: Show enriching benefits of open-ended activities.

When teachers assign open-ended activities, those that allow for choice and creativity, students frequently invest themselves as learners. Both identified and hidden talents emerge (Hertzog, 1998), and teachers can show parents how this works. For example, a teacher who asked students to draw something they learned on a field trip can show parents how their children used their artistic abilities to create intricately detailed and labeled drawings of the layers of rock strata to show the geological history of the visited region. Or a teacher might show parents how he or she uses open-ended journals, such as dialogue journals or reading/writing journals, to get to know students. For example, if a student writes in his dialogue journal that he loves to play soccer, the teacher can show the parents how she or he sparked the child's interest in reading by finding books about soccer for their son to read. The teacher and/or parents might even try to find a way for the child to play on a soccer team.

Targeted Strategy 4: Explain roles and expectations of group work.

Explain to parents the specific roles that students play in collaborative activities, such as recorder, mediator, timekeeper, and researcher, and how they relate to the roles that students currently perform outside the classroom on sports teams or at home, as well as future roles in the workplace and community.

Targeted Strategy 5: Respect parents' social concerns.

Parents may have concerns about how their children are grouped for collaborative activities. Some parents might be concerned about mixed-gender groups or groups made up of children from conflicting tribes or ethnic groups. Teachers should respect these concerns and try to come to a satisfactory agreement, such as agreeing to same-sex groupings for a six-month adjustment period or temporarily avoiding pair work between children of conflicting tribes.

Targeted Strategy 6: Explain grades and other evaluation systems.

Use an orientation meeting and parent-teacher conferences to make sure that parents understand how and why students are graded. Parents may not be familiar with an ABC grade-based system or words such as *satisfactory* and *unsatisfactory*. Some parents may expect all reports to be given in percentages. Some parents may be uncomfortable when all children in a group receive the same collective grade or with a teacher giving comments instead of numerical grades. Other parents may be accustomed to viewing all schoolwork as collaborative and do not consider one child helping another on a test to be cheating.

SITUATION 9 The parents of my ELL children express concern about behavioral problems with their children since coming to the U.S.

SITUATION 10 The parents of my ELL students told me that their children threaten to report them to social agencies or schools if they chastise the children.

Many school systems outside of North America have strict rules of behavior, and teachers are treated with great respect. For example, students may stand up when the teacher enters the classroom and when they respond to a teacher's questions. In some schools, corporal punishment is an accepted practice. Parents of ELL students often see North American classrooms as out of control and North American children as ill-behaved and disrespectful. Conflicts within a family can arise when ELL children begin to pick up what parents perceive to be lax mannerisms and rude behavior. The children, on the other hand, often rebel against what they see as overly strict rules, and sometimes take advantage of their parents' lack of familiarity with North American customs by threatening to report their parents to social agencies. Schools should not shy away from these issues; instead, they should work with parents, children, community agencies, and ethnic groups to address these issues.

Targeted Strategy 1: Work with parent liaisons.

Parent liaisons, especially those coming from the same ethnic community and language background as the families, are in the best position to a) explain to parents a school's rules and behavioral expectations, and b) help parents to understand cultural differences when showing respect or disciplining children in North America.

Targeted Strategy 2: Encourage participation in sports.

Teachers can encourage parents to enroll their children in organized sports, such as soccer, basketball, and martial arts. These activities often help children develop discipline, self-control, and self-esteem.

Targeted Strategy 3: Invite speakers from agencies.

Speakers from social services agencies, such as child protective services, can be invited to parent orientations or PTO meetings. Translators should be available at these meetings, and time and space should be provided so parents can ask confidential questions.

Targeted Strategy 4: Translate local laws about children.

Provide translations of laws pertaining to children, such as how long they can be left unattended, the legal definition of child abuse and maltreatment, and when children can legally work and for how many hours.

Targeted Strategy 5: Help parent support groups.

Schools can provide organizational assistance and facilities for parent support groups. These groups meet on a regular basis to discuss parenting issues (e.g., how to handle children who want to wear clothing that parents consider inappropriate, how to deal with children who are disdainful of their parents because they don't speak much English). The school can help locate speakers from local community and nonprofit organizations, and translators.

Targeted Strategy 6: Include simulations and sensitivity training in classrooms.

Teachers and children can learn more about family life through simulations and role-plays. For example, in a role-play about parents who refuse to let their child attend a sleepover, students can play roles, such as the mother, the father, the grandmother, the child, the sleepover mother, and the sleepover father. After the role-play, the children discuss how they felt in their respective roles. This process can help students understand why their parents may react as they do.

Targeted Strategy 7: Keep siblings together.

For a variety of reasons, because siblings arrive in North America at different times or have varying ELL support needs, children from the same family sometimes end up in different schools. This situation can be very disruptive to families, as they have to deal with different school rules and expectations, in addition to possibly juggling different bus and school schedules. Children are much more likely to feel stable and supported if their siblings are in the same school as they are. We are familiar with cases where behavioral problems were resolved when younger children knew they had the comfort and support of an older sibling in the same building.

References

Achinstein, B., Ogawa, R., & Speiglman, A. (2005). Are we creating separate and unequal tracks of teachers? The impact of state policy, local conditions, and teacher characteristics on new teacher socialization. *American Educational Research Journal, 41*(3), 557–603.

Ada, A. F., & Campoy, F. I. (2000). *Blue and green.* Miami: Santillana USA.

Adger, C. T. (2000). *School/community partnerships to support language minority success* (Paper Research Brief No. 5). Santa Cruz, CA: Center for Research on Equity, Diversity, and Excellence (CREDE). Retrieved from repositories.cdlib.org/cgi/viewcontent.cgi?article=1061&context=crede

Ahlberg, J., & Ahlberg, A. (1978, 1979). *Each peach, pear, plum.* New York: Viking Press.

Ahlberg, J., & Ahlberg, A. (1986). *The jolly postman: Or, other people's letters.* New York: Little Brown.

Allen, R. V. (1976). *Language experiences in education.* Boston: Houghton Mifflin.

Altwerger, B., Arya, P., Jin, L., Jordan, N. L., Laster, B., Martens, P., Wilson, G. P., & Wiltz, N. (2004). When research and mandates collide: The challenges and dilemmas of teacher education in the era of NCLB. *English Education, 36*(2), 119–133.

American heritage dictionary. (1982, 1985). Boston: Houghton Mifflin.

Ammon, P. (1985). Helping children learn to write in English as a second language: Some observations and some hypotheses. In S. W. Freedman (Ed.), *The acquisition of written language* (pp. 65–84). Norwood, NJ: Ablex.

Anderson. C. (2000). *How's it going?: A practical guide to conferring with student writers.* Portsmouth, NH: Heinemann.

Anderson, R. T. (2004). Phonological acquisition in preschoolers learning a second language via immersion: a longitudinal study. *Clinical Linguistics and Phonetics, 18*(3), 183–210.

Asher, J. (2003). *Learning another language through actions* (6th ed.). Los Gatos, CA: Sky Oaks Productions.

Atwell, N. (1998). *In the middle: New understandings about writing, reading, and learning* (2nd ed.). Portsmouth, NH: Heinemann.

August, D., & Shanahan, T. (Eds.). (2006). *Developing literacy in second-language learners: Report of the National Literacy Panel on Language-Minority Children and Youth*. Mahwah, NJ: Lawrence Erlbaum Associates.

Azar, B. S. (1989). *Understanding and using English grammar* (2nd ed.). Englewood, NJ: Prentice Hall.

Barbieri, M. (2002). *"Change my life forever": Giving voice to English-language learners*. Portsmouth, NH: Heinemann.

Baumann, J., Jones, L., & Seifert-Kessell, N. (1993). Using think aloud to enhance children's comprehension monitoring abilities. *The Reading Teacher, 47*(3), 184–193.

Bear, D. R., Invernizzi, M., Templeton, S, & Johnston, F. (2004). *Words their way: Word study for phonics, vocabulary, and spelling instruction* (3rd ed.). Upper Saddle River, NJ: Prentice Hall.

Beeler, S. (2001). *Throw your tooth on the roof*. Boston: Houghton Mifflin.

Blachowicz, C. Z., Fisher, P. L., Ogle, D., & Watts-Taffe, S. (2006). Vocabulary: Questions from the classroom. *Reading Research Quarterly, 41*(4), 524–539.

Bolton, F., & Snowball, D. (1993). *Ideas for spelling*. Portsmouth, NH: Heinemann.

Brewer's dictionary of phrase and fable (15th ed.). (1996). London: Cassell Publishers.

Brown, M. W. (1947). *Goodnight moon*. New York: Harper.

Calkins, L. M. (1986, 1994). *The art of teaching writing*. Portsmouth, NH: Heinemann.

Callanan, M., Alba-Speyer, C., & Tenenbaum, H. (2000). *Linking home and school through children's questions that followed Family Science workshops* (Paper Research Brief No. 8). Santa Cruz, CA: Center for Research on Equity, Diversity, and Excellence (CREDE). Retrieved from http://repositories.cdlib.org/cgi/viewcontent.cgi?article=1082&context=crede

Carle, E. (1979, 1994). *The very hungry caterpillar*. New York: Philomel Books.

Carlo, M. S., August, D., McLaughlin, B., Snow, C. E., Dressler, C., Lippman, D. N., Lively, T. J., & White, C. E. (2004). Closing the gap: Addressing the vocabulary needs of English-language learners in bilingual and mainstream classrooms. *Reading Research Quarterly, 39*(2), 188–215.

Cisneros, S. (1984). *The house on Mango Street*. New York: Random House.

Clark, R. C., Moran, P. R., & Burrows, A. A. (1981). *The ESL miscellany: A cultural and linguistic inventory of American English*. Brattleboro, VT: Pro Lingua Associates.

Clay, M. (2000). *Running records for classroom teachers*. Portsmouth, NH: Heinemann.

Collier, V. P. (1989). How long? A synthesis of research on academic achievement in a second language. *TESOL Quarterly, 23*(3), 509–531.

Collier, V. P. (1992). A synthesis of studies examining long-term language minority student data on academic achievement. *Bilingual Research Journal, 16*(1–2), 187–212.

Cowley, J. (2001). *The monsters' party*. New York: McGraw-Hill.

Crew, Linda. (1989). *Children of the river*. New York: Delacorte Press.

Cummins, J. (1981a). Age on arrival and immigrant second language learning in Canada. A reassessment. *Applied Linguistics, 2*, 132–149.

Cummins, J. (1981b). The role of primary language development in promoting educational success for language minority students. *Schooling and language minority students: A theoretical framework*. Los Angeles: Evaluation, Dissemination and Assessment Center.

Cummins, J. (2000). *Language, power, and pedagogy: Bilingual children in the crossfire*. Buffalo, NY: Multilingual Matters Ltd.

Cummins, J., & Mulcahy, R. (1978). Orientation to language in Ukrainian-English bilingual children. *Child Development, 49*, 1239–1242.

Curran, M. E. (2003). Linguistic diversity and classroom management. *Theory Into Practice, 42*(4), 334–340.

Dahl, R. (1961). *James and the giant peach*. New York: Knopf.

DiMarzio, D., & Coustan, T. (1996). The book bag project for emerging literacy. *TESOL Journal, 5*(4), 36–38.

Dorros, A. (1992). *This is my house*. New York: Scholastic.

Dresser, N. (1993). *Our own stories: Cross-cultural communication practice*. White Plains, NY: Longman.

Dulay, H. C., Burt, M. K., & Krashen, S. D. (1982). *Language two*. New York: Oxford University Press.

Edelsky, C. (1982). Writing in a bilingual program: The relation of L1 and L2 texts. *TESOL Quarterly, 16*(2), 211–228.

Edelsky, C. (1986). *Writing in a bilingual program: Había una vez*. Norwood, NJ: Ablex.

Edelsky, C., & Jilbert, K. (1985). Bilingual children and writing: Lessons for all of us. *Volta Review, 87*(5), 57-72.

Ellis, R. (1994). *The study of second language acquisition*. New York: Oxford University Press.

English, Karen. (1999). *Nadia's hands*. Honesdale, PA: Boyds Mills Press.

Fadiman, A. (1998). *The spirit catches you and you fall down*. New York: Farrar, Straus & Giroux.

Fillmore, L. W., & Snow, C. (2000). *What teachers need to know about language*. Washington, D.C.: Center for Applied Linguistics.

Fountas, I. C., & Pinnell, G. S. (1996). *Guided reading: Good first teaching for all children*. Portsmouth, NH: Heinemann.

Fountas, I. C., & Pinnell, G. S. (2001). *Guided reading: The essential elements* and *Guided reading: The skillful teacher* (Videotapes). Portsmouth, NH: Heinemann.

Fradd, S. H., & Wilen, D. K. (1990). *Using interpreters and translators to meet the needs of handicapped language minority students and their families* (Program Information Guide, 4). Washington, DC: National Clearinghouse for Bilingual Education.

Freeman, D. E., & Freeman, Y. S. (2004). *Essential linguistics: What you need to know to teach reading, ESL, spelling, phonics, grammar*. Portsmouth, NH: Heinemann.

Freeman, Y. S., & Freeman, D. E. (2006). *Teaching reading and writing in Spanish and English in bilingual and dual language classrooms*. Portsmouth, NH: Heinemann.

Freeman, Y. S., Freeman, D. E., & Mercuri, S. P. (2002). *Closing the achievement gap: How to reach limited-formal-schooling and long-term English learners*. Portsmouth, NH: Heinemann.

Fu, D. (1995). *"My trouble is my English": Asian students and the American dream*. Portsmouth, NH: Boynton Cook.

Gattegno, C. (1972). *Teaching foreign languages in schools: The silent way*. New York: Educational Solutions.

Gibbons, P. (2002). *Scaffolding language, scaffolding learning: Teaching second language learners in the mainstream classroom*. Portsmouth, NH: Heinemann.

Gibbs, J. (2007). *Guiding your school community to live a culture of caring and learning* (revised). Revised edition. Windsor, Ontario, Canada: CenterSource Systems.

Graham, C. (1985). *Jazz chants for children*. New York: Oxford University Press.

Graham, C. (1992). *Grammarchants*. New York: Oxford University Press.

Graham, C. (2001). *Jazz chants old and new*. New York: Oxford University Press.

Graham, C. (2002). *Children's jazz chants old and new: Student book*. New York: Oxford University Press.

Graves, D. H. (1983). *Writing: Teachers and children at work*. Exeter, NH: Heinemann.

Graves, D. H. (1994). *A fresh look at writing*. Portsmouth, NH: Heinemann.

Han, J. W., & Ernst-Slavit, G. (1999). Come join the literacy club: One Chinese ESL child's literacy experience in a 1st-grade classroom. *Journal of Research in Childhood Education, 13*(2), 144–154.

Heald-Taylor, G. (1986). *Whole language strategies for ESL students*. Toronto, Ontario, Canada: Ontario Institute for Studies in Education.

Helman, C. (1994). *Culture, health and illness: An introduction for health professionals*. New York: Oxford University Press.

Heredia, R., & Brown, J. (2004). Code switching. In P. Starzny (Ed.), *Encyclopedia of Linguistics*. London: Routledge.

Hertzog, N. (1998). Using open-ended learning activities to empower teachers and students. *Teaching Exceptional Children, 30*(6), 26–31.

Hoobler, D., & Hoobler, T. (1994a). *The Chinese American family album*. New York: Oxford University Press.

Hoobler, D., & Hoobler, T. (1994b). *The Mexican American family album*. New York: Oxford University Press.

Hoyt, L. (1993). How do they learn to read and write?: Literacy instruction in a refugee camp. In K. D. Samway & D. McKeon (Eds.), *Common threads of practice: Teaching English to children around the world* (pp. 67–77). Alexandria, VA: Teachers of English to Speakers of Other Languages.

Hoyt, L. (2003). *Navigating informational texts*. Portsmouth, NH: Heinemann.

Hudelson, S. (1984). Kan yu ret an rayt en Ingles: Children become literate in English as a second language. *TESOL Quarterly, 18*(2), 221–238.

Hudelson, S. (1986). ESL children's writing: What we've learned, what we're learning. In P. Rigg & D. S. Enright (Eds.), *Children and ESL: Integrating perspectives* (pp. 25–54). Alexandria, VA: Teachers of English to Speakers of Other Languages.

Hudelson, S. (1989). A tale of two children: Individual differences in ESL children's writing. In D. M. Johnson & D. H. Roen (Eds.), *Richness in writing* (pp. 84–99). New York: Longman.

Hudelson, S. (1994). Literacy development of second language children. In F. Genesee (Ed.), *Educating second language children: The whole child, the whole curriculum, the whole community* (pp. 129–158). New York: Cambridge University Press.

Huss-Keeler, R. L. (1997). Teacher perception of ethnic and linguistic minority parental involvement and its relationships to children's language and literacy learning: A case study. *Teaching and Teacher Education, 13*(2), 171–182.

Johnson, P. (1997). *Pictures and words together: Children illustrating and writing their own books*. Portsmouth, NH: Heinemann.

Johnston, T. (2003). *Any small goodness: A novel of the barrio*. New York: Scholastic.

Kellogg, S. (1997). *Jack and the beanstalk.* New York: William Morrow & Company, Inc.

Kemp, C., & Rasbridge, L. (2004). *Refugee and immigrant health: A handbook for health professionals.* New York: Cambridge University Press.

Kindersley, A., & Kindersley, B. (1995). *Children just like me.* New York: Dorling Kindersley Publishing.

Kindersley, D. (2002). *A life like mine: How children live around the world.* New York: Dorling Kindersley Publishing.

King, K., & Fogle, L. (2006, April). Raising bilingual children: Common parental concerns and current research. *CAL Digest.* Retrieved from www.cal.org/resources/Digest/RaiseBilingChild.html

Krashen, S. (2006). Read-alouds are good for literacy development: A comment on freakonomics. *Reading Today, 23*(2), 19.

Krashen, S. D. (1985). *The input hypothesis: Issues and implications.* New York: Longman, Inc.

Krashen, S. D., & Scarcella, R. C. (Eds.). (1982). *Child-adult differences in second language acquisition.* Rowley, MA: Newbury House.

Krashen, S. D., & Terrell, T. D. (1983). *The natural approach: Language acquisition in the classroom.* Elmsford, NY: The Alemany Press/Pergamon Press.

Krishnaswami, U. (2003). *Chachaji's cup.* San Francisco: Children's Book Press.

Kubler, A., & Formby, C. (1995a). *Come and eat with us.* Swindon, England: Child's Play International.

Kubler, A., & Formby, C. (1995b). *Come home with us.* Swindon, England: Child's Play International.

Kurtz, J., & Kurtz, C. (1997). *Only a pigeon.* New York: Simon & Schuster.

Lightbown, P. M., & Spada, N. (1993). *How languages are learned.* New York: Oxford University Press.

Lightbown, P. M., & Spada, N. (2006). *How languages are learned* (3rd ed.). New York: Oxford University Press.

López, G. R. (2001). The value of hard work: Lessons on parent involvement from an (im)migrant household. *Harvard Educational Review, 71*(3), 416–437.

Lyman, F. T. (1981). The responsive classroom discussion: The inclusion of all students. In A. Anderson (Ed.), *Mainstreaming Digest.* College Park, MD: University of Maryland Press.

Majidi, M. (1999). *Children of heaven/Bachecha-ye aseman* [Motion Picture]. United States: Miramax.

Marten, C. (2003). *Word crafting: Teaching spelling, grades K–6.* Portsmouth, NH: Heinemann.

May, S., Hill, R., & Tiakiwai, S. (2004). *Bilingual/immersion education: Indicators of good practice.* New Zealand: Ministry of Education.

McCafferty, C. (2001). *The gingerbread man.* New York: McGraw-Hill.

McCarrier, A., Pinnell, G. S., & Fountas, I. C. (2000). *Interactive writing: How language and literacy come together, K–2.* Portsmouth, NH: Heinemann.

Mora, P. (1997). *Tomás and the library lady.* New York: Knopf.

Morris, A. (1989). *Bread, bread, bread.* New York: Lothrop, Lee & Shepard Books.

Morris, A. (1995). *Shoes, shoes, shoes.* New York: Lothrop, Lee & Shepard Books.

Morris, A. (2002). *Grandma Francisca remembers: An Hispanic-American family story.* Brookfield, CT: Millbrook Press

Morrison, S. (undated). *English language learners with special needs.* CAL Resource Guides Online. Retrieved on April 9, 2007, from www.cal.org/resources/archive/rgos/special.html

Mosel, A. (1968, 1989). *Tikki tikki tembo.* New York: Henry Holt & Company.

Moustafa, M., & Land, R. E. (2002). The reading achievement of economically-disadvantaged children in urban schools using Open Court vs. comparably disadvantaged children in urban schools using non-scripted reading programs. In *Yearbook of the Urban Learning, Teaching, and Research* (pp. 44–53). Special Interest Group of the American Educational Research Association.

Nagy, W., & Herman, P. (1987). Breadth and depth of vocabulary knowledge. In M. McKeown & M. E. Curtis (Eds.), *The nature of vocabulary acquisition* (pp. 9–36). Hillsdale, NJ: Lawrence Erlbaum Associates.

Nation, I. S. P. (2001). *Learning vocabulary in another language.* Cambridge England: Cambridge University Press.

National Institute of Child Health and Human Development (NICHD). (2000). *Report of the National Reading Panel: Teaching children to read* (NIH Publication No. 00-4754). Washington, D.C.

Northwest Regional Educational Laboratory. (2001–2004). Riding la fombra mágica: ESL students explore their roots through writing. Retrieved from www.nwrel.org/tapestry/pdf/05_primary_magica.pdf.

Oller, J. (1979). *Language tests at school.* London: Longman.

Olsen, S. (1998). *Look again pictures.* Burlingame, CA: Alta Books.

O'Malley, J., & Valdez-Pierce, L. (1996). *Authentic assessment for English language learners.* Reading, MA: Addison Wesley Publishing Co.

Ortiz, A. A. (1997). Learning disabilities occurring concomitantly with linguistic differences. *Journal of Learning Disabilities, 30,* 321–332.

Oster, L. (2001). Using think-aloud for reading instruction. *The Reading Teacher, 55*(1), 64–69.

Palmer, A., Rodgers, T., & Olsen, J. (1985). *Back and forth: Pair activities for language development.* Hayward, CA: Alemany Press.

Paulsen, G. (1987). *Hatchet.* New York: Bradbury Press.

Pease-Alvarez, L., Samway, K. Davies, Almanzo, M., & Cifka-Herrerra, C. (2007). *Making sense of Open Court: Teachers negotiating top-down reform in literacy instruction for English language learners.* Paper presented at the American Educational Research Association Annual Meeting. Chicago.

Peyton, J. K., & Reed, L. (1990). *Dialogue journal writing with nonnative English speakers.* Alexandria, VA: Teachers of English to Speakers of Other Languages.

Peyton, J. K., & Seyoum, M. (1989). The effect of teacher strategies on students' interactive writing: The case of dialogue journals. *Research in the Teaching of English, 23*(3), 310–334.

Polacco, P. (1988). *The keeping quilt*. New York: Simon & Schuster.

RAND Reading Study Group. (2002). *Reading for understanding: Toward a research and development program in reading comprehension*. Prepared for OERI, U.S. Department of Education.

Ray, K. W. (2001). *The writing workshop: Working through the hard parts (and they're all hard parts)*. Urbana, IL: National Council of Teachers of English.

Reed, B., & Railsback, J. (2003). *Strategies and resources for mainstream teachers of English language learners*. Portland, OR: Northwest Regional Educational Laboratory.

Retish, E. (2000). The world of work. In B. A. Smallwood (Ed.), *Integrating the ESL standards into classroom practice: Grades Pre-K–2* (pp. 43–64). Alexandria, VA: Teachers of English to Speakers of Other Languages (TESOL).

Reyes, M. de la Luz. (1991). A process approach to literacy using dialogue journals and literature logs with second language learners. *Research in the Teaching of English, 25*, 291–313.

Rice, M. L., Huston, A. C., Truglio, R., & Wright, J. (1990). Words from Sesame Street: Learning vocabulary while viewing television. *Developmental Psychology, 26*, 421–428.

Rief, L. (1992). *Seeking diversity: Language arts with adolescents*. Portsmouth, NH: Heinemann.

Rigg, P. (1989). Language experience approach: Reading naturally. In V. Allen & P. Rigg (Eds.), *When they don't all speak English*. Urbana, IL: National Council of Teachers of English.

Rivers, W. M. (1981). *Teaching foreign language skills* (2nd ed.). Chicago: University of Chicago Press.

Rous, E. W. (1993). Using reading and writing process methods to teach English as a foreign language. In K. D. Samway & D. McKeon (Eds.), *Common threads of practice: Teaching English to children around the world* (pp. 120–132). Alexandria, VA: Teachers of English to Speakers of Other Languages.

Rumberger, R. W., & Gandara, P. (2004). Seeking equity in the education of California's English learners. *Teachers College Record, 106* (10), 2032–2056.

Samway, K. (1986). "And you run and you run to catch up with the sun, but it's sinking." *Language Arts, 63,* 352–357.

Samway, K. Davies. (1987a). Formal evaluation of children's writing: An incomplete story. *Language Arts, 64*(3), 289–298.

Samway, K. Davies. (1987b). *The writing processes of non-native English speaking children in the elementary grades.* Unpublished doctoral dissertation, University of Rochester.

Samway, K. Davies. (1993). "This is hard, isn't it?": Children evaluating writing. *TESOL Quarterly, 27*(2), 233–258.

Samway, K. Davies. (2006). *When English language learners write: Connecting research and practice.* Portsmouth, NH: Heinemann.

Samway, K. Davies., & McKeon, D. (1999). *Myths and realities: Best practices for language minority students.* Portsmouth, NH: Heinemann.

Samway, K. Davies., & McKeon, D. (2007). *Myths and realities: Best practices for English language learners.* Portsmouth, NH: Heinemann.

Samway, K. Davies., & Taylor, D. (1993a). The collected letters of two collaborative researchers. In S. J. Hudelson & J. Wells Lindfors (Eds.), *Delicate balances: Collaborative research in language education.* Urbana, IL: National Council of Teachers of English.

Samway, K. Davies., & Taylor, D. (1993b). Inviting children to make connections between reading and writing. *TESOL Journal, 2*(3), 7–11.

Samway, K. Davies., & Whang, G. (1996). *Literature study circles in a multicultural classroom.* York, ME: Stenhouse Publishers.

Samway, K. Davies., Whang, G., & Pippitt, M. (1995). *Buddy reading: Cross-age tutoring in a multicultural school.* Portsmouth, NH: Heinemann.

Saville-Troike, M. (1984). What *really* matters in second language learning for academic achievement? *TESOL Quarterly, 18*(2), 199–219.

Scarcella, R. (2002). Some key factors affecting English learners' development of advanced literacy. In M. J. Schleppegrell and M. C. Colombi (Eds.), *Developing advanced literacy in first and second languages.* Mahwah, NJ: Lawrence Erlbaum Associates.

Scott, J. A., Flinspach, S. L., & Samway, K. Davies. (2007). *Linking word knowledge to the world: The VINE project.* Paper presented at the Annual Meeting of AERA, Chicago.

Selinker, L. (1972). Interlanguage. *International Review of Applied Linguistics in Language Teaching, 10*(3), 209–231.

Sendak, M. (1962). *Chicken soup with rice: A book of months.* New York: Harper & Row.

Serna, I. A., & Hudelson, S. (1993). Emergent Spanish literacy in a whole language bilingual classroom. In R. Donmoyer & R. Kos (Eds.), *At-risk students: Portraits, policies, programs and practices* (pp. 291–321). Albany: State University of New York Press.

Shaw, N. E. (1986). *Sheep in a jeep.* New York: Houghton Mifflin.

Soto, G. (1993). *Too many tamales.* New York: G. P. Putnam's Sons.

Stauffer, R. (1970). *The language experience approach to the teaching of reading.* New York: Harper & Row.

Stewart, D. W. (1993). *Immigration and education: The crisis and opportunities.* New York: Lexington Books.

Storch, N., & Wigglesworth, G. (2003). Is there a role for the use of the L1 in an L2 setting? *TESOL Quarterly, 37*(4), 760–770.

Swanborn, M. S. L., & de Glopper, K. (1999). Incidental word learning while reading: A meta-analysis. *Review of Educational Research, 69*(3), 261–285.

Syvanen, C. (2000). Recyling. In Samway, K. D. (Ed.) *Integrating the ESL standards into classroom practices: Grades 3–5* (pp. 133–149). Alexandria, VA: Teachers of English to Speakers of Other Languages.

Szente, J., Hoot, J., & Taylor, D. (2006). Responding to the special needs of refugee children: Practical ideas for teachers. *Early Childhood Education Journal, 34*(1), 15–20.

Tabors, P., & Snow, C. (1994). English as a second language in preschools. In Genesee, F. (Ed.), *Educating second language children: The whole child, the whole curriculum, the whole community* (pp. 103–125). New York: Cambridge University Press

Tang, F., & Loyet, D. (2003, Fall). Celebrating twenty-five years of jazz chants. *Idiom*, 5–6. Retrieved from www.nystesol.org/pub/idiom_archive/idiom_ fall2003.html

Taylor, D. (1999). The teacher as listener. In J. Lindfors & J. Townsend (Eds.), *Teaching language arts: Learning through dialogue* (pp. 222–231). Urbana, IL: National Council of Teachers of English.

Taylor, D. (2000). Facing hardships: Jamestown and colonial life. In K. D. Samway (Ed.), *Integrating the ESL standards into classroom practice: Grades 3–5* (pp. 53–81). Alexandria, VA: Teachers of English to Speakers of Other Languages.

Taylor, D. M. (1990). Writing and reading literature in a second language. In N. Atwell (Ed.), *Workshop 2: Beyond the basal* (pp. 105–117). Portsmouth, NH: Heinemann.

Thomas, W., & Collier, V. (2001). *A national study of school effectiveness for language minority students' long-term achievement.* Berkeley, CA: Center for Research on Education, Diversity and Excellence (CREDE). Retrieved from crede.berkeley.edu/research/llaa/1.1_es.html

Tierney, R. J., & Parson, P. D. (1981). Learning to learn from text: A framework for improving classroom practice. In R. B. Ruddell, M. R. Ruddell, & H. Singer (Eds.), *Theoretical models and processes of reading* (pp. 496–513). Newark, DE: International Reading Association.

Turkle, B. (1992). *Deep in the forest.* New York: Penguin Books.

Turner, A. (2000). *Grasshopper summer.* New York: Aladdin Paperbacks.

Urzúa, C. (1986). A children's story. In P. Rigg & D. S. Enright (Eds.), *Children and ESL: Integrating perspectives* (pp. 93–112). Washington, D.C.: Teachers of English to Speakers of Other Languages.

Urzúa, C. (1987). "You stopped too soon": Second language children composing and revising. *TESOL Quarterly, 21*(2), 279–304.

Vicens, W. (1995). Let me tell you about our team. *TESOL Journal, 4*(4), 35–36.

Wallace, S. (2004). Effective instructional strategies for English language learners in mainstream classrooms. *New Horizons for Learning.* Retrieved from www.newhorizons.org/spneeds/ell/wallace.htm

Wells, G. (1986). *The meaning makers: Children learning language and using language to learn.* Portsmouth, NH: Heinemann.

Wheeler, J. (1994). The liars' club. *TESOL Journal, 3*(2), 31–32.

White, E. B. (1974). *Stuart Little.* New York: HarperCollins.

White, M., Moore, E., & de Regniers, B. (1988). *Sing a song of popcorn: Every child's book of poems.* New York: Scholastic.

Wilde, S. (2000). *Miscue analysis made easy.* Portsmouth, NH: Heinemann.

Wong-Fillmore, L. (1985). When does teacher talk work as input? In S. M. Gass & C. G. Madden (Eds.), *Input in second language acquisition.* Rowley, MA: Newbury House Publisher, Inc.

Woodson, J. (2005). *Show way.* New York: G. P. Putnam's Sons.

Zimmer, M. (1992). A banking innovation. *TESOL Journal, 2*(1), 36.

Appendix A:

Children's Books About Teasing and Bullying[1]

Allen, Debbie. (2003). *Dancing in the wings*. New York: Puffin Books.

> Written by the actress Debbie Allen, who appeared in *Fame*. A tall, gangly, African American girl studies ballet and triumphs over teasing and put-downs.

Berenstain, Stan & Berenstain, Jan. (1993). *The Berenstain bears and the bully*. New York: Random House.

> This book deals with why bullies bully, and what to do and what not to do when you are the victim of bullying.

Bosch, Carl W. (1988). *Bully on the bus*. Seattle: Parenting Press.

> This book focuses on different decisions a child can make when being bullied.

D'Amico, Carmela. (2004). *Ella, the elegant elephant*. New York: Arthur A. Levine.

> When an elephant moves to a new school, a bully makes fun of her new good-luck hat given to her by her grandmother.

Dolenz, Mickey. (2006). *Gakky two feet*. New York: Putnam.

> Everyone laughs at the monkey who likes to walk on two feet until he saves them from a lion. This book shows the value of being different. The author was in the singing group The Monkees.

Hazen, Barbara Shook. (1985). *Why are people different?* New York: Western Publishing Co.

> This book is about valuing people who are different from ourselves.

Henkes, Kevin. (1991). *Chrysanthemum*. New York: Greenwillow Books.

> Chrysanthemum loves her name until she goes to kindergarten and other children make fun of it. Ultimately, she comes to like her name again.

Leaney, Cindy. (2004). *Long walk to school: A story about bullying*. Vero Beach, FL: Rourke Publishing.

> The Hero kids help a boy who is being bullied, as well as the one doing the bullying (from the Hero Kids series).

Montanari, Eva. (2004). *Dino bikes*. New York: Penguin/Michael Neugebauer.

> Big boys make fun of Dino as he learns to ride a bike—until they begin to have trouble. This book is about learning at your own pace.

---

[1] We would like to thank Karen Peterman and Monica Vorac for their help in compiling this bibliography.

Soto, Gary. (2002). *If the shoe fits*. New York: Putnam.

> Rigo, a 9-year-old Mexican-American boy, usually wears hand-me-downs, so he is excited about his new shoes, until a neighborhood kid makes fun of them. Rigo ends up giving the shoes to his uncle and learns the value of hand-me-downs.

Williams, Karen Lynn. (1992) *First grade king*. New York: Clarion Books.

> A little boy is teased about his name, and a little girl is taunted about her poor vision. They help each other overcome the effects of bullying behavior.

≈ •••

Appendix B:

Children's Videos About Bullying[2]

Bully. (1973). National Instructional Television Center, Box A, Bloomington, IN 47401.

Bullying. (1995). South Carolina Educational Television, P.O. Box 11000, Columbia, SC 29201.

Bully smart. (1995). Street Smart, 105 North Virginia Avenue, Suite 305, Falls Church, VA 22042.

Broken toy. (1993). Summerhills Productions, 846-1/2 McIntire Ave., Zanesville, OH, 43701.

Coping with bullying. (1991). James Stanfield Company, Drawer G, P.O. Box 41058, Santa Barbara, CA 93140.

Dealing with bullies, troublemakers and dangerous situations (Part of the PeaceTalks series). The Bureau for At-Risk Youth, 135 Dupont St., P.O. Box 760, Plainview, NY, 11803-0760.

Don't pick on me. (1993). Sunburst Communications, 101 Castleton St., Pleasantville, NY, 10570.

Groark learns about bullying (Volume 4 in the Prevent Violence with Groark series.) Wisconsin Clearinghouse for Prevention Resources, University Health Services, University of Wisconsin-Madison, Dept. 7B, P.O. Box 1468, Madison, WI 53701-1468.

Michael's story: The no blame approach. 1990. Lame Duck Publishing, 71 South Road, Portshead, Bristol BS20 90Y, England.

Set straight on bullies. (1988). National School Safety Center, 4165 Thousand Oaks Blvd., Suite 290, Westlake Village, CA 91362.

Stamp out bullying. (1990). Lame Duck Publishing, 71 South Road, Portshead, Bristol BS20 90Y, England.

---

[2] Taken from "Bullying Prevention" compiled by Kelly Dunn, school counseling consultant, Office of Student Services, Indiana Department of Education. www.doe.state.in.us/sservices/pdf/bully_manual.pdf

Appendix C:

Selected Children's and Young Adult Books About Diverse Cultures[3]

Picture Books
Fiction

Ada, Alma Flor. (2002). *I love Saturdays y Domingos*. New York: Aladdin.
Told in both Spanish and English, this story introduces readers to the special relationships a young child has with her Mexican American and European American grandparents.

Ai-Ling, Louie. (1993). *Yeh-Shen: A Cinderella story from China*. New York: Scholastic.
This Chinese version of Cinderella dates back 1,300 years.

Altman, Linda J. (1993). *Amelia's road*. New York: Lee and Low Books.
A young Mexican American girl, the daughter of migrant farmworkers, longs for a place she can call home. When she finds a special place, she also discovers a way to keep memories alive.

Bunting, Eve. (1997). *A day's work*. New York: Clarion.
A family of day laborers from Mexico works together to make a living.

Bunting, Eve. (1998). *Going home*. New York: HarperTrophy.
A Mexican migrant family returns to Mexico at Christmas to visit family.

Bunting, Eve. (1999). *A picnic in October*. New York: Harcourt.
An Italian American family takes a ferry for a celebratory picnic on Liberty Island, from which they can see the Statue of Liberty.

Cheng, Andrea. (2000). *Grandfather counts*. New York: Lee and Low Books.
Helen is unable to communicate with her Chinese immigrant grandfather Gong Gong, but through teaching each other how to count train cars in their respective languages, they develop an intergenerational bond.

Chiemruom, Sothea. (1994). *Dara's Cambodian New Year*. New York: Aladdin.
A young Cambodian boy helps his grandfather, who misses his home country.

Choi, Sook-Nyul. (1993). *Halmoni and the picnic*. Boston: Houghton Mifflin.
This book tells the story of Yunmi, a young Korean American girl living in New York and her Korean immigrant grandmother, Halmoni.

Choi, Sook-Nyul. (1997). *Yunmi and Halmoni's trip*. Boston: Houghton Mifflin.
Yunmi accompanies her grandmother, Halmoni, to Korea, where Halmoni was born. Yunmi enjoys her visit, but is concerned that her grandmother will stay in Korea.

---

[3] We appreciate the assistance of Jill Berg, Jen Myers, Rachel Rothman, and Kelly Shulman, who put together bibliographies with Katharine. Some of their entries are included here.

Choi, Yangsook. (2001). *The name jar*. New York: Dell Dragonfly Books.
This story shows the struggles Unhei faces after she moves from Korea to the U.S.

Cisneros, Sandra. (1984, 1994). *Hairs/Pelitos*. New York: Dragonfly Books.
Originally appearing in *The House on Mango Street, Hairs/Pelitos*, a child describes the different kinds of hair people in her family have and how the smell of her mother's hair makes her feel safe.

Climo, Shirley. (1993). *The Egyptian Cinderella*. New York: Scholastic.
This is the retelling of an Egyptian version of Cinderella.

Crews, Donald. (1992). *Shortcut*. New York: Greenwillow Books.
Some children decide to take a shortcut on their way home. The shortcut follows a railroad track, and they almost get hit by a train.

Dooley, Norah. (1995). *Everybody cooks rice*. Boston: Houghton Mifflin.
Carrie goes in search of her little brother at dinnertime. She's invited to share some of the meal in each neighbor's house, where rice is being cooked differently, according to the culture of the family.

Dooley, Norah. (2000). *Everybody serves soup*. Minneapolis: Carolrhoda Books.
Carrie earns money to buy her mother a Christmas present by shoveling snow. She eats with neighborhood families. Each family is eating a soup that is special to their culture.

English, Karen. (1999). *Nadia's hands*. Honesdale, PA: Boyds Mills Press.
A Pakistani American girl is nervous about being asked to be in her aunt's traditional Pakistani wedding.

Friedman, Ina R. (1984). *How my parents learned to eat*. Boston: Houghton Mifflin.
A child narrates how her Japanese mother and American father learned how to eat using unfamiliar utensils, thereby fitting into each other's cultures.

Garland, Sherry. (1998). *My father's boat*. New York: Scholastic.
A Vietnamese refugee fisherman living in Texas longs for his home.

Gibson, Toyomi. (1996). *The two Mrs. Gibsons*. San Francisco: Children's Book Press.
A young girl describes her experiences with her African American grandmother and Japanese mother.

Heide, Florence Parry, & Gilliland, Judith Heide. (1992). *Sami and the time of the troubles*. New York: Clarion.
The author writes about a young boy in war-torn Lebanon.

Hess, Amy. (1997). *When Jessie came across the sea*. Cambridge, MA: Candlewick Press.
A 13-year-old Jewish girl lives in Europe with her grandmother. She arrives alone in New York City, where she sews lace and saves enough money to bring her grandmother to the United States.

Jiménez, Francisco. (1998). *La mariposa*. Boston: Houghton Mifflin.
A migrant boy attends school for the first time. Despite the fact that he speaks only Spanish, he adjusts well.

Keats, Ezra J. (1962). *The snowy day*. New York: Puffin Books.
A little boy spends a day playing in the snow.

Krishnaswami, Uma. (2003). *Chachaji's cup*. San Francisco: Children's Book Press.
A special cup brought from India is a prominent symbol in this story of intergenerational love. The cup helps a young boy learn about his family history and the history of India.

Krishnaswami, Uma. (2006). *The closet ghosts*. San Francisco: Children's Book Press.
The story of a little girl's experience moving into a new house that is haunted with ghosts. Hanuman (an Indian god) helps her get rid of the ghosts.

Kurtz, Jane, & Kurtz, Christopher. (1997). *Only a pigeon*. New York: Simon & Schuster.
Ondu-ahlem, a young boy who lives in Addis Ababa, Ethiopia, raises pigeons.

Kyunchukov, Hristo. (2004). *My name was Hussein*. Honesdale, PA: Boyds Mills Press.
The story of a young Roma boy living in Bulgaria.

Lee, Milly. (1997). *Nim and the war effort*. New York: Farrar, Straus & Giroux.
During World War II, a young Chinese American girl is determined to win a newspaper-collecting competition for the "war effort" in order to prove she's American.

McKay, Jr., Lawrence. (1998). *Journey home*. New York: Lee and Low Books.
Mai is of Anglo Vietnamese heritage, and she accompanies her mother to Vietnam to find her mother's birth family.

Miller, Elizabeth I. (1999). *Just like home: Como en mi tierra*. New York: Albert Whitman & Co.
This book tells about a young girl's first impressions of the United States. Written in Spanish and English, the text uses a repetitive pattern of alternating observations ("Just like home" and "Not like home").

Mora, Pat. (1999). *The rainbow tulip*. New York: Puffin Books.
A Mexican American first grader describes her experiences and expresses her feelings about speaking Spanish and having a home life that is very different from her school life.

Pak, Soyung, & Hartung, Susan Kathleen. (1999). *Dear Juno*. New York: Viking.
A boy corresponds with his grandmother in Korea, even though they don't share a common language. They learn about each other through drawings, photos, and other artifacts.

Polacco, Patricia. (1988). *The keeping quilt*. New York: Simon & Schuster.
Over several generations, a quilt plays a special role in the life of a Jewish immigrant family. This story is based on the author's life.

Rattigan, Jama Kim. (1993). *Dumpling soup*. New York: Little, Brown Young Readers.
This picture book is set in Hawaii on New Year's Eve and is told from the perspective of Marisa, a 7-year-old girl in a multiracial family.

Recorvits, Helen. (2003). *My name is Yoon*. New York: Farrar, Straus & Giroux.
An immigrant child from Korean prefers her name when it is written in Korean.

Ringgold, Faith. (1991). *Tar beach*. New York: Crown Publishers.
A young girl dreams of flying above her Harlem home, claiming all she sees for
herself and her family. Based on the author's quilt painting of the same name.

Rodríguez, Luis. (1998). *América is her name*. Willimantic, CT: Curbstone Press.
América, a young immigrant from Oaxaca, Mexico, lives with her family in Chicago.
She feels out of place and is referred to as an illegal immigrant, even by her teacher.
Poetry is her salvation. (Also available in Spanish.)

Say, Allen. (1999). *Tea with milk*. Boston: Houghton Mifflin.
May's parents return to Japan after living in the United States, where they always felt
like foreigners. In Japan, it is May who feels like a foreigner.

Schanzer, Rosalyn. (2000). *Escaping to America: A true story*. New York: HarperCollins.
In the early twentieth century, a family of Polish Jews comes to a new country.

Shea, Pegi Deitz. (1995). *The whispering cloth*. Honesdale, PA: Boyds Mills Press.
A Hmong child is living in a refugee camp.

Soto, Gary. (1993). *Too many tamales*. New York: G. P. Putnam's Sons.
A little girl loses her mom's wedding ring while making tamales on Christmas Day.
She asks her cousins to help her search for the missing ring.

Soto, Gary. (1997). *Snapshots from the wedding*. New York: Penguin Group.
The flower girl in a Mexican American wedding describes the day's events.

Steptoe, John. (1993). *Mufaro's beautiful daughters*. New York: Scholastic.
This Cinderella story is set in Africa.

Surat, Michele Maria. (1989). *Angel child, dragon child*. New York: Scholastic.
Vietnamese immigrants encounter racism as they adjust to life in the United States.

Suyenaga, Ruth. (1992). *Korean Children's Day*. Cleveland, OH: Modern Curriculum Press.
Young Soo Newton, the adopted son of a European American family, introduces his
friend to Korean culture through a local Korean Children's Day celebration.

Trân Khánh Tuyêt. (1986). *The little weaver of Thai-Yen village* (rev. ed.). San Francisco:
Children's Book Press.
A young Vietnamese girl is injured in a bombing raid and comes to America for
treatment of her injuries.

Wells, Rosemary. (2001). *Yoko's paper cranes*. New York: Hyperion Books for Children.
Yoko lives in the United States, far away from her grandmother in Japan. For her
grandmother's birthday, Yoko makes a gift of origami cranes and sends them to Japan.

Wong, Janet S. (2000). *The trip back home*. New York: Harcourt Children's Books.
A young girl and her mother visit their land of birth.

Woodruff, Elvira. (1999). *The memory coat*. New York: Scholastic.
After a pogrom, two cousins leave their Russian shtetl with their families. They
travel to the United States, where they have to pass through the inspection station
at Ellis Island.

Yin. (2001). *Coolies*. New York: Philomel.
   Chinese immigrants help build the transcontinental railroad across the western
   United States.

Yolen, Jane. (1987). *Owl moon*. New York: Scholastic.
   A boy and his father go out late at night to search for owls.

Yolen, Jane. (1997). *Miz Berlin walks*. New York: Puffin Books.
   A little girl gets to know her neighbor, Miz Berlin, through their daily walks.

Nonfiction

Ancona, George. (1998). *Barrio: José's neighborhood/El barrio de José*. New York: Harcourt.
   Ancona uses colored photos and text to describe the life, experiences, culture, and
   neighborhood of an 8-year-old Latino boy, José Luis, who lives in the Mission District
   of San Francisco.

Badt, Karin Luisa. (1994). *On your feet!* New York: Children's Press.
   All kinds of foot coverings, from across the ages and around the world, are shown in
   photographs, accompanied by text.

Beeler, Selby B. (1998). *Throw your tooth on the roof: Tooth traditions from around the world*.
   Boston: Houghton Mifflin.
   Short accounts of what happens to children's teeth after they have fallen out. Written
   from the perspective of children from all over the world.

Bode, Janet. (1991). *New kids in town: Oral histories of immigrant teens*. New York: Scholastic.
   Teens share their stories of emigrating to the United States and settling into
   communities.

Bridges, Shirin Yim. (2002). *Ruby's wish*. New York: Scholastic.
   The story of the author's grandmother, who became one of the first female students to
   attend university in China.

Brittan, Dolly. (1998). *The Hmong*. New York: PowerKids Press.
   This is one of several books in the series Celebrating the People and Civilizations of
   Southeast Asia.

Cech, John. (1991). *My grandmother's journey*. New York: Simon & Schuster.
   Cech relates the life experiences of a young woman who eventually succeeds in
   emigrating from Russia to the United States with her husband and baby in the
   aftermath of World War II.

Cha, Dia. (1996). *Dia's story cloth*. New York: Lee and Low Books.
   This book tells the history of the Hmong, an ethnic group from the mountains of
   Laos. It is illustrated with traditional story cloths.

Dorros, Arthur. (1998). *This is my house*. New York: Scholastic.
   Drawings of houses from around the world accompany short texts in English and the
   official language of the country.

Fanelli, Sara. (1995). *My map book*. New York: HarperCollins.
This is a collection of labeled, hand-drawn maps of real and imagined places, such as the young author's family, day, tummy, playground, bedroom, colors, and school.

Freedman, Russell. (1980). *Immigrant kids*. New York: Dutton Juvenile.
This picture book with photos explores the lives of young immigrants living in urban areas in the late 1800s and early 1900s.

Garza, Carmen Lomas. (2000). *In my family/En mi familia*. San Francisco: Children's Book Press.
A bilingual text and illustrations provide insights into the author's childhood in a Mexican American community in Texas.

Garza, Carmen Lomas. (2005). *Family pictures/Cuadros de familia*. San Francisco: Children's Book Press.
Detailed pictures of scenes from the author's life growing up in a Mexican American community in Texas illustrate the bilingual text.

Gordon, Ginger. (1993). *My two worlds*. New York: Clarion.
Color photographs and text show how 8-year-old Kirsy Rodriguez prepares for and goes on a visit with her big sister to their home town in the Dominican Republic.

Hoobler, Dorothy, & Hoobler, Thomas (1994a). *The Chinese American family album*. New York: Oxford University Press.
Text and black-and-white photos tell the stories of Chinese immigrants to the United States through the 1980s.

Hoobler, Dorothy, & Hoobler, Thomas (1994b). *The Mexican American family album*. New York: Oxford University Press.
Text and black-and-white photos tell the stories of Mexican Americans, from the annexation of Mexican land at the end of the U.S.-Mexican War, in 1848, to movement across the border in search of work through the 1990s.

Hoobler, Dorothy, & Hoobler, Thomas (1995). *The African American family album*. New York: Oxford University Press.
Text and black-and-white photos tell the stories of African Americans, from 1526, when the first Africans arrived as slaves, through the 1990s.

Jackson, Ellen. (1994). *The winter solstice*. Brookfield, CT: Millbrook Press.
Jackson writes about the shortest day of the year, its scientific explanation, and how people around the world have responded to it over time.

Katsuyo, Howard (Ed.). (1990). *Passages: An anthology of the Southeast Asian refugee experience*. San Mateo, CA: AACP Inc.
First-person accounts are divided into three sections: "Children, we must leave!" "Living in two worlds," and "Moving on."

Knight, Margy Burns. (1993). *Who belongs here? An American story*. Gardiner, ME: Tilbury House Publishers.
This is the story of Nary, a young refugee boy from Cambodia, who comes to the United States.

Teaching English Language Learners: Strategies That Work, K–5

Krull, Kathleen. (2003). *Harvesting hope: The story of César Chávez*. New York: Scholastic.
The biography of César Chávez, a Hispanic American who founded the National
Farm Workers Association.

Kubler, Annie, & Formby, Caroline (Illus.). (1995). *Come home with us!* Wiltshire,
England: Child's Play.
An Oxfam book with flaps illustrates how homes around the world vary according to
the climate and other contextual factors.

Kuklin, Susan. (1992). *How my family lives in America*. New York: Simon & Schuster.
Photo essays show three children with a parent who comes from another country.
(Note: The author refers to the parent from Puerto Rico as an immigrant to the
United States; however, the island is a commonwealth of the United States.)

Levine, Ellen. (1994). *If your name was changed at Ellis Island*. New York: Scholastic.
A question-and-answer format is used to describe the experiences of immigrants who
passed through Ellis Island between 1892 and 1914.

McKissack, Patricia C., & McKissack, Frederick L. (1994). *Christmas in the big house,
Christmas in the Quarters*. New York: Scholastic.
Set in 1859 on a plantation in Virginia, this story tells how Christmas was celebrated
in the slave quarters and the slave owner's house just prior to the Civil War.

McMahon, Patricia, & McCarthy, Conor Clarke. (2005). *Just add one Chinese sister:
An adoption story*. Honesdale, PA: Boyds Mills Press.
The story of a little girl's adoption from China is told from the adoptive mother's
point of view and from her new little brother's viewpoint.

Mochizuki, Ken. (1997). *Passage to freedom: The Sugihara story*. New York: Lee and
Low Books.
Hiroki Sugihara tells the story of how his father, Chiune Sugihara, a Japanese
diplomat in Lithuania in 1940, helped save the lives of thousands of Polish Jews
fleeing from the Holocaust.

Mora, Pat. (1997). *Tomás and the library lady/ Tomás y la señora de la biblioteca*. New York:
Knopf.
Books allowed Tomás Rivera, a young migrant farmworker, to discover new worlds.
Rivera later became chancellor of the University of California, Riverside.

Morris, Ann. (1989). *Bread, bread, bread*. New York: HarperCollins.
Photographs illustrate the many forms of bread and how it is enjoyed around
the world.

Morris, Ann. (1990). *Loving*. New York: HarperCollins.
Photographs illustrate some of the ways that love is expressed in many different
cultures, particularly the parent-child relationship.

Morris, Ann. (1995). *Shoes, shoes, shoes*. New York: HarperCollins.
Photos and short accompanying texts explore foot coverings.

Morris, Ann. (2002a). *Grandma Esther remembers: A Jewish-American family story.*
Brookfield, CT: Millbrook Press.
Pamela and Allison live in New York. They learn about their heritage from their
grandma, Esther, when she tells them how she escaped from Lithuania during
World War II.

Morris, Ann. (2002b). *Grandma Francisca remembers: An Hispanic-American family story.*
Brookfield, CT: Millbrook Press.
Angelica lives in San Francisco with her parents, siblings, and grandma, Francisca.
A native of New Mexico, Francisca shares some of her life experiences.

Morris, Ann. (2003). *Grandma Hekmatt remembers: An Arab-American family story.*
Brookfield, CT: Millbrook Press.
Three Arab American sisters in New Jersey learn about their cultural heritage from
their grandparents, who came from Egypt.

Murphy, Nora. (1997). *A Hmong family.* Minneapolis: Tandem Library.
Murphy provides historical and cultural information about the Hmong, an ethnic
group from Laos, and shares the experiences of a Hmong family that comes to
the U.S. (from Journey Between Two Worlds, a series that looks at the lives of
refugee families)

Paterno, Maria Elena. (1994). *A first look at Philippine trees.* Wiltshire, England: Bookmark.
This book is one in a series of books about Philippine flora and fauna.

Paterno, Maria Elena. (1999a). *A first look at Philippine birds.* Wiltshire, England: Bookmark.
This book is one in a series of books about Philippine flora and fauna.

Paterno, Maria Elena. (1999b). *A first look at Philippine fishes.* Wiltshire, England:
Bookmark.
This book is one in a series of books about Philippine flora and fauna.

Pérez, Amada Irma. (2002). *My diary from here to there/Mi diario de aquí hasta allá.*
San Francisco: Children's Book Press.
The author relates her experience in immigrating with her family to the United States
from Mexico. Writing in Spanish and English, Pérez uses a diary format.

Sandler, M. W. (1995). *Immigrants.* New York: HarperTrophy.
Photographs and short texts describe the lives and contributions of immigrants who
came to the United States from 1870–1920. It focuses on European immigrants.

Say, Allen. (1993). *Grandfather's journey.* Boston: Houghton Mifflin.
Say writes about his grandfather's life in Japan and the United States and his love for
both countries.

Sing, Rachel. (1992). *Chinese New Year's dragon.* New York: Aladdin.
A young girl describes how her family celebrates Chinese New Year.

Smith, David J. (2002). *If the world were a village: A book about the world's people.*
Tonawanda, NY: Kids Can Press.
Smith presents factual information on a range of global issues, including the
distribution of safe water, electricity, schooling, and food.

Winter, Jeanette. (2004). *Calavera abecedario: A day of the dead alphabet book*. San Diego, CA: Voyager Books.

The book is based on the life of Don Pedro Linares, an artist who became famous in Mexico for his papier-mâché art—especially his *calaveras*.

Wolf, Bernard. (2003). *Coming to America: A Muslim family's story*. New York: Lee and Low Books.

This is the story of the Mahmoud family, who left Egypt to live in New York City.

Woodson, Jacqueline. (2005). *Show way*. New York: G. P. Putnam's Sons.

The making of "show ways," or quilts that once served as secret maps for freedom-seeking slaves, is a tradition passed from mother to daughter in the author's family.

Xiong, Ia. (1996). *The gift: The Hmong New Year*. El Monte, CA: Pacific Asia Press.

This may be the first American picture book by a Hmong writer.

Poetry, Proverbs, and Diaries

Alarcón, Francisco X. (1999). *Angels ride bikes*. San Francisco: Children's Book Press.

The renowned Mexican American poet revisits and celebrates his childhood memories of Los Angeles in this collection of bilingual poems.

Gonzalez, Ralfka, & Ruiz, Ana. (1995). *My first book of proverbs/Mi primer libro de dichos*. San Francisco: Children's Book Press.

Mexican American proverbs/dichos are presented in both Spanish and English.

Grimes, Nikki. (2006). *Thanks a million*. New York: HarperCollins.

These 16 poems by Nikki Grimes vary in form.

Gunning, Monica. (2004). *America, my new home*. Honesdale, PA: Boyds Mills Press.

Gunning writes about a young Jamaican girl's immigrant experiences.

Hopkins, Lee Bennett. (1992). *Through our eyes: Poems and pictures about growing up*. New York: Little Brown and Company.

This collection of 16 poems by various poets—many from underrepresented groups—describes childhood.

Johnston, Tony. (1996). *My Mexico/México mío*. New York: Penguin Putnam Books.

A collection of poems in English and Spanish about life in Mexico.

Moss, Marissa. (2000). *Hannah's journal: The story of an immigrant girl*. San Diego: Harcourt.

A Jewish girl emigrating from Lithuania to the U.S. in the early 1900s keeps a journal.

Paschen, Elise. (Ed). (2005). *Poetry speaks to children*. Naperville, IL: Sourcebooks Inc.

This poetry anthology includes a wide range of poems, historically, poetically, and visually. There are 95 poems from 73 poets. Fifty-two of the poems are on an accompanying audio CD.

Rampersad, Arnold, & Roessel, David (Eds.) (2006). *Poetry for young people: Langston Hughes*. New York: Scholastic.

This anthology is an introduction to poetry by Langston Hughes. The 26 poems offer a glimpse into the racial and social history of American culture.

Novels and Short Stories

Bagdasarian, Adam. (2000). *The forgotten fire*. New York: Dorling Kindersley Publishing.
Written by the grandnephew of a survivor of the 1915 Armenian genocide, this book describes how over one and a half million Armenians living in Turkey lost their lives.

Crew, Linda. (1989). *Children of the river*. New York: Delacorte.
Teenager Sundara flees Cambodia with family members in 1975, endures enormous hardships on a refugee boat, and settles in Oregon. There, she encounters both prejudice and love.

Estes, Eleanor. (1944). *The hundred dresses*. New York: Harcourt.
This short novel is about a Polish American girl who is teased by other girls in her class.

Giff, Patricia Reilly. (2000). *Nory Ryan's song*. New York: Delacorte.
Set in 1845 on the west coast of Ireland, this book explains how the potato famine and British land removal led to the deaths and emigration of millions of Irish.

Hansen, Joyce. (1994). *The captive*. New York: Scholastic.
Kofi, the son of an African chief, is kidnapped twice and sold into slavery. His story is set in Africa and Boston.

Ho, Minfong. (1991). *The clay marble*. New York: Farrar, Straus & Giroux.
Twelve-year-old Dara and her family flee their home in Cambodia. The setting is a refugee camp on the Thai-Cambodian border in 1980.

Ho, Minfong. (2003). *The stone goddess*. London: Orchard Books.
In Cambodia during the Khmer Rouge era, a young girl named Nakri survives life in a forced labor camp. She finds her way to a refugee camp and then comes to the U.S.

Houston, Jeanne Wakatsuki. (2002). *Farewell to Manzanar*. Boston: Houghton Mifflin.
Houston writes about Japanese American internment during World War II.

Jiménez, Francisco. (1997). *The circuit/Cajas de cartón*. Boston: Houghton Mifflin.
This is a collection of largely autobiographical stories told by a young migrant boy.

Jiménez, Francisco. (2001). *Breaking through*. Boston: Houghton Mifflin.
In this sequel to *The Circuit*, the narrator is a teenage migrant boy who succeeds in school due to hard work and personal resilience, family love and support, and some help from others.

Lasky, Kathryn. (2003). *A journey to the new world: The diary of Remember Patience Whipple*. New York: Scholastic.
Twelve-year-old Mem and her family travel on the *Mayflower* in 1620. This book recounts their experiences during their first year in the New World.

Lawlor, Laurie. (1998). *Voyage to a free land: 1630*. New York: Aladdin.
Hannah and her family set sail from London in 1630. After a series of adventures, they finally arrive in America and settle in the Massachusetts Bay Colony (from the American Sisters series).

Lord, Betty Bao. (1984). *In the year of the boar and Jackie Robinson*. New York: Harper & Row.

A young girl is initiated into life in the United States through baseball.

Lowry, Lois. (1989). *Number the stars*. Boston: Houghton Mifflin.

During the German occupation of Denmark during World War II, Jewish people are smuggled to safety in Sweden.

Na, An. *A step from heaven*. Asheville, NC: Front Street.

First-person narration tells about the experiences of a Korean girl, Young Ju, and her immigrant family from the time she was 4 until she goes to college.

Newth, Mette. (1989). *The abduction*. New York: Farrar, Straus & Giroux.

In the 17th century, Inuit Eskimos in Greenland are enslaved and taken to Norway.

Ryan, Pam Muñoz. (2000). *Esperanza rising*. New York: Scholastic.

Esperanza and her family fall on hard times during the Great Depression. They go to California, where they are hired as farmworkers.

Shaw, Janet. (1986). *Kirsten learns a lesson*. Middleton, WI: Pleasant Company Publications.

Kirsten, an immigrant girl from Sweden, has a secret friendship with a Native American girl. The setting is the late 1880s.

Uchida, Yoshiko. (1971) *Journey to Topaz*. New York: Scribner Books.

Uchida writes about the internment of Japanese Americans during World War II.

Uchida, Yoshiko. (1978). *Journey home*. New York: Margaret K. McElderry.

At the end of World War II, interned Japanese Americans return to their homes.

Yep, Laurence. (1975). *Dragonwings*. New York: Harper & Row.

In the early 1900s, Young Moon Shadow is sent from China to join his father, Windrider. Windrider makes his living doing laundry, but dreams of flying a plane.

Yep, Laurence. (1993). *Dragon's gate*. New York: HarperCollins.

Fourteen-year-old Otter is sent to California from China in 1867. He joins his father and uncle in building a tunnel for the transcontinental railroad through the Sierra Nevada mountains.

Appendix D:

Videos for Children About Diverse Cultures

Dinner for two/Dîner intime. (1996). Montreal, Quebec, Canada: National Film Board of Canada.

One of six short animated films without words in the ShowPeace series on conflict resolution (www.onf.ca/webextension/showpeace/?lg=en), *Dinner for Two/Dîner Intime* is about mediation. In this film, disaster occurs when two lizards are caught in a sticky conflict. With help from a frog who serves as a mediator, the situation is resolved and peace comes once again to the rain forest. The other five films in the series are *When the Dust Settles* (about managing anger), *Bully Dance* (about bullying), *Elbow Room* (about conflict styles and negotiation), *Dominoes* (about diversity), and *Tête à Tête à Tête* (about tolerance).

Just a little red dot. (1996). Toronto, Ontario, Canada: Sandalwood Productions.

This 36-minute documentary is about a 10-year-old Tamil child who, as a new student in her class, unleashes great curiosity about the red dot she wears on her forehead. A discussion on respect ensues. After an incident in the playground, the class explores the term *racist* and what racism does to people. Further incidents, including bullying, lead to a conclusion that challenges the negative attitudes of some students and allows for the development of sensitivity, tolerance, and respect for all people. The filmmaker, Mitra Sen, was the teacher of this class.

The peace tree. (2005). Toronto, Ontario, Canada: Sandalwood Productions.

This film about tolerance features three young girls, two Muslim and one Christian, who want to share their special festivals, Eid and Christmas, respectively. When their parents object, the girls persuade their parents to let them participate in each other's celebrations. In the process, the girls teach their parents about the importance of tolerance and celebrating diversity. They also create a peace tree, which includes symbols reflecting a range of cultures and faiths. This film is based on the experiences of the filmmaker, Mitra Sen, when she was a teacher in Toronto and encountered some parents who wouldn't allow their children to participate in multicultural celebrations.

Appendix E:

Children's Books About Diverse Health Practices

Calderón, E., Cowan, R., Douglas, S., & Sharon, F. (2004). *Eduardo el curandero: the words of a Peruvian healer*. Berkeley, CA: North Atlantic Books.

Krishnaswami, U. (2005). *The happiest tree: A yoga story*. New York: Lee and Low Books.

Onyefulu, I. (2006). *My grandfather is a magician: Work and wisdom in an African village*. London: Frances Lincoln.

Rivera-Ashford, R. C. (2002). *My nana's remedies/Los remedios de mi nana*. Tucson, AZ: Arizona-Sonora Desert Museum Press.

Appendix F:

Booksellers and Distributors of Books About Diverse Cultures and Books Written in Languages Other Than English

AACP, Inc (Asian American Curriculum Project, Inc.)
83 W. 37th Ave., San Mateo, CA 94403
Tel: (650) 357-1088 or (800) 874-2242
Fax: (650) 357-6908
E-mail: aacp@asianamericanbooks.com
Web: www.AsianAmericanBooks.com

> This is a not-for-profit organization dedicated to educating the public about Asian American experiences, and to fostering cultural pride among Asian Americans. It sells books by and about Asian Americans, including Cambodian, Chinese, Filipino, Hawaiian, Hmong, Iu Mien, Japanese, Korean, Laotian, Samoan, South Asian, Tongan, and Vietnamese Americans.

Arkipelago
953 Mission Street, San Francisco, CA 94103
Tel: (415) 777-0108
Fax: (415) 777-0113
Web: www.arkipelagobooks.com

> Arkipelago sells Filipino books, recordings, and other heritage materials.

AWAIR (Arab World and Islamic Resources and School Services)
P.O. Box 174, Abiquiu, NM 87510
Tel/Fax: (505) 685-4533
E-mail: awair@igc.org (Audrey Shabbas) requests@awaironline.org (books and materials)
Web: www.awaironline.org

> This not-for-profit organization was founded by Audrey Shabbas. It is devoted to fostering an understanding of the Arab world and Islam. AWAIR distributes books, videos, and instructional materials for teachers and students from kindergarten to college. It also offers fully funded staff development.

Children's Book Press
1461 Ninth Avenue, San Francisco, CA 94122
Tel: (510) 655-3395
Fax: (510) 655-1978
Web: www.childrensbookpress.org

> This press publishes books written in both English and another language and audiocassettes.

Mariuccia Iaconi Book Imports

Iaconi Book Imports specialized in Spanish language literature and resource materials, and was one of the first places to go when looking for books in Spanish. Sadly, after more than 50 years in business, it closed its doors in early 2007.

Oyate

2702 Mathews Street, Berkeley, CA 94702

Tel: (510) 848-6700

Fax: (510) 848-4815

E-mail: oyate@oyate.org

Web: www.oyate.org

Oyate distributes children's, young adult, and teacher books and materials, with an emphasis on texts written and illustrated by Native people.

Shen's Books and Supplies

40951 Fremont Blvd. Fremont, CA 94538

Tel: (800) 456-6660

Fax: (510) 668-1057

Web: www.shens.com

This company distributes books in English about world cultures and languages, books in languages other than English, and books written by American authors from diverse cultural backgrounds. Asian cultures and languages are a focus of the company.

Appendix G:

Authors and Illustrators From Underrepresented Groups Who Write for Children and Young Adults: An In-Process List

(Other terms used in the professional literature include: parallel cultures, primary writers, and people of color)

Indicates that the person has written and/or illustrated picture books. May have written extended texts, also.

African/African American/Afro Caribbean Authors and Illustrators

Angelou, Maya*
Bambara, Toni Cade
Barber, Barbara
Battle-Lavert, Gwendolyn*
Berger, Terry
Berry, James
Bolden, Tonya (Ed.)
Bontemps, Arna
Boyd, Candy Dawson
Brooks, Gwendolyn*
Bryan, Ashley (Illus.) *
Bundles, A'Lelia
Burden-Patmon, Denise*
Burroughs, Margaret
Butler, Octavia
Byard, Carole (Illus.)*
Caines, Jeannette*
Charles, Oz
Childress, Alice
Christie, Gregory (Illus.)
Clifton, Lucille*
Collier, Bryan (illus)
Collier, Eugenia
Cook, Trish
Cooper, Floyd*
Crews, Donald*
Cummings, Pat (Illus.)*
Davis, Ossie
Deveaux, Alexis
Dillon, Diane (Illus.)
Dillon, Leo (Illus.)
Dingle, Derek T.
Douglass, Frederick

Ellis, Veronica Freeman*
Evans, Mari
Feelings, Muriel*
Feelings, Tom (Illus.)*
Fields, Julia
Flournoy, Valerie*
Gibson, Toyomi*
Gilchrist, Jan Spivey*
Giovanni, Nikki*
Graham, Lorenz
Graham, Shirley
Greene, Bette
Greenfield, Eloise*
Grimes, Nikki*
Guy, Rosa
Haley, Alex
Hamilton, Virginia*
Hamlin, Willie T.
Hansen, Joyce
Haskins, Francine*
Haskins, James
Havill, Juanita*
Holbert, Raymond*
Howard, Elizabeth Fitzgerald*
Hudson, Wade
Hughes, Langston*
Humphrey, Margo
Hunter, Kristen
Jackson, Jesse
Johnson, Angela *
Johnson, Dolores*
Johnson, James Weldon
Jonas, Ann
Jones, Angela
Lawrence, Jacob (Illus.)

Lester, Julius
Marshall, Paule
Mathis, Sharon Bell*
McKissick, Patricia*
McKissick, Frederick*
Medearis, Angela Shelf
Mendez, Phil*
Miranda, Robin*
Monceaux, Morgan
Moore, Emily
Morninghouse, Sundaira
Musgrove, Margaret*
Myers, Christopher
Myers, Walter Dean
Newton, Deborah M.
Patrick, Denise
Patterson, Lillie
Pinkney, Andrea*
Pinkney, Brian (Illus.)*
Pinkney, Jerry (Illus.)*
Price, Leontyne*
Ransome, James (Illus.)
Reynolds, Barbara
Ringgold, Faith*
Robinson, Adjai*
Safari, Mcheshi Aenda
St. James, Synthia*
Steptoe, John (Illus.)*
Strickland, Claudia
Tate, Eleanora*
Taylor, Mildred
Thomas, Ianthe
Thomas, Joyce Carol
Walker, Alice*
Walter, Mildred Pitts
Wilkinson, Brenda
Williams-Garcia, Rita
Wilson, Johnniece Marshall
Woodson, Jacqueline
Yarborough, Camille*

Cambodian/Cambodian American Authors and Illustrators
Chia, Dia
Chiemroum, Sothea*
Lee, Huy Voun*
Mam, Teeda Butt
Wall, Lina Mao*

Chinese/Chinese American Authors and Illustrators
Ai-Ling, Louie
Carling, Amelia Lau
Chan, Harvey
Chan, Jennifer*
Chang, Monica
Chin, Charlie*
Chin, Frank
Chin-Lee, Cynthia*
Chong Lau, Allen
Ho, Minfong*
Hom, Nancy (Illus.)
Hong, Lily Toy*
Hou-Tien, Cheng*
Hsu-Flanders, Lillian (Illus.)
Huang, Chen Zhi
Krach, Maywan Shen
Lee, Dom
Lee, Gus
Lee, Keunhee
Lee, Milly*
Lee, Wendy*
Liu, Saho Wei
Lord, Betty Bao
Louie, Ai-Ling*
Mah, Adeline Yen
McCunn Lum, Ruthanne
Namioka, Lensey
Sing, Rachel*
Tan, Amy*
Wang, Rosalind
Wong, Jade Snow
Wong, Janet
Wong, Shawn
Wu, Di
Yang, Belle
Yee, Paul
Yen, Clara*
Yep, Lawrence*
Young, Ed*

Filipino/Filipino American Authors and Illustrators
Angel, Carl (Illus.)
Aruego, Ariane*
Aruego, Jose*
Ligasan, Darryl (Illus.)
Robles, Anthony D.

Urge, José and Ariane
Villanueva, Marie*

Indian/Indian American Authors and Illustrators (from the Indian subcontinent)

Bhaha, Shiraaz (Illus.)
Gavin, Jamila
Gilmore, Rachna
Goden, Ruma
Hidier, Taniya Desai
Khan, Rukhsana
Krishnaswami, Uma*
Sitaraman, Soumya
Sreenivasan, Jyotsna

Japanese/Japanese American/Japanese Canadian Authors and Illustrators

Akaba, Suekichi*
Anno, Mitsumasa*
Aliki*
Arai, Tomie (Illus.)
Finch, Linda (Illus.)
Gibson, Toyomi*
Hamanaka, Sheila*
Hayashi, Akiko (Illus.)
Hidaka, Masako*
Hoshino, Felicia (Illus.)
Ichikawa, Satomi*
Igus, Toyomi
Ikeda, Daisaku
Iko, Momoko
Isami, Ikuyo*
Ishii, Takayuki
Ito, Yoriko (Illus.)
Iwamura, Kazuo*
Iwasaki, Chihiro*
Kanome, Kayoko*
Kasja, Tejma*
Kawaguchi, Sanae*
Kikuchi, Isao*
Kimura, Yasuko*
Kishida, Eriko
Kitamura, Satoshi*
Kobayashi, Yugi*
Kobeyashi, Robert*
Koide, Tan*
Komaiko, Leah*

Lee–Tai, Amy*
Maruki, Toshi
Matsuno, Masaka*
Matsutani, Miyoko
Miyazawa, Kenji
Mizumura, Kazue*
Mochizuki, Ken
Mori, Kyoko
Mori, Toshio
Morimoto, Junko*
Murayama, Milton
Nakatani, Chiyoke*
Namachi, Saburo*
Otani, June
Sakai, Kimiko*
Sakuri, Rhoda*
Say, Allen*
Shikegawa, Marlene*
Soya, Kiyosha*
Takashima, Shizuye*
Takeshita, Fumiko*
Tamanaka, Lois-Ann
Tejima, Keraburo
Tomioka, Chiyoko
Tsuchida, Yoshiharu
Tsuchiya, Yukio*
Tsutsui, Yoriko
Uchida, Yoshiko*
Watanabe, Chigo*
Watkins, Jeanne Wakatsuki
Watkins, Yoko
Yagawa, Sumiko*
Yamada, Takahiro*
Yamaguchi, Tohr*
Yashima, Mitsu
Yashima, Taro*
Yoshi*

Korean/Korean American Authors and Illustrators

An Na
Choi, Sook Nyul
Choi, Yangsook *
Lee, Marie G.
Kim, Young Sook
Paek, Min*
Pak, Soyung*
Park, Frances*
Park, Ginger*

Park, Linda Sue
Rattigan, Jama Kim
Shin, Sun Yung
Wong, Janet

Latino/Chicano/Mexican/Mexican American/Puerto Rican/Central American Authors and Illustrators

Acuna, Rudy
Ada, Alma Flor*
Alarcón, Francisco X.
Algeria, Ricardo
Alvarez, Cecilia Concepción (Illus.)
Alvarez, Julia
Anaya, Rudolfo*
Ancona, George
Anzaldúa, Gloria*
Argueta, Jorge
Argueta, Manlio*
Bernardo, Anilú
Bernier-Grand, Carmen
Bertrand, Diane González
Blanco, Alberto*
Brusca, María Cristina*
Campoy, Isabel
Canales, Viola
Castañeda, Omar
Castillo, Ana
Castro, Elena*
Cedeño, Maria E.
Chagoya, Enrique (Illus.)
Chow, Octavio*
Cisneros, Sandra*
Coffer, Judith Ortiz
Colón, Raul (Illus.)
Colorado, Antonio
Corpi, Lucha
Cruz, Manuel
Cuevas, Ernesto, Jr. (Illus.)
Cumpiano, Ina
Deedy, Carmen Agra
De Garza, Patricia
Delacre, Lulu*
De Lucio-Brock, Anita (Illus.)
Díaz, Jorge*
Dole, Mayra L.*
Felipe, Juan*
Flores, Barbara*
Flores, Enrique (Illus.)

Galvez, Daniel (Illus.)
Garay, Luis
García, María*
García, Richard*
Garza, Carmen Lomas*
Gomez, Cruz*
Gómez, Elizabeth (Illus.)
González, Lucía
González, Maya Christina (Illus.)
González, Ralfka
González, Rigoberto*
Griego, Margaret
Hermanes, Ralph
Hernandez, Eddie*
Hernández, Irene Beltrán
Herrera, Juan Felipe
Ibarra, Rosa (Illus.)
Jaramillo, Nellie Palacio
Jiménez, Francisco*
Lasanta, Miriam
Lopez, Loretta
López de Mariscal, Blanca
Maestro, Jorge
Martel, Cruz
Martin, Patricia Preciado
Martinez, Ed* (Illus.)
Martinez, Victor
Mendez, Consuelo*
Mendoza, George
Mohr, Nicholasa
Montoya, Malanquias (Illus.)
Mora, Pat*
Morales, Rodolfo
Olivera, Fernando (Illus.)
Ordóñez, María Antonia (Illus.)
Orozco, José-Luis*
Ortiz Cofer, Judith
Peña, Sylvia Cavazos
Perez, Gloria Osuna (Illus.)
Perez, Irma Amada
Perez, Lucia Angela (Illus.)
Pico, Fernando
Ramírez, José (Illus.)
Ramirez, Mary* (Illus.)
Ramirez, Michael*
Rifo, María (She was secretary to César Chávez.)
Rodriguez, Luis
Rosa-Casanova, Sylvia

Rosairo, Idalia
Ruiz, Ana
Ryan, Pam Muñoz
Sáenz, Benjamin Alire
Sánchez, Enrique O.
Sandoval, Ruben
Santiago, Danny
Solá, Michele
Soto, Gary*
Tapia, Honorio Robledo (Illus.)
Tonel (a.k.a. Antonio Eligio
    Fernandez) (Illus.)
Torres, Leyla
Vargas, Cirilo Toro
Zubizarreta, Rosalma*

Laotian/Laotian American Authors and Illustrators
Xiong, Blia*

Middle Eastern (including Arab, Arab American, Iranian) Authors and Illustrators
Barakat, Ibtisam
Ghazi, Suhaib Hamid
Nye, Naomi Shihab*
Rayyan, Omar (Illus.)

Native American/Canadian Authors and Illustrators
Ata, Te*
Bagay
Black Elk
Blue Eagle, Agee
Bluenose, Philip
Brown, Dee
Bruchac, Joseph*
Campbell, Maria
Deloria, Vine
Dorris, Michael
Ekoomiak, Normee*
Erdrich, Louise*
Harper, Maddie*
Highwater, Jamake
Hungry Wolf, Beverly
Kakkak, Dale (Illus.)
King, Edna and Jordan Wheeler
King, Sandra*
Kusugak, Michael Arvaarluk*

Littlechild, George*
Manintonquat
Momaday, Scott
Ortiz, Simon*
Parker, Arthur
Peters, Russell M.*
Regguinti, Gordon*
Sanderson, Esther*
Sandoz, Mari
Smith, Cynthia Leitich
Sneve, Virginia Driving Hawk*
Sterling, Shirley
Tapahonso, Luci
Taylor, Drew Hayden
Thompson, Sheila*
Tremblay, Gail
Wallis, Velma
Walters, Anna Lee
Whipple, Catherine* (Illus.)
White Deer of Autumn*
Wittstock, Laura Waterman *
Yamane, Linda*

South Sea Islanders (e.g., Hawaiian, Tongan, Samoan) Authors and Illustrators
Chock, Eric

Thai/Thai American Authors and Illustrators
Vathanaprida, Supaporn

Vietnamese/Vietnamese American Authors and Illustrators
Huynh, Quang Nhuong
Lee, Jeanne M.*
Mai, Vo-Dinh (Illus.)
Phong, Ann (Illus.)
Quyen, Van Duong
Thai, Ed (Illus.)
Tran, Kim-Lan*
Tran, Truong*
Tran-Khan-Tyuet*
Vo-Dinh Mai*

Appendix H:

Cultural Differences in Student Behavior[4]

Perceived Behavior	Possible Cultural Explanation
The student avoids eye contact.	Keeping eyes downcast may be a way of showing respect. In some cultures, direct eye contact with a teacher is considered disrespectful and a challenge to the teacher's authority.
The student tends to smile when disagreeing with what is being said or when being reprimanded.	A smile may be a gesture of respect that children are taught to employ to avoid giving offense in difficult situations.
The student shrinks from or responds poorly to apparently inoffensive forms of physical contact or proximity.	There may be taboos on certain types of physical contact. Buddhists, for instance, regard the head and shoulders as sacred and would consider it impolite to ruffle a child's hair or give a reassuring pat on the shoulder. There are also significant differences among cultures with respect to people's sense of what is considered an appropriate amount of personal space.
The student appears to be overtly affectionate with other students.	In many cultures it is not uncommon for friends (girls and/or boys) to link arms, hold hands or greet each other with a hug or kiss on the cheek.
The student refuses to eat with peers.	Some students may be unaccustomed to eating with anyone but members of their own family.
The student refuses to eat certain kinds of foods or doesn't eat at all at certain periods.	Many religions have food taboos and fasting periods. Young children are often exempt from fasting, but many choose to participate.
The student does not participate actively in group work or collaborate readily with peers on cooperative assignments.	Cooperative group work is never used by teachers in some cultures. Students may thus view sharing as "giving away knowledge" and may see no distinction between legitimate collaboration and cheating.
The student displays uneasiness, expresses disapproval, or even misbehaves in informal learning situations or situations involving open-ended learning processes (e.g., exploration).	Schooling in some cultures involves a strict formality. For students who are used to this, an informal classroom atmosphere may seem chaotic and undemanding, while teachers with an informal approach may seem unprofessional. Such students may also be uncomfortable with process-oriented learning activities and prefer activities that yield more tangible and evident results.

---

[4] Based on, but modified and expanded from, the ESL Learner Web site of the Ministry of Education, Government of British Columbia. Retrieved from www.bced.gov.bc.ca/esl/policy/learnclass.htm

Perceived Behavior	Possible Cultural Explanation
The student talks loudly and sometimes overlaps speech with the others in the group or class.	In some classrooms around the world, students have more freedom to speak. They're not as closely regulated. Students talk a lot more, and they talk more loudly. What is considered interruptive or rude behavior in many North American classrooms would be considered task-oriented behavior in their home country's schools.
The student refuses to participate in extracurricular or in various physical education activities (e.g., swimming, skating, track and field).	Extracurricular activities may not be considered a part of learning or may even, along with some physical education activities, be contrary to a student's religious or cultural outlook. Some students may also be required to use after-school hours to generate income.
The student seems inattentive and does not display active listening behaviors.	In some cultures, the learning process involves observing and doing or imitating rather than listening and absorbing (e.g., through note-taking).
Performance following instruction reveals that the student does not understand the instruction, even though he/she refrained from asking for help or further explanation.	In some cultures, expressing a lack of understanding or asking for help from the teacher is interpreted as a suggestion that the teacher has not been doing a good enough job of teaching and is considered impolite.
The student is unresponsive, uncooperative, or even disrespectful in dealing with teachers of the other gender.	Separate schooling for boys and girls is the norm in some cultures. Likewise, in some cultures the expectations for males and females are quite different. The idea that females and males should have the same opportunities for schooling and play comparable roles as educators will therefore run contrary to some students' cultural conditioning.
The student appears reluctant to engage in debate, speculation, argument, or other processes that involve directly challenging the views and ideas of others.	In some cultures, it is considered inappropriate to openly challenge another's point of view, especially the teacher's. In other cases, there may be a high value attached to being prepared, knowledgeable, and correct when one opens one's mouth.
The student exhibits discomfort or embarrassment at being singled out for special attention or praise.	To put oneself in the limelight for individual praise is not considered appropriate in some cultures, where the group is considered more important than the individual.
The student fails to observe the conventions of silent reading.	Some students may be culturally predisposed to see reading as essentially an oral activity and will therefore read aloud automatically. For others reading aloud is associated with memorization.
The student refuses to take off headwear.	Many religions have prescripted headwear, such as yarmulkes, turbans, and headscarves for boys or girls.

Appendix I:

Patterned Language Books to Support ELL Writers

Alexander, Sue. (1978). *Marc the magnificent*. New York: Pantheon.

Carle, Eric. (1979, 1994). *The very hungry caterpillar*. New York: Philomel Books.

Carle, Eric. (1985). *The very busy spider*. New York: Philomel.

Carle, Eric. (1987). *Have you seen my cat?* New York: Scholastic.

Carle, Eric. (1996). *The grouchy ladybug*. New York: HarperCollins.

Carle, Eric. (1997). *From head to toe*. New York: HarperCollins.

Carle, Eric. (2000). *Does a kangaroo have a mother too?* New York: HarperCollins.

Charlip, Remy. (1986). *Fortunately*. New York: Four Winds Press.

Donamska, Janina. (1996). *If all the seas were one sea*. New York: Aladdin.

Druce, Arden. (1991). *Witch, witch, come to my party*. Wiltshire, England: Child's Play.

Fox, Mem. (1987). *Hattie and the fox*. New York: Simon & Schuster.

Ginsburg, Mirra. (1987). *The chick and the duckling*. New York: Simon & Schuster.

Joslin, Sesyle. (1958, 1986). *What do you say, dear?* New York: Harper & Row.

Joslin, Sesyle. (1961, 1985). *What do you do, dear?* New York: Harper & Row.

Kalan, Robert. (1978). *Rain*. Illus. by Donald Crews. New York: Scholastic.

Kent, Jack. (1973). *The ten days of Christmas*. New York: Parents' Magazine Press.

Kraus, Robert. (1970, 1986). *Whose mouse are you?* New York: Aladdin.

Kroll, Steven. (1976). *That makes me mad*. New York: Pantheon.

Martin, Bill Jr. (1970). *A ghost story*. Holt, Rinehart, & Winston.

Mayer, Mercer. (1974). *What do you do with a kangaroo?* New York: Four Winds Press.

Raskin, Ellen. (1973). *Who, said Sue, said whoo?* New York: Atheneum.

Sendak, Maurice. (1962). *Chicken soup with rice: A book of months*. In *The Nutshell Library*. New York: Harper & Row.

Sendak, Maurice. (1962). *Pierre: A cautionary tale in five chapters and a prologue*. In *The Nutshell Library*. New York: Harper & Row.

Shaw, Charles G. (1947). *It looked like spilt milk*. New York: HarperCollins.

Shulevitz, Uri. (1974). *One Monday morning*. New York: Atheneum.

Viorst, Judith. (1972, 1987). *Alexander and the terrible, horrible, no good, very bad day*. New York: Aladdin.

Viorst, Judith. (1978, 1988). *Alexander, who used to be rich last Saturday*. New York: Aladdin.

Westcott, Nadine Bernard. (1980, 2003). *I know an old lady who swallowed a fly*. Boston: Little Brown.

Williams, Linda. (1986). *The little old lady who was not afraid of anything*. New York: HarperCollins.

Williams, Sue. (1990). *I went walking*. San Diego: Gulliver / Harcourt.

Appendix J:

Selected Wordless Picture Books

Anno, Mitsumasa, (1997). *Anno's journey*. New York: Putnam.
> A traveler begins alone, traveling across many intricately detailed scenes. This is one of several wordless books by Anno, each with intricate details that will be appreciated by older children.

Baker, Jeannie. (1993). *Window*. New York: Puffin / Penguin.
> A little boy grows up looking at the landscape outside his window as it changes from forest and animals to houses and factories. The story ends with the boy, now a man, holding up his own son to a completely difference landscape. This book can inspire discussions about the changing environment with older children.

Bang, Molly. (1980). *The grey lady and the strawberry snatcher*. New York: Aladdin / Simon & Schuster.
> This is an intriguing story about a grey lady who buys strawberries and then must elude a blue figure who tries to snatch them away. The book is mysterious, with beautiful colors and artistry. It will appeal to both young and older children.

Banyai, Istvan. (1995). *Zoom*. New York: Penguin.
> Pictures zoom in or zoom out, and sometimes what you think you are seeing is actually something else as the picture zooms out. *Zoom* can be read forward or backward with different results. Istvan has done other wordless books, including the sequel, *Re-zoom*, and *The Other Side*.

Briggs, Raymond. (2006). *The snowman*. New York: Puffin / Penguin.
> A snowman comes to life, and he and a young boy share each other's worlds until the snowman melts.

Carle, Eric. (2007). *1,2,3 to the zoo*. New York: Penguin.
> A counting book in which ten different zoo animals are introduced one by one. Carle has illustrated other wordless books, including *Do You Want to Be My Friend?*

dePaola, Tomie. (1978). *Pancakes for breakfast*. New York: HarperCollins.
> A little old lady who decides she wants pancakes for breakfast goes to a great deal of trouble to gather the ingredients.

Johnson, Crockett. (1996). *Harold and the purple crayon*. London, England: Bloomsbury.
> This classic book tells the story of a boy who creates a world with his purple crayon.

Lehman, Barbara. (2004). *The red book*. Boston: Houghton Mifflin.
> A girl in a city finds a red book about a boy on an island, who also finds a red book. This book is a story within a story within a story. Older children, as well as younger ones, will find it intriguing.

Mayer, Mercer, & Mayer, Marianne. (2003). *A boy, a dog, and a frog*. New York: Penguin
> A little boy and his dog try to catch an uncooperative frog. This is one of several wordless pictures books by Mayer with the same characters.

Popov, Nikolai. (1996). *Why?* New York: Michael Neugebauer / North South Books.
War escalates from a simple encounter between a frog and an umbrella-wielding mouse. This story can open up interesting discussions about the devastation of war, but should be used very carefully with refugee children who have suffered the traumas of war.

Rogers, Gregory. (2004). *The boy, the bear, the baron, the Bard.* New Milford, CT: Roaring Brook Press.
A young boy playing soccer winds up on stage in a Shakespeare play and then has adventures in England. This story can be appreciated by older children.

Rohmann, Eric. (1997). *Time flies.* New York: Dragonfly Books / Crown Publisher Inc.
A bird flies into a dinosaur museum. A dinosaur comes to life and eats the bird, but the bird escapes when the dinosaur becomes a skeleton again.

Sis, Peter. (1990). *Beach ball.* New York: Greenwillow / HarperCollins.
When the wind takes a little girl's ball, she chases it through pictures of numbers, shapes, and colors. *Beach Ball* is a good book for children learning basic vocabulary. Sis has created other wordless pictures books, including *Trucks, Trucks, Trucks* and *Dinosaur!*

Spier, Peter. (1997). *Rain.* New York: Yearling / Random House.
A brother and sister enjoy themselves in the rain. *Rain* has wonderful details.

Tafuri, Nancy. (1991). *Have you seen my duckling?* New York: HarperCollins.
A mother duck loses her eighth duckling and goes to other animals to search for it. Young children enjoy finding the missing duckling, which is hidden on each page.

Turkle, Brian. (1992). *Deep in the forest.* New York: Puffin / Penguin.
The story of Goldilocks is turned around when a bear cub enters the hunting cabin of a human family. ELL children may not be familiar with the Goldilocks story and may therefore be unable to appreciate the irony of the role reversal, so it's a good idea to read "Goldilocks and the Three Bears" first.

Ward, Lynd. (1992). *The silver pony.* Boston: Houghton Mifflin.
This book, lengthier than many picture books, has black-and-white illustrations and is appropriate for older children. The story involves a boy who travels to distant places on the back of a winged pony.

Weitzman, Jacquelan Priess. (2001). *You can't take a balloon into the Metropolitan Museum.* New York: Puffin / Penguin.
A little girl and her grandmother go to the Metropolitan Museum. The little girl's balloon, which she is not allowed to take into the museum, escapes and has several adventures around New York City while the girl and her grandmother are looking at the paintings in the museum. This story can be appreciated by older children.

Wiesner, David. (2006). *Flotsam.* Boston: Clarion / Houghton Mifflin.
When a boy finds a camera and develops the film, he discovers fantastical pictures of undersea life—and also pictures of children from all over the world holding pictures of other children. Wiesner has created other wordless pictures books, including *Tuesday* and *Sector 7.*

Appendix K:

Picture/Visual Dictionaries

Addison-Wesley picture dictionary. (1984). Upper Saddle River, NJ: Pearson.
  Available in a Spanish-English edition, in addition to a monolingual English edition.

Clark, J., & Ashworth, J. (1999). *Longman picture dictionary of American English*. Upper
  Saddle River, NJ: Pearson.

Corbeil, J. (1986). *The facts on file visual dictionary*. New York: Facts on File.

Ultimate visual dictionary of science. (1998). New York: Dorling Kindersley Publishing.

Ultimate visual dictionary. (2006). New York: Dorling Kindersley Publishing.

Goodman, M. (2003). *Let's learn English picture dictionary*. New York: McGraw-Hill.

Graham, C. (2002). *Longman children's picture dictionary*. Upper Saddle River, NJ: Pearson.
  (Includes songs and chants by Carolyn Graham.)

Iosa, A. (2003). *Word play: Spanish-Inglés*. Carlsbad, CA: Penton Overseas, Inc.

Kauffman, D., & Apple, G. (2000). *The Oxford picture dictionary for the content areas*.
  New York: Oxford University Press.

Keyes, J. R. (1998) *The Oxford picture dictionary for kids*. New York: Oxford University Press.

Merriam-Webster's visual dictionary. (2006). Springfield, MA: Merriam-Webster.

Moran, P. (2001). *Lexicarry: Pictures for learning languages* (3rd ed.). Brattleboro, VT:
  Pro Lingua Associates.

Parnwell, E. C. (1989). *The new Oxford picture dictionary*. New York: Oxford University Press.
  In addition to a monolingual English edition, it is available in bilingual editions.
  Bilingual editions include English and Cambodian, Chinese, Japanese, Korean, Navajo,
  Polish, Russian, Spanish, and Vietnamese.

Scarry, R. (1980). *Richard Scarry's best word book ever*. New York: Golden Books / Random
  House.

Schimpff, J. (1983). *Open sesame picture dictionary*. New York: Oxford University Press.
  Provides pictures and words for more than 550 high-frequency words. Can be used
  alone or with their Open Sesame children's series. Bilingual editions are available in
  English and Spanish, Chinese, Japanese, and Polish.

Shapiro, N., and Adelson-Goldstein, J. (1998). *The Oxford picture dictionary*. New York:
  Oxford University Press.
  In addition to a monolingual edition in English, bilingual editions are available in
  English and Spanish, Japanese, Thai, Brazilian Portuguese, Arabic, French, Polish,
  Korean, Russian, Chinese, Vietnamese, Haitian Creole, and Cambodian.

Zwier, L. J. (1999). *Basic English for everyday activities: A picture process dictionary*. Syracuse,
  NY: New Readers Press.

Appendix L:

Guidelines for Cloze Activities

Cloze activities can be used for reading practice and/or for assessment purposes. Follow these guidelines to prepare cloze activities.

    a. Select or write a passage that is about 250 words long.

    b. Leave the first and last sentences intact.

    c. Beginning with the second sentence, delete every fifth (or seventh or tenth) word throughout the passage. (Remember to leave the last sentence intact.)

    d. Replace the deleted words with a blank space that is about 1 to 1½ inches long. Each blank space should be the same length.

    e. If a word to be deleted is a number, skip to the next word and delete that word.

- It is possible that more than one word may go in a space, and students should be encouraged to think of alternatives, while maintaining the meaning of the passage.

- Students completing a cloze should not work under a time limit. Instead, they should be encouraged to complete it thoughtfully.

- It can be very useful for students to work together in pairs or triads. However, partnerships should be arranged carefully so all students are actively involved.

- After students have completed the cloze, it is important to go through it with them and talk about their responses.

Appendix M:

Example of a Cloze Text With Every Five Words Deleted[5]

A Visit to a Coastal Science Center

The class spent two days at a coastal science center, where students learned about marine life. When the boys and _____ returned from their field trip, _____unloaded their specimen bags. There _____ lots of shells, most _____ them very small, but _____impressively large. Some children _____ collected a variety of _____ and stones. Other children _____ quite a collection of _____, which was now dry _____no longer glistened as_____had in the water. _____ some of the shells, _____were still fragments of _____remains of shellfish.

Once _____ bags were empty, the _____ began to classify their _____. Children sorted _____ shells according to color, _____, and shape. One student _____ knew a lot about _____ sorted his shells according _____ the shellfish family to _____ the shell belonged, such _____mussels and clams. When _____ sorted their _____ of seaweed, they often _____ shape to help them _____. For example, some were _____ and wide, whereas others _____ bobbles at the end. _____who sorted stones also _____ color, size, and shape _____guide them. Some students _____ to sort their rocks _____ to the type of _____, so they borrowed a _____ from the library to _____ them. After sorting their _____, the class generated a _____ of questions about life _____ the seashore. They spent _____ next two weeks investigating _____ topic.

_____

[5] See Appendix P, p. 303, for the text without deletions.

Appendix N:

Example of a Cloze Text With Every Ten Words Deleted[6]

A Visit to a Coastal Science Center

The class spent two days at a coastal science center, where students learned about marine life. When the boys and girls returned from their field _____, they unloaded their specimen bags. There were lots of _____, most of them very small, but some impressively large. _____ children had collected a variety of pebbles and stones. _____ children had quite a collection of seaweed, which was _____ dry and no longer glistened as it had in _____ water. Inside some of the shells, there were still _____ of the remains of shellfish.

Once their bags were _____, the children began to classify their specimens. Children sorted _____ shells according to color, size, and shape. One student _____ knew a lot about shellfish sorted his shells according _____ the shellfish family to which the shell belonged, such _____ mussels and clams. When students sorted their fragments of _____, they often used shape to help them categorize. For _____, some were flat and wide, whereas others had bobbles _____ the end. Students who sorted stones also used color, _____, and shape to guide them. Some students wanted to _____ their rocks according to the type of rock, so _____ borrowed a book from the library to help them. _____ sorting their specimens, the class generated a list of _____ about life at the seashore. They spent the next _____ weeks investigating their topic.

---

[6] See Appendix P, p. 303, for the text without deletions.

Appendix O:

Example of a Selected Feature Cloze Text: Past Tense Verbs[7]

A Visit to a Coastal Science Center

The class spent two days at a coastal science center, where students learned about marine life. When the boys and girls _____ from their field trip, they _____ their specimen bags. There _____ lots of shells, most of them very small, but some impressively large. Some children _____a variety of pebbles and stones. Other children _____ quite a collection of seaweed, which _____ now dry and no longer _____ as it _____in the water. Inside some of the shells, there _____still fragments of the remains of shellfish.

Once their bags _____ empty, the children _____ to classify their specimens. Children _____ their shells according to color, size, and shape. One student who _____ a lot about shellfish _____ his shells according to the shellfish family to which the shell _____, such as mussels and clams. When students _____ their fragments of seaweed, they often _____ shape to help them categorize. For example, some _____ flat and wide, whereas others _____ bobbles at the end. Students who _____ stones also _____ color, size, and shape to guide them. Some students _____ to sort their rocks according to the type of rock, so they _____ a book from the library to help them. After sorting their specimens, the class _____ a list of questions about life at the seashore. They _____ the next two weeks investigating their topic.

_____

7 See Appendix P, p. 303, for the text without deletions.

The Cloze Text Without Deletions

A Visit to a Coastal Science Center

The class spent two days at a coastal science center, where students learned about marine life. When the boys and girls returned from their field trip, they unloaded their specimen bags. There were lots of shells, most of them very small, but some impressively large. Some children had collected a variety of pebbles and stones. Other children had quite a collection of seaweed, which was now dry and no longer glistened as it had in the water. Inside some of the shells, there were still fragments of the remains of shellfish.

Once their bags were empty, the children began to classify their specimens. Children sorted their shells according to color, size, and shape. One student who knew a lot about shellfish sorted his shells according to the shellfish family to which the shell belonged, such as mussels and clams. When students sorted their fragments of seaweed, they often used shape to help them categorize. For example, some were flat and wide, whereas others had bobbles at the end. Students who sorted stones also used color, size, and shape to guide them. Some students wanted to sort their rocks according to the type of rock, so they borrowed a book from the library to help them. After sorting their specimens, the class generated a list of questions about life at the seashore. They spent the next two weeks investigating their topic.

Appendix Q:

Picture Books to Help Spark Students' Memories

Altman, Linda J. (1993). *Amelia's road*. New York: Lee and Low Books.
A young Mexican American girl, the daughter of migrant farm workers, longs for a place she can call home. When she finds a special place, she is able to keep memories alive.

Choi, Yangsook. (2001). *The name jar*. New York: Dell Dragonfly Books.
This story shows the struggles Unhei faces after she moves from Korea to the U.S.

Cisneros, Sandra (1984, 1994). *Hairs/Pelitos*. New York: Dragonfly Books.
In *Hairs/Pelitos*, a child describes the different kinds of hair people have in her family and how the smell of her mother's hair makes her feel safe. This story originally appeared in *The House on Mango Street*.

Crews, Donald. (1991). *Big mama's house*. New York: Greenwillow Books.
This story focuses on a family and the adventures they have while spending the summer with the grandparents.

Crews, Donald. (1992). *Shortcut*. New York: Greenwillow Books.
A group of children takes a shortcut home and faces danger when they find themselves on the railroad tracks.

DePaola, Tomie. (1973). *Nana upstairs, Nana downstairs*. New York: Putnam.
This poignant story tells about three generations of the same family who live together.

DePaola, Tomie. (1981). *One foot, now the other*. New York: Putnam.
DePaola writes about the special relationship between a young boy and his grandfather.

English, Karen. (1999). *Nadia's hands*. Honesdale, PA: Boyds Mills Press.
A Pakistani American girl is nervous about being asked to be in her aunt's traditional Pakistani wedding.

Fanelli, Sara. (1995). *My map book*. New York: HarperCollins.
Written by a young girl, this is a collection of labeled, hand-drawn maps of real and imagined places, such as the young author's home, playground, bedroom, and school.

Gibson, Toyomi (1996). *The two Mrs. Gibsons*. San Francisco: Children's Book Press.
A young girl describes her experiences with her African American grandmother and Japanese mother.

Hoffman, Mary. (1991). *Amazing Grace*. New York: Dial Books.
Grace wants to play Peter Pan in the school play, but her classmates think she cannot because she is African American and a girl.

Keats, Ezra Jack. (1962). *The snowy day*. New York: Puffin Books.
A young boy has adventures in the snow.

Keats, Ezra Jack. (1964). *Whistle for Willie*. New York: Puffin Books.
A young boy learns to whistle, but not without a great deal of hard work and some funny adventures along the way.

Krishnaswami, Uma. (2003). *Chachaji's cup*. San Francisco: Children's Book Press.
In this story of intergenerational love, a special cup brought from India features symbolically. The cup helps a young boy learn about his family history and the history of India.

Kurtz, Jane, & Kurtz, Christopher. (1997). *Only a pigeon*. New York: Simon & Schuster.
A young boy, Ondu-ahlem, lives in Addis Ababa, Ethiopia, and raises pigeons.

Kyuchukov, Hristo. (2004). *My name was Hussein*. Honesdale, PA: Boyds Mills Press.
Set in Bulgaria, a Roma (Gypsy) boy, Hussein, is a Muslim and is forced to change his name after soldiers occupy his village. This story is based on the author's life.

Mora, Pat. (1997). *Tomás and the library lady/ Tomás y La Señora de la Biblioteca*.
New York: Knopf.
The young migrant farmworker boy, Tomás Rivera, later becomes chancellor of the University of California, Riverside. In his childhood, books (and a librarian) allowed him to discover new worlds.

Mora, Pat. (1999). *The rainbow tulip*. New York: Puffin Books.
A Mexican American first grader describes her experiences with and expresses her feelings about speaking Spanish and having a home life that is very different from her school life.

Perez, Amada I. (2002). *My diary from here to there/Mi diario de aquí hasta allá*.
San Francisco: Children's Book Press.
The author describes her feelings as a young girl when her family decides to leave its home in Mexico to look for work in the United States.

Pilkey, Dave. (1999). *The paperboy*. New York: Orchard Books.
A young boy describes the daily adventure of delivering newspapers.

Soto, Gary. (1993). *Too many tamales*. New York: G. P. Putnam's Sons.
A little girl loses her mom's wedding ring on Christmas Day while making tamales. She asks her cousins to eat all the tamales in the search for the missing ring.

Viorst, Judith. (1971). *The tenth good thing about Barney*. New York: Macmillan.
After his cat dies, a little boy remembers all the good things about his pet.

Winter, Jeanette. (2004). *Calavera abecedario: A Day of the Dead alphabet book*. San Diego: Voyager Books.
This ABC book is based on the life of Don Pedro Linares, an artist who became famous all over Mexico for his papier-mâché art—especially his *calaveras*. It tells about the process of making calaveras.

Winter, Jeanette. (2005). *The librarian of Basra: A true story from Iraq*. New York: Harcourt.
The actions of a chief librarian who, along with neighbors, saves the books in the Central Library in Basra, Iraq, during the 2003 invasion.

Woodson, Jacqueline. (2005). *Show way*. New York: G. P. Putnam's Sons.
The making of "show ways," or quilts, which once served as secret maps for freedom-seeking slaves, is a tradition passed from mother to daughter in the author's family.

Yolen, Jane. (1987). *Owl moon*. New York: Scholastic.
A boy and his father go out late at night to search for owls.

Yolen, Jane. (1997). *Miz Berlin walks*. New York: Puffin Books.
A little girl gets to know her neighbor, Miz Berlin, through their daily walks. On their walks, Miz Berlin tells the little girl fantastic stories from her past.

Appendix R:

What I Like to Do Throughout the Year: Two Locations

Activity   **Location**

In *January*, I like to _____ in _____ ,

but I like to _____ in _____ .

In *February*, I like to _____ in _____ ,

but I like to _____ in _____ .

In *March*, I like to _____ in _____ ,

but I like to _____ in _____ .

In *April*, I like to _____ in _____ ,

but I like to _____ in _____ .

In *May*, I like to _____ in _____ ,

but I like to _____ in _____ .

In *June*, I like to _____ in _____ ,

but I like to _____ in _____ .

In *July*, I like to _____ in _____ ,

but I like to _____ in _____ .

In *August*, I like to _____ in _____ ,

but I like to _____ in _____ .

In *September*, I like to _____ in _____ ,

but I like to _____ in _____ .

In *October*, I like to _____ in _____ ,

but I like to _____ in _____ .

In *November*, I like to _____ in _____ ,

but I like to _____ in _____ .

In *December*, I like to _____ in _____ ,

but I like to _____ in _____ .

Appendix S:

Types of Written Reflection in the Classroom

Logs/Journals:

• Subject and topic are chosen by the writer (e.g., an end-of-the-day log or a personal journal).

• Subject is selected by the teacher, but the topic is selected by the writer (e.g., a mathematics log, but writers select their topics).

• Subject and topic are selected by the teacher (e.g., a social studies log in which writers must respond to a prompt).

Dialogue Journals:

• Content may be entirely open-ended or focused on a particular subject (e.g., a reading log).

• Two or more people correspond in a journal (e.g., student and teacher, two students).

Field Notes:

• Writers report and reflect on events that they are studying (e.g., the behavior of an animal, family language patterns, the literacy development of a younger student).

• Writers keep notes similar to the notes an anthropologist might keep.

Questionnaires:

• May be completed at the beginning and end of a period of study in order to note change over time

• Are generally focused (e.g., on content and processes)

• May be followed up with a discussion/interview

Field Trip Permission Slip

We are planning a class field trip on **October 15** to the **zoo**.

We need your approval for your child to participate.

We will **go** to the zoo at **9:00 a.m.**

We will **return** to school at about **1:00 p.m.**

We will be traveling by bus.

The trip will be appropriately supervised.

Please call me if you have any questions.

I need this **form returned** to the school by **October 8**.

_____ has my permission.
      (child's name)

_____

Appendix U:

Homework Journal

Name _____   Date _____

Subject	Assignment	Parent Checked	Teacher Checked	Comments
123 Math	Exercise 5 on page 23: Dividing whole numbers	✔	☺	*All correct!*
Reading	Read for 15 minutes. Write title here: <u>The Snowy Day</u>	✔	☺	*Good book for winter!*
ABC Spelling	1. Choose 6 spelling words and draw a picture. 2. Write a sentence with the other 6 spelling words.	✔	☹	*Only wrote 4 sentences. Needs to write 2 more sentences.*
Social Studies	Complete your work sheet on different services in the community.	*She no understand*	☺	*Thank you! I explained it to her. She can show it to you.*

Fiction, Nonfiction, and Poetry Touchstone Texts[8]

Fiction:

Choi, Yangsook. (2001). *The name jar.* New York: Dell Dragonfly Books.
> This story shows the struggles Unhei faces after she moves from Korea to the U.S.
> *Craft elements*: character development; dialogue; internal monologue; movement through time; infusion of non-English words (e.g., *kimchi, chinku*); plot that uses problem-and-solution format

Cisneros, Sandra. (1984, 1994). *Hairs/Pelitos.* New York: Dragonfly Books.
> A child describes the different kinds of hair people have in her family and how the smell of her mother's hair makes her feel safe (originally appeared in *The House on Mango Street*).
> *Craft elements*: written in English and Spanish; figurative language (e.g., *my father's hair is like a broom*; *my mother's hair, like little rosettes, like little candy circles*); rhythmic language, such as sets of three (e.g., *the snoring, the rain, and Mama's hair that smells like bread*)

Crews, Donald. (1992). *Shortcut.* New York: Greenwillow Books.
> One day, some children decide to take a shortcut. The shortcut is along a train track, and they almost get hit by a train.
> *Craft Elements:* strong lead (creates suspense); strong ending (use of short sentences for impact/emphasis); varied punctuation; fonts (enlarged and capitalized for emphasis); sounds (shown by emphasizing font to illustrate the train getting closer and closer); tension; exploded moment

English, Karen. (1999). *Nadia's hands.* Honesdale, PA: Boyds Mills Press.
> A Pakistani American girl is nervous about being asked to be in her aunt's traditional Pakistani wedding.
> *Craft elements*: infusion of Urdu words in the English text; glossary with pronunciation guide for Urdu words; rhythmic language, such as sets of three (e.g., repetition of a phrase: *She sat watching the door . . . She sat watching out the window . . . Finally, she sat watching the big kitchen clock over the stove*)

Keats, Ezra Jack. (1962). *The snowy day.* New York: Puffin Books.
> A little boy spends a day playing in the snow.
> *Craft Elements:* circular story; varied punctuation (commas, colons, dashes); rhythmic language; repetition; sounds used for emphasis; powerful adjectives

Krishnaswami, Uma. (2003). *Chachaji's cup.* San Francisco: Children's Book Press.
> In this story of intergenerational love, a special cup brought from India features symbolically and helps a young boy learn about his family history and the history of India.
> *Craft elements*: rhythmic language, such as sets of three (e.g., *using sticks and stones and blocks*); evocative and precise verbs (e.g., *thundered, giggled, whispered*); infusion of some non-English words (e.g., *masala chai, beta*); circular story (begins with great uncle Chachaji making tea and ends with the mom and dad making tea)

---

8 This annotated list was developed by Katharine Davies Samway, Jill Berg, and Kelly Shulman.

Krishnaswami, Uma. (2006). *The closet ghosts.* San Francisco: Children's Book Press.
The story of a little girl's experience moving into a new house that is haunted by ghosts. Hanuman [an Indian God] helps the little girl get rid of the ghosts.
Craft Elements: illustrations that depict emotions and movement; strong lead (character, plot, and setting development); circular story; dialogue; italicized font for thoughts; different use of fonts to show songs; varied punctuation; thought bubbles

Kurtz, Jane, & Kurtz, Christopher. (1997). *Only a pigeon.* New York: Simon & Schuster.
A young boy, Ondu-ahlem, lives in Addis Ababa, Ethiopia, and raises pigeons.
Craft elements: lyrical, poetic language; powerful descriptions; respectful integration of cultural information; pictures complement and support the text very effectively; varied sentence length (e.g., *The night holds many dangers. As he turns from the coop, he stoops to look with fear at something on the ground. Footprints.*); infusion of some non-English words; glossary for pronunciation and meaning of non-English words; author's note about raising pigeons

Kyuchukov, Hristo. (2004). *My name was Hussein.* Honesdale, PA: Boyds Mills Press.
In Bulgaria, Hussein, a Roma [Gypsy] boy and a Muslim, is forced to change his name after soldiers occupy his village.
Craft elements: rhythmic language, such as sets of three and four (e.g., *They are happy when they see me. They hug me and hold me on their laps. They give me candies that smell nice like roses.);* author's note about Bulgaria since WWII

Pak, Soyung. (1999). *Dear Juno.* New York: Puffin Books.
A little boy writes to his grandmother, who lives in another country. They write to one another through pictures because he cannot read yet.
Craft elements: descriptive lead (developing the setting); authentic-sounding dialogue (e.g., *C'mon*); rhythmic language (listing in threes); descriptive language

Pilkey, D. (1999). *The paperboy.* New York: Orchard Books.
The author describes a paperboy's daily routine.
Craft Elements: circular story; strong lead (statement that includes setting and character); varied punctuation; descriptive language; rhythmic language; bumpy font for emphasis

Polacco, Patricia. (1988). *The keeping quilt.* New York: Simon & Schuster.
A family heirloom, a quilt, that was made from pieces of fabric that each told a little bit about family members, has been passed down through generations of the author's family.
Craft elements: rhythmic language, such as sets of three (e.g., *Shhhhhh . . . Shhhhhh . . . Shhhhhh; He gave Anna a gold coin, a dried flower, and a piece of rock salt, all tied in a linen handkerchief. The gold was for wealth, the flower for love, and the salt so their lives would have flavor.*); infusion of Russian and Yiddish words (e.g., *babushka, challah, huppa, kulich)*; circular text structure focusing on leaving home

Ringgold, Faith. (1991). *Tar beach.* New York: Crown Publishers.
A young girl dreams of flying above her Harlem home, claiming all she sees for herself and her family (based on the author's quilt painting of the same name).
Craft elements: strong lead; voice; historical information about labor unions and the building of the Brooklyn Bridge embedded

Soto, Gary. (1993). *Too many tamales*. New York: G. P. Putnam's Sons.
A little girl loses her mom's wedding ring on Christmas day and asks her cousins to eat all the tamales in the search for the missing ring.
Craft elements: lead that describes the setting; infusion of non-English words (e.g., *masa*); dialogue; internal dialogue; conventions (e.g., commas in a series); plot that uses cause-and-effect structure

Yolen, Jane. (1987). *Owl moon*. New York: Scholastic.
A boy and his father go out late at night to search for owls.
Craft elements: sensory language; strong lead (powerful, interesting statement); descriptive, poetic language; italicized words for sounds; repetitive sentences

Yolen, Jane. (1997). *Miz Berlin walks*. New York: Puffin Books.
A little girl gets to know her neighbor, Miz Berlin, through their daily walks. Miz Berlin tells the little girl fantastic stories from her past.
Craft elements: strong lead; sensory language; italicized font for emphasis and sounds; dialogue; punctuation; circular story

Nonfiction/Literary Nonfiction

Ajmera, Maya. (1999). *To be a kid*. Watertown, MA: Charlesbridge.
Text and photographs from countries around the world illustrate some of the activities children everywhere have in common.
Craft elements: world map, foreword, labels, repetitive language, commas in a series

Beeler, Selby B. (1998). *Throw your tooth on the roof: Tooth traditions from around the world*. Boston: Houghton Mifflin Company.
Brief statements relate what children from around the world do with a tooth that has fallen out. Includes facts about teeth.
Craft elements: varied punctuation; voice; world map; subtitles; author's note

Bridges, Shirin Yim. (2002). *Ruby's wish*. New York: Scholastic
The story tells about the author's grandmother, who became one of the first female students to attend university in China.
Craft elements: descriptive lead; strong setting; vivid language; varied punctuation; groups of three; dialogue

Cameron, Eileen. (2002). *Canyon*. New York: Mikaya Press.
The author describes the making of a canyon over millions of years.
Craft elements: poetic language (e.g., *cascades through the rocks, slide into creeks that tumble downhill*); vivid photographs that complement the text; laid out as a slanting, non-rhyming poem

Fanelli, Sara. (1995). *My map book*. New York: HarperCollins.
This collection of labeled, hand-drawn maps shows real and imagined places, such as the young author's family, day, tummy, playground, bedroom, colors, school.
Craft elements: child's humorous voice; wide spectrum of map possibilities; intersection of drawings and labels; handwritten text

Krull, Kathleen. (1996). *Wilma unlimited: How Wilma Rudolph became the world's fastest woman*. San Diego: Voyager Books.
This biography explores how Wilma Rudolph overcame polio as a child to become the first woman to win three gold medals in track in a single Olympics.
Craft elements: strong lead; varied punctuation; descriptive language; voice; author's note; illustrations that combine photographs, watercolors, and acrylics

Krull, Kathleen. (2003). *Harvesting hope: The story of César Chávez*. New York: Scholastic.
This biography of César Chávez, a Hispanic American, includes his founding of the National Farm Workers Association.
Craft elements: vivid language; setting; Spanish words embedded in text; varied punctuation; author's note

Mora, Pat. (1997). *Tomás and the library lady/Tomás y la señora de la biblioteca*. New York: Knopf.
Tomás Rivera, a young migrant farmworker boy, later becomes chancellor of the University of California, Riverside.
Craft elements: descriptive lead (*It was midnight. The light of the full moon followed the tired old car.*); repetition (e.g., *Tomás was tired too. Hot and tired.*); sound words (e.g., *The wind was howling, whoooooooooo, and the leaves were blowing, whish, whish . . .*); figurative language (e.g., *Its tall windows were like eyes glaring at him*); infusion of Spanish words and phrases; circular story; engaging closure (*Tomás closed his eyes. He saw the dinosaurs drinking cool water long ago. He heard the cry of the wild snakebird. He felt the warm neck of the dinosaur as he held on tight for a bumpy ride.*)

Pérez, Amada I. (2002). *My diary from here to there/Mi diario de aquí hasta allá*. San Francisco: Children's Book Press.
The author describes her feelings as a young girl when her family decides to leave their home in Mexico to look for work in the United States.
Craft elements: diary format; English and Spanish; descriptive language; author's note; varied punctuation

Schaefer, Lola M. (2001). *This is the rain*. New York: Greenwillow Books.
Craft elements: cumulative text (e.g., *This is the ocean, blue and vast, that holds the rainwater from the past. This is the sunshine, hot and bright, that warms the ocean, blue and vast, that holds the rainwater from the past.*); poetic language; use of colored print to help in conveying meaning; use of rhyme; rich language; afterword (about the water cycle)

Swinburne, Stephen R. (2005). *Turtle tide: The ways of sea turtles*. Honesdale, PA: Boyds Mills Press.
This story follows a mother sea turtle and her offspring, from prenatal to life to early death.
Craft elements: an informational book written like a story; afterword, About Sea Turtles, and Suggested Reading provide background information; rich, poetic language (e.g., *pulled by a rich longing to come ashore*; *a giant yellow moon sleeping on the sea*); watercolor illustrations complement the text

Winter, Jeanette. (2004). *Calavera abecedario: A Day of the Dead alphabet book*. San Diego, CA: Voyager Books.
This ABC book is based on the life of Don Pedro Linares, an artist who became famous all over Mexico for his papier-mâché art—especially his *calaveras*.
Craft elements: strong lead; infusion of Spanish words; varied text placement on the page; groups of three; glossary of Spanish words; author's note

Winter, Jonah. (2002). *Frida*. New York: Scholastic.
This biography features the Mexican artist Frida Kahlo.
Craft elements: written poetically; strong lead; short sentences; Spanish words embedded in text; author's note and artist's note

Woodson, Jacqueline. (2005). *Show way.* New York: G. P. Putnam's Sons.
"Show ways" are quilts that once served as secret maps for freedom-seeking slaves. Woodson explores the making of these quilts.
Craft elements: repetitive language; varied sentence length; various uses of fonts; powerful ending; circular storyline; historical events from African American history embedded

Poetry

Ada, Alma Flor, & Campoy, F. Isabel. (2000). *Laughing crocodiles.* Miami: Santillana.
This book includes poems written by Hispanics and poems about Hispanics; it also includes short descriptions of the authors' lives.
Craft elements: repetitive language; personification; rhyme; infusion of non-English words; voice; free verse; onomatopoeia; table of contents; subtitles

Alarcón, Francisco X. (1999). *Angels ride bikes.* San Francisco: Children's Book Press.
In this collection of poems, Alarcón writes in both English and Spanish.
Craft elements: Free verse; varied punctuation; similes; onomatopoeia; Spanish words embedded in English poems; informational footnotes; afterword

Grimes, Nikki. (2006). *Thanks a million.* New York: HarperCollins.
These 16 poems by Nikki Grimes vary in form.
Craft elements: haiku; free verse; rebus; riddles; metaphors; dialogue; personification; repetitive language; rhyme; table of contents

Hopkins, Lee Bennett (Ed.). (1992). *Through our eyes: Poems and pictures about growing up.* Boston: Little Brown and Company.
This collection of 16 poems written by various authors describes childhood.
Craft elements: rhyme; free verse; repetition; varied punctuation; alliteration; descriptive language; table of contents

Janeczko, Paul B. (2005). *A kick in the head: An everyday guide to poetic forms.* New York: Scholastic Inc.
This collection of poems by various authors illustrates 29 different poetic forms from acrostic to haiku, ballad to ode, and sonnet to cinquain.
Craft elements: many forms of poetry; table of contents; glossary/notes about the different forms; author's introduction

Johnston, Tony. (1996). *My Mexico/México mío.* New York: Penguin Putnam Books.
Johnston writes in English and Spanish about life in Mexico.
Craft elements: similes, onomatopoeia; Spanish embedded in English poems; circular poems; table of contents; glossary

Myers, Walter Dean. (1997). *Harlem.* New York: Scholastic Inc.
This narrative poem describes life in Harlem from the perspective of an African American.
Craft elements: free verse; descriptive language; important historical figures mentioned; strong emotions; powerful illustrations; one-word ending

Paschen, Elise. (Ed.). (2005). *Poetry speaks to children.* Naperville, IL: Sourcebooks Inc.
Many of the 95 poems from 73 poets are read by the poets on the accompanying CD; information on the origins of the poems is included, such as Langston Hughes explaining how he wrote "The Negro Speaks of Rivers."
Craft elements: many poetic forms and elements; editor's introduction; table of contents

Index

DUE DATE
